CHANGING STATES

What unites Yeats, Heaney, Synge, Beckett, Joyce and Máirtín Ó Cadhain, Robert Welch argues, is their attempt to respond to the transformation of Irish life from Gaelic to twentieth-century, post-industrial culture. Writing against a sense of loss, their work is distinguished by an intense awareness of the power of language; a provisionality in regard to the concept of the self; a preoccupation with change; and an obsession with the past and its meanings.

Robert Welch draws attention to the hidden aspects of Irish literature and examines what makes it so distinctive and so powerful. He provides an account of all the major writers of modern Ireland and presents his readers with an overview of this very varied body of work.

Changing States will be an indispensable text for anyone interested in Irish life and literature, as well as those interested in language and translation.

Robert Welch is Professor of English at the University of Ulster at Coleraine. He is the author of a number of books on Irish literature; editor of *The Oxford Companion to Irish Literature* and a poet and translator. *Muskerry*, a volume of his poetry, appeared in 1991.

CHANGING STATES

Transformations in Modern Irish Writing

Robert Welch

London and New York

First published 1993
by Routledge
11 New Fetter Lane, London EC4P 4EE

Simultaneously published in the USA and Canada
by Routledge
29 West 35th Street, New York, NY 10001

Printed in Great Britain by Clays Ltd, St Ives plc.

British Library Cataloguing in Publication Data
Welch, Robert
Changing States: Transformations in
Modern Irish Writing
I. Title
891.6209

Library of Congress Cataloging in Publication Data
Welch, Robert,
Changing states: transformations in modern Irish writing / Robert Welch.
p. cm.
Includes bibliographical references and index.
1. English literature - Irish authors - History and criticism.
2. English literature - 20th century - History and criticism.
3. English literature - 19th century - History and criticism.
4. Literature and society - Ireland - History. 5. Irish literature - History and criticism. 6. Ireland in literature. I. Title.
PR8755.W44 1993
820.9′9415—dc20 92-24801

ISBN 0-415-08666-3
0-415-09361-9 (pbk)

FOR:

Rachel

Killian

Egan

Tiernan

CONTENTS

PREFACE
Translation for the Irish

> For Don Juan it was not only visions of past cultures that held a dangerous element in them; anything which was the object of an obsessive concern had a harmful potential.
> Carlos Castaneda, *The Eagle's Gift* (Harmondsworth, 1982), p. 23

> 'Wait a minute,' I protested. 'What about the sorcery stories? Aren't you going to tell them to me?'
> 'Of course I am,' he said. 'But they are not stories that one can tell as if they were tales. You've got to think your way through them and then rethink them and relive them so to speak.'
> Carlos Castaneda, *The Power of Silence*: *Further Lessons of Don Juan* (London, 1988), pp. 20–1

How do we approach the past? How do we avoid fetishizing it, making it the object of our obsessive concern? If particular works or periods or figures become an obsessive concern then not only do we cease to understand those things, we also cease the continuous activity of questioning and requestioning necessary to learning, self-development and self-knowledge. Stasis ensues, a perfect lock between an immobile perceiver and the petrified object: Medusa. Much satisfaction can be gained from this lock: stasis has its own pleasures, mostly to do with self-fixation and the ego. Medusa is really Narcissus. The lock is apparently fierce and unyielding, but underneath it is really as soft as putty because the object of concern is the ego all the time, and egoists always go easy on themselves.

All writers or artists have a choice: they can choose the activity of the will, or as Coleridge would call it, the creative imagination; or they may choose inertia. The one is life, the other death. The choice is never made once and for all; it is constantly renewed, and the temptations to inertia increase in direct proportion to the increase in potentiality in the arena of the will. In choosing activity, will, imagination, the artist opts for the kind of concern for interaction with reality, including the past, which is the direct antithesis of Castaneda's 'obsessive concern'; he or she opts for an activity the nature of which may be loosely embraced within the term 'translation'.

The past is dangerous; ruins can fall on you. There may be trapdoors, secret labyrinths, torture chambers, such delectations. All very entrancing and alluring, but dangerous. Or we may take a fragment to shore against *our* ruins; or convert it to an icon which can be used to console ourselves and terrify others, for instance Edward Walsh the schoolmaster-poet, on his knees before John Mitchel on Spike Island in Cork Harbour, before Mitchel's transportation to Van Dieman's land for revolutionary activity in 1848. Such a scene can be used for all kinds of purposes, to serve various ideologies. It is not just the telling of the story, but how it is told.

If a story is told with a fixed view then nothing stirs; we are in the realms of petrifaction, which, as has been said, has its own allurements, primarily to do with ego. But if the story is told as if it were happening again, as if it were entering reality once more, then something will stir. Telling a story like this is translating it, carrying it over into the present, making it live again. To translate a story from the dead world of custom and fixed idea into the unpredictability of an emerging contingency where it once again is subjected to the conditionality of chance, is to make the past contemporary. This re-creation of the past is not the rewriting of history so feared by Orwell for good reason in the 1940s and early 1950s. The kind of rewriting Orwell had in mind, particularly in *1984*, was conducted according to a fixed set of ideas and therefore the opposite of the discipline of translation and re-creation imagined here. A totalitarian rewriting of history accepts the impossibility of any movement or change: all must be made to conform with the fixed ideology; so there is no discipline because there is no search, therefore no method. The method of activity of the engaged will involves approaching the past in complete openness, to retell a story in such a way that that story lives again. Such a method is true historical enquiry and a legitimate method, because it frees the past into its own contours and intricacies, while at the same time making it an actual encounter in the present. The past is moved, and this movement requires us to move.

All legitimate intellectual enquiry is translation of one kind or another: it takes a text, a phase of history, an event, an instant of recognition, and proceeds to understand it by reliving it in the process of re-creating it. In doing so it renews the unpredictability of the event or text by subjecting it once again to the challenges and opportunities of contingency. The thing is lived again, and it re-enacts its completeness in the new context. There is a state of change, but the thing, in the course of the re-enactment, reveals itself more completely than ever before. It confirms itself as belonging to its own time and place by displaying its ability to move in the present time. Life shows itself as being a concrete and actual reality in its ability to transform its very self by means of what we may call translation.

In certain cultures, the Irish amongst them, translation is a crucial activity. There are obvious reasons for this, in that before the nineteenth century to speak of Irish culture is to speak of a different language and entirely different ways of seeing. Irish culture, for two hundred years, has, in this very obvious sense, been in the business of translating itself to itself and to the outside world. It has, of course, been remarkably successful in accomplishing this act of communication. But also, in Ireland, historical narratives, stories, legends, the past, have a tendency to become objects of Castaneda's 'obsessive concern'; so that translation, in the broader sense of freeing those narratives from the lock of fixed idea and the petrifactions of ego, becomes necessary, not just from time to time, but continually. Ireland, like some other countries, is continually in need of transformation *precisely because* it is so traditional. Irish people, it may be said, are amongst those who are, at one and the same time, deeply archaic and immediately contemporary.

ACKNOWLEDGEMENTS

I would like to thank the British Academy for the award of a personal research grant; the Faculty of Humanities, the University of Ulster, for leave of absence in 1989 and for its support during the writing of this book; Dr Joseph McMinn, Dr Paul Davies, Dr Mike Patterson, Dr John Pitcher, Dr Declan Kiberd, Dr Bruce Stewart, Dr Elmer Andrews and Mr Alan Peacock, all of whom read chapters in draft; Rosemary Savage, Cindy McAllister, Beth Holmes, Lyn Doyle and Mary McCaughan, who typed the book at various stages; and most of all my wife, Angela, agus ár ceathrar álainn: Rachel, Killian, Egan and Tiernan. A special thanks, for their kindness, to Tomás Ó Murchadha and Seán Ó Ríordáin (nach Maireann), Jeanne Jeffares, Francis Stuart, Brian Friel, Pearse Hutchinson and Seamus Heaney.

Cúl Rathain, 1991

1

CHANGE AND STASIS IN IRISH WRITING

We think of Irish culture as deeply divided. There are good reasons for this: the main one being that the Irish went through a profound shift in cultural orientation in surrendering one language for another, Irish for English, in the nineteenth century. Ireland, unlike most other European countries, did not have the opportunity of fully experiencing the experiments of individualism, enterprise, collectivity and modernization that are known as the Renaissance and the Enlightenment. Being a colony of England, Ireland was cut off; her people experienced Europe, in the modern period, that is to say from about 1600, through an English transmission. There were exceptions, such as the Irish propagandists of the Counter-Reformation trained in Louvain and elsewhere, who returned to Ireland to promote the Catholic interest; or the sons of those Catholic houses who were sent to study at Salamanca and Lisbon. But these men could not be said to have constituted themselves into a body of settled opinion, back in Ireland, that affected Irish life and thought. There were waves of rumour and agitation, depending on what crisis was at hand, for which poets and apologists, trained in Counter-Reformation propaganda techniques, were often responsible; but these were frequently contradictory, as between one occasion and another.

There was no consensus: how could there have been when the basic structure of Irish life had been torn apart by Mountjoy's defeat of the Irish at Kinsale? We are dealing, in Ireland's case, with an example of an almost completely successful colonial takeover. There was no settled body of Irish life and thought in the modern, secular, urbanized and predominantly middle-class sense in which that phrase tends to be applied. When we use it we think of the established norms of polite society, of theatres, perfume, salons, cafés; its business and its art; its eating and its drinking; Moll Flanders' interiors, Zola's kitchens and drawing rooms. We think of newspapers, a publishing industry, authorship, artists and their modern dependence upon and conflict with materialistic society. We think of parliaments and courts; of the power language may have in these environs, to persuade, affect, deceive and stultify. All of this large arena of modern European culture, so dependent on the way language creates and reflects society, is, to a great extent, absent from Irish life up to the nineteenth century. There were, of course, theatres in eighteenth century Dublin. There was a tradition of political thought upon which Swift built; but even that, when it came closest to defining distinct forms of Irish life, did so in a spirit of exasperation with the customary English assumption that everything that mattered happened in London and on the 'mainland', to use a word which still comes readily to some lips in Ireland.

From Kinsale to the end of the nineteenth century one cannot say that there was such a thing as 'Irish life and thought': there was English life and thought which sometimes accommodated an Irish accent for added vitality. Ireland, cut off from Europe, mastered by Britain, was not in a position to evolve modern forms of life which would develop from the pre-existent forms, patterns, social organizations and emotional predispositions that were there in Gaelic Ireland.

This is a catastrophic and, for that very reason, satisfying reading of Irish cultural history. It is a traumatic reading in the precise sense of that word. Something went wrong: what went wrong, it is often argued, is traceable to the English presence in Ireland. It is easy to see this line of thinking deployed by cultural nationalists. The only way in which the damage can be undone, the argument goes, is by openly admitting that Irish culture from Kinsale onwards has been, in all major respects, English; and that in the last twenty years it has become Anglo-American. The logic here leads to setting up the Irish language as the only true icon of Irishness: everything else is pussyfooting and special pleading. We see writers like Alan Titley, Michael Hartnett and Nuala ní Dhomhnaill either explicitly or implicitly making this analysis and taking appropriate action. They write in Irish because no other language will do; no other language will convey, for them, those interior states of being that all writers who are real writers want to talk about. They experience the trauma of the fracturing of Irish culture and attempt the healing process in their own work and language.

These writers make a simple straightforward analysis and they act upon it. In their writings occur some of the most significant insights that are being re-created in contemporary Irish writing. One of the main sources of the power that writers such as Nuala ní Dhomhnaill display is the intensity with which they approach the entire question of language itself, seeing it as comprising latencies and persuasions that determine modes of thought and behaviour. For ní Dhomhnaill and for Hartnett the loss of the Irish language was a cataclysmic blow to the psyche of the Irish people in that it ripped out and tore asunder all the secret interiors that sponsor the manifold activities that go to make up a culture. That such interiors are not immediately accessible to our thinking to begin with is only evidence of their intrinsic and radical nature: what is at the root of a situation takes tremendous trouble to keep itself hidden.

On the other side of the coin are the linguistic or cultural behaviourists. They say: language is merely a set of counters; and those mysteries to which the cultural nationalists lay claim are romanticism, mantra-seeking, bog-digging for treasure-troves of words. The cultural behaviourists would argue that Irish people should get on with what they have. In any case, they say, whatever it is to be Irish now is involved with the capitalisms of the West and the emerging capitalisms in post-Communist eastern Europe. Why trouble ourselves over traumas that may or may not have taken place a century ago? This view, in its robust common sense, has certain attractions.

But which is right? It may be that we do not need to back either of these two horses. It may be that the way we pose the question about tradition is itself part of the problem. Irish culture, now, and for the last one hundred years, has been preoccupied with the question of continuity, and this at a time when it seems that the idea of continuity and the related one of community are cracking up irremediably. One response to this breakdown is to lament it and to try for wholeness and integrity. But what if cultures do have within them periods of fracture and cleavage, even to the point of trauma? And what if the test of a culture is its capacity to survive these cleavages and even to be strengthened by them? A culture either survives or it does not. If it does not then it does not have the ability to reactivate itself by means of those things which seem to threaten it by demanding so much. Think of what Shaw says about 'creative evolution' in the preface to *Back to Methusalah*:

> the will to do anything can and does, at a certain pitch of intensity set up by conviction of its necessity, create and organize new tissue to do it with. . . . Evolution shews us . . . vitality doing all sorts of things: providing the centipede with a hundred legs, and ridding the fish of any legs at all; building lungs and arms for the land and gills and fins for the sea.[1]

This could equally be applied to culture and its evolution and transformations. If a culture cannot make the adaptation that necessity demands, then it will die and probably deserves to die, in that it has not answered life's call.

One of the most striking examples of cultural survival in Ireland is in music. Indeed, it is scarcely correct to talk of survival here because there is ample evidence of robust cultural health. In the 1970s, '80s and '90s there has been a burgeoning of new talent, a standard of musicianship and excellence, that no one would have foretold in the early 1960s. And the extraordinary thing is that this new phase of Irish music entirely carries over, effectively translates, the traditions, techniques and very airs that Edward Bunting found in Belfast in 1792. Two hundred years have passed since then and listening to Nioclás Tóibín singing 'Bán Chnoic Eireann Ó' or Peadar Ó Riada's Cúil Aodha choir chanting 'Abha an tSulláin' it is as if time has been set aside, and we hear back two, three, four hundred years.

Music is freer to do this than the other arts are because it does not have the responsibility of denotation. Words signify, they denote; we traffic with time in the arts of language, and with history and its events. And when we deal with history we come back to fracture and cleavage, the 'nightmare' of Stephen Dedalus. We come back to the stumbling block of discontinuity. When we listen to Seán Ó Riada's 'Mairseáil Rí Longsigh' we experience no sense of discontinuity; there is wholeness, unity; but always in the arts of language there is consecutiveness, and that reminds us of the cultural failures and abortions of the nineteenth century, the century of 'silence' as Thomas Kinsella, following Sean de Fréine, has called it.[2] And yet we experience

Irishness; we know that there is such a thing, now, as an 'Irish way of life' and even though, as with the rest of the elements that comprise that complex, there is much that is tawdry in it, we know it is there. It is there because we have not yet ceased to will it to be there, in Shaw's language of creative evolution.

What is this Irish way of life, and how may it be described? History will not really help here, because history, with its correct insistence on consecutiveness, events, discontinuities, fractures, leads us back into the dilemma. If Irish culture has survived, and a good deal of evidence tends to suggest it has, then it will have done so by preserving itself through change. It will have been able to change because it will have held on to the basic patterns, the deep structures; it will have held on to them by changing them in ways that help to accomplish fuller and more extensive expression.

Irish culture is preoccupied by continuity. But that does not mean that it will always be continuous. Indeed, we may suspect that if a culture is preoccupied by continuity it may have acquired a very highly developed awareness of the presence and pressure of discontinuity. Joyce's Citizen in the 'Cyclops' episode of *Ulysses* is fanatical in his insistence on the continuity and purity of Irish culture. He is the apotheosis of the cultural nationalist. He wants Ireland to be a fixed thing, defined by him, and there is only one opinion on all matters pertaining to Ireland: his. He wants to annihilate all variations of opinion and subject them to his ordinances and prejudices. There is a superb ironic play going on in Joyce's text: the inflexibility of the nationalist Citizen, the Cyclops, comes out of a fixation with Britain that dominates every aspect of his thought. He becomes what he hates. His nationalism is a mirror image of the imperialist authority he professes to despise. The one-eyed Cyclops really wishes to convert all the problematic twists and turns of Irish life and history into a continuous narrative of his own devising, which he can weave and unweave on the spot, picking up a personal irritation, a private spleen, and making it part of the overall pattern. The Cyclops dominates through his language; he must, in each of his words, preside over the moment, and seek to prevent his story from straying too far away from a fixed and determined view. This is a strain, a code, a method, very dominant in Irish culture. In music it is repetition; in bardic verse it is the emphasis upon formal perfection, where this aspect of poetry dominates almost completely. When one reads a conventional bardic poem addressed to a chieftain the pleasure resides not in the originality of the approach, or in the shocks of surprise that the linguistic effects may offer; rather the pleasure resides in the very lack of these. Each quatrain aspires to be a repetition, with some variation, of a previous quatrain. The reading of the poem, or its recital, is merely an occasion to facilitate the moment when the unity of Irish culture, its singleness, its one-eyed coherence, may be seen.

This is a highly original poetry in the proper meaning of the term, in that it is preoccupied by harking back to the origin. It takes its situation, often the situation of inauguration, where the chief's assumption of authority is celebrated, and links it with other inaugurations; compares its subject with other heroes in Irish or classical tradition; and generally establishes the event which is the occasion of the poem as one with many precedents in myth or history. As an art it is entirely traditional, and deeply attentive to continuity.

All literature, it may be said, will have a tendency to move towards stasis, the negation of that very activity of spirit and mind that we expect in works of imaginative vision. However, if we think more closely, this negation, this movement towards stasis, is actually a powerful element in the complex interactions between stasis and activity, between death and life, that go on and that announce themselves in the rhythms of poetry and in the designs of art. But what is remarkable in Ireland, as, for example, in Japan, are the long periods during which an art will not develop at all, or develop only slightly, so strong and powerful are the attractions of the rapture of stasis. Only a culture of great antiquity can allow itself these long static ecstasies of negation, and still survive. Such a culture knows that stasis is one side of the question; that the other side is all frenetic activity and manifold experience. And it is this manifold nature of being itself that is announced to us in that speech of Manannan's in the seventh century *Immram Brain* (*The Voyage of Bran*), where he speaks of the different ways of seeing that are possible. Bran is sailing in his coracle when the sea god speaks:

> The light of the sea you are on,
> the brilliance on which you row,

has put forth yellow and green;
it is solid land.

Salmon leap from the womb
of the white sea on which you gaze,
they are calves, lambs of pure white,
in amity, without hate.[3]

Manannan's vision is the opposite of the Cyclopean fixedness. It is related to the voyaging forth which is the mark of the *immram*, or voyage tale, which itself is a genre of tale that concentrates a characteristic tendency to formulaic repetition and stasis. In Manannan's vision the signifiers float into the realm of metaphoric free play. To find an opposite for Manannan in Irish mythology one could look to Balor who, in *Cath Maighe Tuireadh* (*The Battle of Moytura*) is opposed to Lugh. Balor, a Fomorian, is associated with darkness, negation; while Lugh, one of the Tuatha Dé Danann, is linked to the sun god (Lughnasa: August) and is known as the Samildanach – 'possessing many arts together'. Balor is a Cyclops with a poisoned eye; Lugh is manifold and is related to the Manannan of the *Immram Brain*.

We may sum up and say that the preoccupation with continuity in Irish culture and literature is linked to a desire for stasis and negation, a human desire, by no means confined to Ireland. Against this, in Irish culture, in culture generally, and continually begot by and begetting its opposite, there is a desire for variation and ceaseless change. A tension of this kind probably underlies all creative activity, and indeed probably lies at the root of language itself.

In language there is a desire to mean, which involves a desire to restrict the play of the possibility of variance in signification; on the other hand there can be no meaning without the arbitrary nature of the sign. Change and stasis continually re-create one another.

My proposition is very simple: the validity of any culture, its strength, will depend on how thoroughly it remains attentive to the interaction between change and stasis. The validity will not depend on local circumstances, otherwise there could be no general statement about the nature of culture, although the 'minute particulars of mankind'[4] will be taken up and revealed and filled with wonder in the interplay of change and stasis. If this is true then the actual language itself in which literature is made at any time matters less than that the interaction we have been speaking of should take place. But the interaction may not take place if one of the poles, of change or stasis, is at any time too dominant. A culture may receive a shock, as we may say that Irish culture did in the nineteenth century; and its reaction may be to seek to be static, or to hand over its being, temporarily, to another culture, in Ireland's case that of Britain. All venture for change then, all the free play of the signifiers in such a circumstance, may be inhibited; or the impulse to stasis may convert them into dead repetition, negative cyclicity, Cyclops.

Such a period of stasis occurred in Ireland in the nineteenth century in certain areas of culture. But again, students of literature should always remember that culture comprises many things. There was a great deal of other kinds of cultural activity in nineteenth century Ireland; a period of stasis, admittedly, in the literary arts. The arts of language were being worked and deployed in other areas: politics, propaganda, social organization. Those interiors to which the creative arts pay attention may not have been voiced, but O'Connell, Davis, Parnell, in their different ways, were developing what would become the modern Irish way of life. By the end of the century those interiors to which literature and its culture turn, and without which any culture is incomplete, were ready to break from stasis and voyage forth again in variance, difference and change. This is what we call the Irish Literary Revival. It came with such force and strength because of the waiting. At last the waiting could no longer continue and silence had to be broken. The full interchange between change and stasis had to take place again in the literary arts. Yeats arrived and opened up the interplay between change and stasis.

Yeats promoted change by seeking radical continuity, and in searching for that he was venturing into areas of experience, mythology, folklore, and so on with a freshness of address not hitherto seen. He linked these enquiries to the search for the interior that was taking place again in the culture of Europe in the late nineteenth century. He made continuity all the stronger and more radical, all the more charged by change, *because* of the effort of will required to accomplish it. The tendency to stasis and that to change, the need for continuity and the desire to sally forth and open unforeseen ways of being arrive together in his language, which strains to accommodate a full complex apprehension of what it is like to be.

All of this may be summed up in section III of 'Meditations in Time of Civil War' - the section called 'My Table'. Yeats has been writing of the problems surrounding continuity, of what can be handed on through the generations. Ancestral houses are built by wild and bitter men, trying to find continuity and stillness, but their heirs may grow soft in leisure. He comes to his own case, his own house, the Tower at Ballylee, which is not a place for soft leisure, but a place to 'exalt the mind', a 'befitting emblem of adversity'. Then he considers his writing table, where a Japanese sword lies, a symbol of changelessness. He thinks of the highly formal, continuous and often static culture that produced it - that of Japan - and is excited by the capacity for stasis and for waiting in that culture. And then the awareness of the poetry opens out, sallies, into the realization that changelessness must embody change, each must charge the other. As the awe of the poetry mounts he considers how a Japanese aristocrat walking in the countryside, in all his formality and sternness, carries an excitement because his mind continuously awakens into difference and variation. As the section concludes, Yeats says: 'it seemed/Juno's peacock screamed': a scream of wonder, excitement, terror and joy, to celebrate the interaction of stasis and change that underlies being and language. This poetry, highly formal, carefully worked, is a kind of fury of wonder at life itself:

> Two heavy trestles, and a board
> Where Sato's gift, a changeless sword,
> By pen and paper lies,
> That it may moralise
> My days out of their aimlessness.
> A bit of an embroidered dress
> Covers its wooden sheath.
> Chaucer had not drawn breath
> When it was forged. In Sato's house,
> Curved like new moon, moon-luminous,
> It lay five hundred years.
> Yet if no change appears
> No moon; only an aching heart
> Conceives a changeless work of art.

Our learned men have urged
That when and where 'twas forged
A marvellous accomplishment,
In painting or in pottery, went
From father unto son
And through the centuries ran
And seemed unchanging like the sword.
Soul's beauty being most adored,
Men and their business took
The soul's unchanging look;
For the most rich inheritor,
Knowing that none could pass Heaven's door
That loved inferior art,
Had such an aching heart
That he, although a country's talk
For silken clothes and stately walk,
Had waking wits; it seemed
Juno's peacock screamed.[5]

There is such a thing as Irish culture, and it realizes itself deeply (something cultures need to do, otherwise they disappear) when it can activate and be attentive to basic patterns of being. One of these is the interplay between stasis and change, something to which Irish culture has been and is highly attuned. The nineteenth century is a long period of stasis, generally speaking, but there are breakthroughs and ventures there too. Callanan, Hardiman, Ferguson, Carleton – all have something to say, but it is a phase of waiting. There is a rupture, but one of the contentions advanced here is that Irish linguistic and literary culture is all the stronger for the waiting: 'still the indomitable Irishry'.[6]

2

LANGUAGE AND TRADITION IN THE NINETEENTH CENTURY

To speak of tradition in nineteenth century Irish literature is to be conscious of an absence. In an eloquent and deeply influential lecture by Thomas Kinsella, on 'Irish Poetry and the Nineteenth Century', delivered at the Merriman Festival in Ennis in 1968, the lecturer went over the names of the nineteenth century poets who have assumed a place in the roll-call of honour. This was his verdict:

> Callanan, nothing. From Thomas Davis, Thomas D'Arcy McGee, Speranza . . . rhetorical fluency, savage indignation, high purpose . . . Mangan and Ferguson, with Moore and perhaps Allingham . . . it all amounts to very little. . . . From John Todhunter . . . nothing . . . waste characterizes the scene.[1]

Waste, silence, absence. This way of writing about the state of Irish culture in the nineteenth century is familiar. George Petrie, in 1855, writing in the preface to his *Collection of the Native Music of Ireland,* of the effects of the Famine on Ireland, spoke of the *absence* of the dimension of celebration in Irish life which was once there and to which the *Collection* itself bears witness. There is a break; there is a gap. There is something broken, hesitant and uncertain about the work of writers as various as Thomas Moore, Callanan, Ferguson, Carleton, Davis, Griffin and Le Fanu.

That uncertainty is caused by a great number of factors – political, economic, cultural, social – but for the moment we might rest on one: the linguistic. In nineteenth century Ireland one of the most devastating shifts that can take place in a culture, the shift from one language to another, came about in a very short time. This sudden shift is all the more remarkable when we consider that it had been a part of imperial policy since the days of the Tudor conquest, and before, to get rid of the Irish language. It all happened very quickly at the end. The Irish, to adopt a phrase of David Greene's, committed linguistic suicide. Why did it happen? A community has to feel it has a competence. It must feel that it has the ability to express itself in its art, institutions, food, general way of life, and, most of all, language. A culture becomes a community through the system of signs, codes, transmissions that it organizes to give meaning and coherence to its life-experience. A culture that is not a colonized culture will find ways of continuously developing such a system of signs. It may look to its neighbours for examples, it may fall into inertia, but a *free* culture will have the privilege of communicating to and for itself its sense of itself by its own system of significances. In as much as it is drawn to life it will do this, because once life draws and attracts then a culture responds by making; by creating institutions, by building, by developing pathways and interconnections, by creating a representation of corporate life. There may be many foreign influences on a culture; indeed a sign of cultural health is just this ability to absorb and transform other experience, but such an ability rests upon a culture's sense of self-possession, which has to do with its refusal to depart from its own ways of seeing and expressing.

Gaelic culture had its systems of law, inheritance, organization and learning. It was an adaptable and flexible culture as any is when it is in a healthy state. The old Gaelic world had accommodated Christianity, and one of the great achievements of Europe is the Irish missionary movement in the so-called Dark Ages. But Irish culture was deeply hierarchical and aristocratic, and when the Tyrone rebellion was put down and when the chieftains left in the seventeenth century, Gaelic culture began to lose touch with its centre.

By the time we are considering, the beginning of the nineteenth century, that culture, while still active in many respects, was, in many other important ways, vestigial. Brian Merriman, the last major Gaelic poet until Seán Ó Ríordáin, Pearse Hutchinson and Nuala ní Dhomhnaill in our own time, died in Limerick in 1805.

A language is the most comprehensive and satisfying of all the systems that a culture has in which to represent itself to itself. What language was there for Irish writers at the beginning of the nineteenth century? There was English, and the tradition of Anglo-Irish prose embodied in the work of Swift, Berkeley, Burke and Goldsmith; and the tradition of Anglo-Irish drama that stretched from Lording Barry from Bandon to R.B. Sheridan. But before we leave that statement, that there was the English language, and the tradition of Anglo-Irish drama and prose, we should pause and confess an unease about the nature and kind of continuity that that leaves unsaid. If we think of language as simply a tool, a technological device for the transmission of information (which is often the way it is thought of, even in the universities) then, to a certain extent, the language a writer uses to communicate to his or her community is a matter of accident. But if we think of a language not as something subject to our will and caprice, like the control panel of a microcomputer, but as something on which we are dependent, something that represents for us an ability to establish for ourselves a clearing to be in, then you cannot think any more that writers, turning to what lies before them in their cultural system of language, are not affected by what is there. And what was there for the poet at the beginning of the nineteenth century was a language system, English, associated with the English imperium, its established constitutional life, its power. In that system there were the different, often challenging voices of Swift, Goldsmith, Burke and Berkeley; and within it as well there were the English voices of difference, challenge and dissent: Milton and Marvell, for example. But the mention of Milton serves to remind us of a very significant consideration: that English liberty was grounded on what Burke loved to call 'traditionary' rights,[2] rights which were put to the test and sustained in the century of English revolution – the seventeenth; a testing and sustaining in which Milton had his part to play. The Irish writer could look to Swift, who also had a part to play in defining English constitutional liberty, especially as it referred to Ireland, but there was no *Irish* achievement in parliamentary systems and constitutional freedom which had established itself firmly in the 'traditionary' rights of the imperium. Far from it, the Irish parliament voted itself out of existence in 1800 in the Act of Union.

There was, however, the voice of Ulster dissent, to be found, for example, in the work of William Drennan. Radical

Presbyterianism, which looked to France, and which was a major strand in the ecumenical weave of the United Irishmen, carried forward into the late Enlightenment the thinking of Milton on individual liberty and the prerogative it should have in a reformed and renewed state. The radical Presbyterians, in making this connection, were remaining in touch with their own intellectual and theological origins in seventeenth century controversy and debate, and were offering a totally different view of British constitutional history and continuity from that of Burke, and one which might have generated another system had the United Irish rebellion been successful. But it was not, and in case there is a danger of becoming entranced by the alluring prospect of radical Presbyterian liberty (which never was) as the salve to all Irish woes (which were and are), it is necessary to recall that the ecumenical euphoria of the United Irishmen, while admirable, had many tensions within it, the most inescapable being the fact that Ulster Dissenters looked to Cromwell as the liberator, while the Catholic Irish could never see him quite in that light. And what mixed feelings did the Dissenters have about William of Orange, and would they have shared these in any way with their Catholic fellow-countrymen?

All of this has to do with how an Irish writer would have thought and felt about English at the beginning of the nineteenth century. English was the language of power and liberty, Wordsworth's and Burke's liberty, not that of Milton or of Blake. Had the Anglo-Irish tradition of Swift, or the United Irish radicalism of Tone been successful; had the Irish parliament achieved independence and become more representative of the people of Ireland – then the English language, and all the world of liberty and power associated with it would have been closer, less foreign, less 'out there'.

A culture has a system of representation, by means of which it confirms itself to itself in spontaneous and often unconscious acts of recognition: that coffee shop, that piece of pottery, that dish of food, that facial contexture, that gesture, all co-ordinate in a sense of relationship, which adds up to meaning, significance, identity. We know ourselves in and through the things we see and hear around us. The everyday particulars of life give back to us our sense of ourselves, our sense of location and presence. All of these form in themselves a kind of language (remember Bloom's comment in *Ulysses*, 'everything speaks in its own way'), but it is language itself that is the mesh in which all the particularity of the everyday is connected in our cultural systems. One of the most important of the sub-codes within language, one of the most significant of the systems of meshes that go to make up the corporate life of a culture, is the institution of government, and its constitution, which is the activity, the living body, of a state. What constitution did the Irish people have after the Union? There was a constitution, certainly, for the United Kingdom of Great Britain and Ireland, but Ireland did not have anything like its own way of representing itself to itself within that system. Its sense of itself as a state was not a living thing; it was without a means of representation, a means of embodying its own particular sense of its conscious and unconscious life. It felt itself to be second-rate, a feature of Irish life still in evidence. This goes back, in the Irish situation, to that huge shift in mentality and in feeling that took place in the move from one language to another. With Irish, there was no problem; even with English, had the Anglo-Irish parliamentary system broadened to include a greater range of Irish life, to include Dissenter and Catholic (a range Burke longed for), then there could have been a life for the Irish themselves as themselves; but with the Union all that disappeared and life, as Desmond Fennell would say, was 'elsewhere'.[3] The Irish became full provincials.

The Act of Union followed upon a period of questioning and debate in England upon the state and the rights and privileges of its citizens. England had been going through since the French Revolution one of its periodic bouts of self-definition and self-renewal. At the end of the eighteenth century English constitutional thinking was taking its modern form, in reaction to the drama in France as it unfolded. English nerves were very alert to those events, and there were none more alert than those of the man who gave English constitutional liberty its most forceful and persuasive language: the Irishman Edmund Burke. There is an irony here the depth of which it is hard to fathom.

Burke hated what he called the 'new conquering empire of light and reason' which strips life of its moral and emotional clothing, to leave it naked and shivering. He endows 'traditionary' rights and privileges with a sacral and humane aura, and sees those who would dissolve that aura as 'sophistors', mechanicals, Jacobins. They are without dignity because they insult the instinct life has, according to Burke, to make and sustain codes:

> All the decent drapery of life is to be rudely torn off. All the super-added ideas, furnished from the wardrobe of the moral imagination, which the heart reveres, and the understanding ratifies, as necessary to cover the defects of our naked shivering nature, and to raise it to dignity in our own estimation, are to be exploded as a ridiculous, absurd, and antiquated fashion.[4]

Burke argues that it is a meddling and profane intelligence that refuses to acknowledge the legitimacy of codes and of their continuance. It is meddling because it does not know tact; and it is profane because it cannot see that the codes and systems a people evolves in which to represent itself to itself have what he considers a sacred and 'awful' quality, a gravity; because it is through them and in them that we have our relationship with life itself. It is through these codes and languages that we respond to the call life makes to us; these codes and languages are a *creative* and *natural* response. We are impelled into making them by life itself and in making them we are imitating nature. To break them is to be mechanized and Jacobinical, to be out of nature, to be monstrous. It is blasphemy because such an attitude is an affront to the secrecy of life itself in its 'great mysterious incorporation of the human race':

> Our political system is placed in a just correspondence and symmetry with the order of the world, and with the mode of existence decreed to a permanent body composed of transitory parts; wherein, by the disposition of a stupendous wisdom, moulding together the great mysterious incorporation of the human race, the whole, at one time, is never old, or middle-aged, or young, but in a condition of unchangeable constancy, moves on through the varied tenour of perpetual decay, fall, renovation, and progression.[5]

The placing and disposition of these phrases is not just windy rhetoric. The writing is straining to realize, as it reflects upon the revolution in France, that renovation of the system of English liberty which will not be revolution. Watch again the movement and rhythm of the last clause in the passage above, which is all one sentence: 'moves on through the varied tenour of perpetual decay, fall, renovation, and progression'. Burke wants his speech to be visited by and to enact that principle of nervous yet flexible self-possession and constancy that he sees embodied in the British constitution. He wants to give that principle a language. And, of course, he succeeded, remarkably well. Poise, passion, gravity, dignity, he has all of these things. He provides a language, a system of representation, in which the English can see, defined and renovated, the liberty which they, Burke insists, must feel proud to inherit. He makes a system for a system. He shows that English can expand to accommodate the immediacy of the events in France and react to them, and measure them because it itself, the language, is grounded in an affiance with life. It is empty-headed meddling, and dangerous blasphemy, to be attracted by the kind of views advanced in the sermon given by Richard Price in the Old Jewry, the immediate stimulus to the *Reflections*. The English system, redefined and renovated, ensures that the English people will enjoy a sure and 'domestic' (one of Burke's favourite words) relation with the things of life. Things are dear to us because we can rest upon an assurance of continuity; take continuity away and things lose their substance; they become chimeras and fantasies. This is Burke's argument and it is one of the most capacious statements of conservative thought ever made. And it was made by an Irishman, defining the nature of English freedom to the English; just as Burke's opposite, Shaw, showed the nature of the confinements of English life over a hundred years later.

With the passing of the Act of Union Ireland lost its own system of representation and Burke's model of the constitution was now the one that served for Ireland as well. If a community of people does not have a system of representation, a code, which will reflect its life and show that life to be of value and of significance, then its people will get the sense that real life is being lived elsewhere, so they lose touch with the particular evidences, the facts, of day to day life as they stand there before them. They lose poise, attention to detail, and they lose self-respect. They become preoccupied and vacant, because they are in two places at once and therefore nowhere. This is the world of absence that gives us so much vapid verse in the nineteenth century, but it is the dispossession out of which springs also the work of Sheridan Le Fanu, Flann O'Brien, and Beckett, to name but three Irish writers who have chronicled the obsessions of futility.

In the nineteenth century the strategy was to invent as many Irelands as possible. Because there *was* no Ireland, because there was no language, no system for it, then it was as well to try out as many possibilities as the brain could invent. And in any case it is a fact of psychological behaviour that if a person does not have a solid life-image the tendency will be to invent ceaselessly, to contradict, to venture as many versions as possible, anything rather than try to face the absence, the emptiness, the lack of continuity.

It is the same for a community. The absence of a satisfactory set of representations rooted in continuity will drive a community to extremes of self-abasement and self-assertion. There will be a plethora of images but they will not co-ordinate. And yet there will be a desire to make a system, to make it all cohere. So there will be a strong, insistent, even strident emphasis on difference, difference from the dominant life-image. In the case of Irish literature in the early nineteenth century the dominant life-image was the cultural set, the constitutional pattern, the confident power of English tradition and of the English way of life.

Ireland became mysterious not just to the English, to whom it is ever a source of bafflement or irritation, but to the Irish themselves. And they even came to develop an English tendency to exasperation over the inefficiency and silliness of their benighted fellow-countrymen. Ireland had no language, no established way of life, no set of representations: it was a mood, a cloudy intimation, a dream. It could be sensed in Irish music; that at least was non-verbal. Music allowed access to something that had to do with the core of Irish experience, but it was not troubled with precise identifications and relationships. The early nineteenth century was the period in which a good deal of Irish musical tradition was taken down from recital, by Edward Bunting from Belfast and by others. But when we consider the work of the poet, the friend of Robert Emmet, who was excited by the Bunting *Collection* of 1796 into wishing to do something 'truly national',[6] we see how poetry of the time cannot convey the sense of the centre from which music emanates. The poet is, of course, Thomas Moore; the enterprise which was to be 'truly national' was the *Irish Melodies*, which appeared in ten numbers from 1808 to 1834. In one of these *Melodies*, the one 'On Music',

Moore himself gives us an account of the poetic psychology that underlies his approach:

> Music! oh! how faint, how weak,
> Language fades before thy spell!
> Why should feeling ever speak,
> When thou canst breathe her soul so well?[7]

Feeling becomes disembodied. There is no language for it. Music, for Moore, was associated with the centres of feeling, and Irish music in particular seemed to him to derive its 'tone of sorrow and depression' from the core of Irish experience. There being no system in which to represent that experience, to embody it, music offered a mood which could float free from the constraints of the actual. Moore was inspired by the United Irishmen of 1798 and was influenced by what he called the 'democratic principle'[8] that spread throughout Europe and to Ireland in the 1790s, the very thing Burke abominated most. But he went to London, away from the country for which he wished to do something 'truly national'. He went, because, as a poet, he would want daily life to incorporate certain things: a community of interests, a sense of the relationship between the past and present, but most of all a set of representations that would be adequate for people to *be* where they were. All of this was missing in Ireland. There was no language, no continuity, no national assembly, no imagery of corporate life, no system within which a community could rejoice in the common impressions and transactions of the everyday. There was no sense of relationship in Irish life, so little sense of significance.

In 1808 Moore published two verse epistles, *Corruption and Intolerance*, 'addressed to an Englishman by an Irishman'. These poems in harsh pentameters are an attack on the corruption that facilitated the passing of the Union, and on the intolerance that Moore sees as characterizing relations between Ireland and England. The rhetoric of this writing conveys a kind of nervous hysteria, a blind unco-ordinated rage, that takes the reader, accustomed to the idea of Moore as a bland innocuous writer, the smiling weeper mocked by Hazlitt and others, by surprise:

> But oh, poor Ireland! if revenge be sweet
> For centuries of wrong, for dark deceit

And withering insult – for the Union thrown
Into this bitter cup, when that alone
Of slavery's draught was wanting – if for this
Revenge be sweet, thou *hast* that daemon's bliss;
For, oh! 'tis more than hell's revenge to see
That England trusts the men who've ruin'd thee . . .
All that devoted England can oppose
To enemies made friends, and friends made foes,
Is the rank refuse, the despised remains
Of that unpitying power, whose whips and chains
Made Ireland first, in wild, adulterous trance,
Turn false to England's bed, and whore with France.[9]

The Union is the culmination of a history of oppression and intolerance, the final bitterness. (It is odd that Seamus Heaney too is drawn to the phrase from *Hamlet* which Moore has in mind here, in 'Shelf Life' in the 1984 *Station Island.* See Chapter 14.)

In an appendix which he wrote to *Corruption and Innocence* Moore expands further on the sorry state of affairs between Ireland and England, and on the historical background. An early lack of constitutional and parliamentary independence weakened moral fibre and resolve, he argues, and made Ireland a cipher:

> The loss of independence very early debased our character. . . . It is true this island has given birth to heroes . . . but success was wanting to consecrate resistance, their cause was branded with the disheartening name of treason, and their oppressed country was such a blank among nations that . . . the fame of their actions was lost in the obscurity of the place where they achieved them.[10]

Moore is here registering a fear that underlies much nineteenth and twentieth century Irish writing, even work of the most explicitly nationalist and defensive kind: that Ireland does not matter, that it is a 'blank', a non-place, and that being, life, vivacity are elsewhere. Further on in the appendix he outlines the entire strategy of his Irish poetry, in particular the *Melodies*: because the Ireland of history is a non-place, the poet is drawn to seek his images from legend or from those pristine times before the 'conquerors had divided, weakened and disgraced us', the time 'when our Malachies wore collars of gold'. In addition, the appendix makes the case that music and song are best equipped to convey the sense of unavailing sorrow that seems, to Moore, the predominant fact of Irish life and feeling. Such a mood can be, he argues, effective, and he cites the story of Theodosius and Antioch. The reign of Theodosius 'affords the first example of a disqualifying penal code enacted by Christians against Christians'. The implication is clear, the inference all too obvious. He then tells how the people of Antioch made Theodosius relent by getting their minstrels to teach the Emperor's own musicians the sad songs of Antioch, which they played to him at dinner. The sad songs from Asia Minor had their effect in Rome. Here, in essence, is the strategy of the *Melodies* in general, and of 'Oh! Blame not the Bard' in particular. 'Success was wanting to consecrate resistance', he wrote, and anyone taking up Ireland's cause is accused of treason:

> But, alas for his country! – her pride has gone by,
> And that spirit is broken, which never would bend;
> O'er the ruin her children in secret must sigh,
> For 'tis treason to love her, and death to defend.
> Unprized are her sons, til they've learned to betray;
> Undistinguish'd they live, if they shame not their sires;
> And the torch, that would light them through dignity's
>   way,
> Must be caught from the pile where their country expires.
> Then blame not the bard, if in pleasure's soft dream
> He should try to forget what he never can heal.[11]

These last two lines give us an indication as to where Moore's imagination is tending: towards the 'soft dreams' of pleasure, repression, sadness, a kind of masochistic longing for an energy and vitality seen to be out of reach. 'Oh! Blame not the Bard' appeared in the third number of *Melodies,* in 1810, and in 1817 Moore's masterpiece, *Lallah Rookh,* a prolonged reverie of 'soft' pleasure was published. The poem is an intensely atmospheric evocation of imagined oriental luxury, shot through with Irish references and notations, but the power of the poem resides not in the nationalist allegory that may be extracted, but in the sheer volubility of the writing, its ceaseless inventiveness, and a sad sense that all the riches that are described are illusory. An emptiness lies at the core, a 'blankness' that the erotic languishing of the poem tries to fill. *Lallah Rookh* is a kind of pornography, not without its attractions, but essentially sad and out of touch with the scenes and objects it strives to present. It is a 'soft dream'. In the following extract two 'lightsome maidens' dance, embodying the desire of Azim for an Arab girl who has just sung to him:

> Around the white necks of the nymphs who danced
> Hung carcanets of orient gems, that glanced
> More brilliant than the sea-glass glittering o'er
> The hills of crystal on the Caspian shore;
> While from their long dark tresses, in a fall
> Of curls descending, bells as musical
> As those that, on the golden-shafted trees
> Of Eden, shake in the Eternal Breeze,
> Rung round their steps, at every sound more sweet,
> As 'twere the ecstatic language of their feet!
> At length the chase was o'er, and they stood wreathed
> Within each other's arms; while soft there breathed
> Through the cool casement, mingled with the sighs
> Of moonlight flowers, music that seemed to rise
> From some still lake, so liquidly it rose;
> And, as it swell'd again at each faint close
> The ear could track through all that maze of chords
> And young sweet voices, these impassion'd words.[12]

And so on. The poem is a 'maze of chords', through which the ear attempts to track a centre, a core of vision, or a cluster of associated perceptions that would vivify the work. But the writing is all activity, no life; all invention, no power.

Moore went to London and brooded upon 'vanquished Erin' and her woes. J.J. Callanan, the Cork poet, went to West Cork to try to realize his life-image. He was one of the first of those in Ireland, who, disappointed with city life, 'fly to the mountains'.[13] This last is a phrase he used in a letter to John Windele, the Cork antiquary. He planned a series of *Munster Melodies* along the Moore line, which he tried to research himself in Bandon, Clonakilty, Bantry and Gougane Barra. Nothing much remains: a few stray letters in a collection gathered by his friend Windele; a handful of translations; and a longish poem in imitation of Byron. There may be more as yet undiscovered, but it is unlikely. There is one superb poem, a poem which summarizes much of what has been said so far about a sense of absence and the lack of a system to represent how people are in their lives. That is 'The Outlaw of Loch Lene'. Purporting to be a translation (it is in fact an amalgam, drawn from various sources), it re-creates in English a certain kind of Irish love song – the kind where the man bewails the loss of his woman, and in which the world of nature seems to sympathize with his plight. But more interesting than that is the consideration that the speaker of the poem is *outside* the law, he has no system, no set of signs. And the language that Callanan uses, while inspired by the imagery and runs of the love songs, itself goes astray into a serial progression of images, that move outside the ordinary and the normal to create a sense of continuous shift and difference. It is a writing continuously evading the requirement that writing such as this, which has a strong narrative overtone, leads the reader to expect that a clear story be told. It continuously breaks the sense-expectation and yet retains an impassioned and forceful rhetorical drive:

O many a day have I made good ale in the glen,
That came not of stream, or malt, like the brewing of men.
My bed was the ground, my roof, the greenwood above,
And the wealth that I sought – one far kind glance from my
  love.

Alas! on that night when the horses I drove from the field,
That I was not near from terror my angel to shield.
She stretched forth her arms, – her mantle she flung to the
  wind,
And swam o'er Loch Lene, her outlawed lover to find.

O would that a freezing sleet-winged tempest did sweep,
And I and my love were alone far off on the deep!
I'd ask not a ship, or a bark, or pinnance to save, –
With her hand round my waist, I'd fear not the wind or the
  wave.

'Tis down by the lake where the wild tree fringes its sides,
The maid of my heart, the fair one of Heaven resides –
I think as at eve she wanders its mazes along,
The birds go to sleep by the sweet wild twist of her song.[14]

In this poem we do not know what the terror is, nor how it is that the girl lives by the lakeside. It may be that she is dead, and that this is why the outlaw is living in the glen. But the reader will see that these kinds of consideration have nothing to do with the effect of the poetry: this derives from a sense of strangeness that the writing conveys, a hidden secret mystery, towards which the poetry gestures, but which it does not explicate. Such a quality is frequently found in Gaelic love song:

> Tá crann ann san ngáirdín
> Ar a bhfásann duilleabhar a's bláth buí,
> An uair leagaim mo lámh air
> Is láidir nach mbriseann mo chroí.[15]
>
> There's a tree in the garden
> On which grows foliage and yellow flowers,
> When I put my hand on it
> My heart nearly breaks.

But in 'The Outlaw' Callanan takes this quality of sudden sharp realization and converts it into the organizing principle of the entire poem, so the piece drives forward with an excitement all the more effective for the strange, mysterious images in which it is presented. It is highly successful but it is very odd. It is intriguing because of the way it slides *off* its theme or narrative, to concentrate on the rhetorical drive. A central meaning remains unsaid, which does not matter in such a powerfully compacted poem as this, but when Callanan attempts to write analytical and historically responsible verse, as in 'The Recluse of Inchydoney', he fails to find a form for his emotion.

Callanan turned away from Moore's example and the imperial model of Burke. He sought out a community in West Cork, but he became a provincial. An unruly temperament, he searched for an alternative tradition to the dominant one with which he was confronted in the prosperous, mercantile Cork of the early nineteenth century. Again, given the circumstances, given his attitude, it was inevitable. There was a community in West Cork to which the poet wished to relate, but it was without the power of expressing itself to itself, publicly. There were West Cork poets writing in Gaelic, for their own people, but that community had become a closed system within the larger closed-off system of Ireland itself.

Callanan longed for continuity and he looked for a source,

identifying it, in another poem of his, 'Gougane Barra', with the lake of that name, a black circle of water at the bottom of a cauldron of mountains in West Cork. Here, he says, the legends 'darkly' slept. It was his ambition to awaken them, but he failed. No renovation takes place because, for this to happen, there would need to be not just an audience for Callanan's work but a community, from which, through which, and to which he could speak. He lacked, in other words, a language, a system of adequate representation. His talent, lyrical and impulsive, needed a strong network of codes within which, against which, to work.

Daniel O'Connell's Catholic Association provided an objective for the majority of the people of Ireland at this time: Emancipation. His organization, based on the parish and supported by the Catholic clergy, gave Irish people the sense that they could effect change purposefully and coherently. Emancipation came in 1829, but still, we must remind ourselves, government was in Westminster. O'Connell won the concession from Westminster constitutionally, but the constitution was that defined by Burke. Emancipation was meant to be the prelude to Repeal, which would give the Irish people their own system of representing themselves to themselves, but Repeal never came. There was a good deal of literary activity in the years up to and soon after Emancipation. Carleton's *Traits and Stories* began to appear in the *Christian Examiner*; Hardiman's *Irish Minstrelsy* was published in 1831; Samuel Ferguson was trying to think out a reconciliation of nationalism and Unionism; and Banim published *The Boyne Water*.

It would be wrong to lump all of this writing together: Hardiman's cultural analysis showed that Irish literature had a long and distinguished history and aimed to present that literature in a way which would emphasize its archaic nature and civilized qualities. He stressed the integrity and dignity of Irish tradition and pulled no punches in accusing the English of, at best, blind indifference to that tradition; at worst, outright hostility. He is a supremely confident spokesman for Gaelic culture and knows full well that a great deal had been lost. However, when it came to presenting the poetry of that culture to an audience lacking Gaelic he handed over the responsibility for translation to men such as John D'Alton and Thomas Furlong, who were non-poets, whose models were Moore's *Melodies*, and whose language entirely lacks emotional bite or any sting of reality or gravity.

Hardiman was a Catholic nationalist. Ferguson was a Protestant Unionist, with strong nationalist sympathies, and unlike Hardiman's poetaster translators, someone with a gift for forceful, clear and effective language. He tried, in the 1830s, with all the energy of his youthful enthusiasm, to create a cultural space in which the Gaelic past would collaborate with the modern British imperial present, where Irish Catholic and Protestant could come to an accommodation through a better understanding of their respective traditions. At the root of his thinking in the 1830s is the concern to find a way of being in Ireland for Irish people, Catholic and Protestant, so that they can feel at home in the present and attached to the past. He is very conscious that Ireland does not have an adequate system whereby it can represent itself to itself. There has not been a civil evolution, as in England, of the kind described by Burke in the *Reflections*, when he reflects upon what was tested and sustained in the seventeenth century. The Irish Protestants, Ferguson says, have forgotten the liberty to which they are attached as part of the kingdom of Great Britain and Ireland; but the native Irish did not participate in this civil evolution in any way. Protestant and native Irish are 'unable to amalgamate from the want of these intermediate steps upon the civil scale - steps forgotten by the one and never taken by the other'.[16]

Now the Protestants must show the lead. The responsibility is all the greater in that the opportunism of Rome has shown itself in the way the Catholic priests have allied themselves with O'Connell. The Protestants must, if the country is not to be taken over by another Bonaparte, another meddling Jacobinical democratizing tyrant, present their case, and show their countrymen a way of thinking about Ireland which will be inclusive and significant - that is, capable of signifying for now, for the present. Protestant industry must develop a method of enquiry which will have for its object a system of signs, rooted in the country's past, whereby Irish people can 'live back in the land they live in'. In the passage from which this is taken, from the *Dublin University Magazine* in 1840, he is speaking of the enlargement of our 'portion of space, of time, of feeling' that is 'the true source of intellectual pleasure':

> And all this doubling, and trebling, and infinite multiplying of the shares of time, and space, and feeling, originally placed at our disposal, is the result of the observation and recording of facts. All must be set down at first in strict (not dry) detail. . . . What we have to do with, and that to which these observations properly point, is the recovery of the mislaid, but not lost, records of the acts, and opinions, and condition of our ancestors – the disinterring and bringing back to the light of intellectual day, the already recorded *facts,* by which the people of Ireland will be able to *live back,* in the land they live *in,* with as ample and as interesting a field of retrospective enjoyment as any of the nations around us.[17]

Ferguson is imagining a method whereby the 'facts' can be found and one in which past and present, living and dead, can interact. This ideal is what impelled Ferguson to study Irish and to translate the poems he found in Hardiman in ways that make them stand out, lucidly declaring their ability to realize what life is like and how it feels to Irishmen or women. Ferguson is a good translator of Irish verse not just because he is faithful to the originals: it is because he sees them as part of a system of being to which Irish people must have access, must be able to talk about and read and enjoy, if they are to be themselves. He sees the importance of a system of meanings and signs, and mourns the inability of the Hardiman translations to carry it over from one language to another. To do that is to enlarge the possibility of being for any Irishman or woman:

> A plenteous place is Ireland for hospitable cheer,
> Uileacan Dubh O!
> Where the wholesome fruit is bursting from the yellow barley ear;
> Uileacan Dubh O!
> There is honey in the trees where her misty vales expand,
> And her forest paths, in summer, are by falling waters fanned,
> There is a dew at high noontide there, and springs in the yellow sand,
> On the fair hills of holy Ireland.[18]

Ireland is holy to him, because it has the possibility of wholeness.

It is holy because in the small system of this poem the little things, the fruit, the ear of barley, acquire a sacral quality as they link into the expansion of spirit the poem charts in its loving enumeration. The language is renovating the relationships between individual history, place and 'fact'. The things before the eyes of the mind acquire more resonance because of the sacral activity of the poem's language. This is Ferguson's achievement, and it led him to much larger enterprises in poetry and scholarship.

Throughout his life he continued to work to make Irish tradition more of an effective presence in the minds of his contemporaries. His work is full of wild images, huge brooding forms, savage action, declamation. In Ferguson's handling the Gaelic materials, the historical facts of the Gaelic world as well as the insights into the emotions and world view that inform Gaelic literature are transposed into an Irish Victorian idiom. It is an unlikely accommodation, and at times it can produce a sense of strain, but it can also realize bold and startling effects, as in the following passage from 'The Welshmen of Tirawley', where the Lynotts, blinded by having needles driven into their eyeballs, stagger across the stepping-stones of Clochan-na-n'all in Co. Mayo:

> O'er the slippery stepping-stones of Clochan-na-n'all
> They drove them, laughing loud at every fall,
> As their wandering footsteps dark
> Fail'd to reach the slippery mark
> And the swift stream swallow'd stark,
> One and all,
> As they stumbled –
> From the vengeance of the Welshmen of Tirawley.[19]

The stubborn difficult music of this poem derives from the thrill that material of this kind gave Ferguson. But this thrill carried with it a constitutional health warning; wildness of this kind was associated with the Gael, and it was Protestant, Anglo-Irish duty to exercise civic control over passions such as these, very effective in art, vivifying within Irish tradition, but dangerous to civic life.

'Conary' is a poem composed out of those very psychological materials which the Union should strive to incorporate and civilize. Conary is a good king. Since his installation no 'harsh wind ruffled hair upon the side/of grazing beast'. But now his foster-brothers, aided by a British pirate, are going to overthrow him. They experience misgivings about what they are to do and argue that continuity, without which no state can maintain itself, is embodied in the crown and its institutions. The constitutional model here is Burke's, the materials are from the Gaelic saga *Togail Bruidne Da Derga* (*The Destruction of Da Derga's Hostel*), but there are all kinds of narrative tensions. Conary represents stability, and his rule is described in language that derives from Burke, but he is a Gaelic king. The usurpers are British *and Irish*; the world Ferguson's saga-adaptation presents is one riven by conflict, division, superstition, taboo; and the mood is one of savage desperation. One of the usurpers has second thoughts, and describes the effect that killing Conary will have as follows (he is addressing the British pirate):

> We gave thee not
> Licence to take the life, the soul itself
> Of our whole nation, as you now would do,
> For, slay our reverend sages of the law,
> Slay him who put the law they teach in act;
> Slay our sweet poets, and our sacred bards,
> Who keep the continuity of time
> By fame perpetual of renowned deeds;
> Slay our experienced captains who prepare
> The youth for martial manhood, and the charge
> Of public freedom, as befits a state
> Self-governed, self-sufficing, self-contained;
> Slay all those who minister our loftier life,
> Now by this evil chance assembled here,
> You leave us but the carcass of a state,
> A rabble ripe to rot, and yield the land
> To foreign masters and perpetual shame.[20]

The thought here is that of Burke, modified by the ideas of Thomas Davis. Yeats echoes the line about self-government in a surprising place, in 'A Prayer for my Daughter', which asks that in a time of anarchy, his daughter may be allowed to recover innocence in 'one dear perpetual place' (the word 'perpetual' is echoed also; Yeats *studied* Ferguson):

> Considering that, all hatred driven hence,
> The soul recovers radical innocence

> And learns at least that it is self-delighting
> Self-appeasing, self-affrighting.[21]

Ferguson's ideal of the state becomes a statement about the soul, which takes up too Davis's notion of a nation's spirit and converts it to a private spiritual significance.

Irishness was a quality to be admired and understood, but it should have, to Ferguson's way of thinking, a British framework otherwise it would remain outlandish and outside the law. This is the Burkean, Unionist approach to the problem of Irish identity within the British Isles. The continuity of Irish tradition could be sustained in this compromise, by being translated into the larger body of the Empire, just as Irish poetry and saga can be translated into English, if the translator is faithful to his originals and sensitive to the new language. But Irish people felt differently; they experienced a difference from England, and that difference would not go away. It is there in Ferguson's harsh stanza forms, and in the narrative strains of 'Conary'.

Ferguson cannot see Ireland simply as a place to be, and his language is agitated by so many considerations, political, cultural, propagandist, sectarian, that it cannot open out to become a system of representation for a mind fully engaged with, fully informed by, life. This is not to deny that he wrote some very fine poems, but simply to recollect that with Ferguson we are with one of the major figures of nineteenth century Irish literature, and yet we cannot even begin to compare him with, say, Victorian writers and cultural commentators such as Ruskin, Carlyle or Tennyson. He simply does not have access to a language capable of representing the broad conspectus of experience and of relating past and present in a confident assumption that there is such a thing as a coherent tradition. It is in these assumptions and confidences that Victorian authority is grounded, but for an Irish Victorian there would be, continually, for all the desire to anneal and compromise, a profound sense of rupture, unease and strain. In the twentieth century, ironically, artistic authority is grounded in just these discontinuities: 'we sing in our uncertainty', wrote Yeats.

James Clarence Mangan, in whom Yeats had an interest for a time, sang in uncertainty. He emerged in the 1830s as a writer with manifold interests, and as one with special insight into extreme Romanticism, particularly that of Germany. There were certain affinities between Ireland and Germany in the early nineteenth century which had to do with the fact that both cultures felt themselves to be under pressure from an imperial threat, in Germany's case that of Napoleon. Mangan was attracted to Germanic nationalism, to the emotional power of the *Stürm und Drang*, and to the emphasis, in the poetry of Herder, Schiller, Goethe and Freiligarth, on spiritual essences. Translation attracted Mangan for all kinds of complex reasons, but mostly because it allowed him a 'cloak' (he used to call himself the 'Man in the Cloak' in the *Comet* and elsewhere) under which he could find a means of expression.

Indirection was temperamental. In Mangan there is a radical sense that self or identity is simply not there: in a long prose piece, 'An Extraordinary Adventure in the Shades', the theme revolves around the idea that it is impossible to speak to anyone because speech presupposes a self, and seeing as there is no such thing as a central self then there can be no direct approach, no open speech. The manifold identities that he saw translation offering was a way out of the difficulty. He translated extensively from German, French, Italian, but also (even though he did not know the languages) from Persian and from Irish.

His translations from Irish are especially interesting because he saw them as allowing him to identify with a cause rather than anatomize his own personal angst. He knew Charles Gavan Duffy, Davis and Mitchel, and wrote for the *Nation*, contributing translations and also propaganda pieces. His version of 'O'Hussey's Ode to the Maguire' is well known, and the conclusion shows how he is drawn emotionally to extremism and violence (in his *Autobiography* he tells us that he loved news of disasters and revolutions):

> Hugh marched forth to the fight – I grieved to see him so
> depart;
> And Lo! tonight he wanders frozen, rain-drenched, sad
> betrayed
> – *But the memory of the lime-white mansions his right*
> *hand hath laid*
> *In ashes warms the hero's heart.*[22]

This translation bears little resemblance to the original austere bardic poem by Eochaidh Ó hEodhusa.

Perhaps Mangan's best poem is the one where he confronts

directly his own fearfully acute sense of non-self and relates it directly to the state of being in Ireland itself. Things are bad, not just on an individual level, but on the level of collective society. There is no mode of signification, no speech; the reality is oppression, suffering, terrible silence and spiritual cold. The poem is 'Siberia', first published in the *Nation* on 18 April 1846, the year of famine:

In Siberia's wastes
Are sands and rocks
Nothing blooms of green or soft,
But the snow-peaks rise aloft
And the gaunt ice-blocks.

And the exile there
Is one with those;
They are part, and he is part,
For the sands are in his heart,
And the killing shows.

Therefore, in those wastes
None curse the Czar
Each man's tongue is cloven by
The North Blast, that heweth night
With sharp scymitar.[23]

In questions of culture and tradition everything comes back to language. Whenever there is a sense of crisis, of something vital being transacted, the words a person uses, in speech or in writing, become crucial. Language is not just a medium for the communication of ideas, as if ideas were some kind of solid substance that can be moved from one brain into another: the language used in a particular situation derives from all the elements that go to make up that situation - politics, sex, hatred, private persuasions and prejudices, memory, and so on. In a critical situation of difficulty or challenge the management that language makes of all these elements will matter greatly; if someone is pleading a special case (as, for example, when Samuel Johnson voices his reservations about Milton as writer and man in his *Life* of the poet), then the style, the disposition of the clauses, the choice and placing of verb and noun, the way abstract is balanced with concrete, will all be crucial. If the balance and co-ordination are not effected then the idea does not communicate, the dignity and authority of the writer or speaker is called into question. Fullness of utterance, a convincing style, depends as much upon the tradition of language the writer inherits as it does upon individual talent. There is a great deal of sense in the apparently paradoxical axiom of Heidegger's that it is language, not man, which speaks.

For nineteenth-century Irish writers the language available to them was, of course, English, but English associated with the authority and power of Burke's definition of the British constitution. They had no language of their own.

This is a baffling statement, at face value. But one must consider that we are here not speaking of language simply as a medium of communication, but as a cultural system, full of signs and referents, which call up associations and relations that are rooted in the past and are activated by the disposition and evocative power of the words we use. Each entry into speech, if we consider closely enough, is a remaking of the past and our past selves. Such a delicate operation will only take place successfully if one of two preconditions are met: either the tradition of thought and feeling which the language represents is well and truly established, so that the individual speech act can link up with given persuasions and feelings, prejudices of the mind or the emotions; or, the individual speech act is so forceful as to make its own history and establish itself.

In the nineteenth century there were good Irish poets, but none with the sheer downright force of personality to establish his or her own traditions. Ferguson, Hardiman, Callanan, Mangan and others looked for a tradition and what was there before them was Burke, the British/Irish constitutionalist. There was no Irish way of being, apart from that in the Irish countryside, which they were prepared to sentimentalize, but hardly to live out. When they wished to speak of any matters of serious concern they did not have that 'retrospective field', of which Ferguson wrote in 1840, into which their words could move. Swift, the dissenting Republicans, the United Irishmen of 1798, these were now a world away (Moore spoke of the men of '98 as the *ultimi Romanorum*). What was present and defined, with a very secure sense of its legitimacy, was the modern British Empire, with its language, into which Irishness, somehow, would have to be translated. Ireland had gone, for a time. It was re-forming itself in the O'Connellite masses, who had their own powerful popular culture in English and in Irish, but that had little or no effect on literary culture and its ideas of tradition for some considerable time.

3

GEORGE MOORE

'The law of change is the law of life'

'Life has no other goal but life, and art has no other end but to make life possible, to help us to live.'

George Moore to Eduoard Dujardin, June 1903

Many pictures, even caricatures, of George Moore have been created, and he himself has contributed to the range, his own being often the most farcical. There is George Moore the aesthete, the finical young man in Paris, with a python in the corner of his room, trying to be an artist, and friend to Renoir, Monet, Pissarro, Berthe Morisot. He became a Wagnerite, and made the pilgrimage to Bayreuth with his cousin Edward Martyn. He admired Zola intensely for his unrelenting realism, his readiness to describe the squalor of the lives of those deprived by fate, or burnt up by the furnaces of nineteenth century capitalist enterprise. He loved Flaubert, for his cold, incisive appraisal of the meanness of the human heart, the narrowness of its designs. He became an enthusiast for the Celtic Twilight, and went out in search of the old pagan deities with A.E. (George Russell), finding only, incidentally, a pair of serious, black-suited Presbyterians from the North of Ireland. He wrote novels about women, that could be called feminist in tone and politics. He developed the interior monologue independently of Joyce, adapting Eduoard Dujardin's mechanistic attempts to convey the flurry of thought in *Les Lauriers sont Coupés* to a subtle and sinuous stylistic impressionism, that depicts the pulses and shifts of the mind as it moves around a problem, an idea or an obsession. He wrote a comic autobiography where Moore himself is subject, narrator, and the butt of many of the jokes. His deeply religious temperament led to novels exploring the nature of the spiritual impulse in men and women, as well as a version of the gospel story, the latter of which is amongst his greatest achievements. His flair as a storyteller, learnt in the stables of Moore Hall and the houses around Ballinrobe and Lough Carra as a boy, matured into a strange and unique finesse in his later work, breathing an airy freedom of pure narrative invention.

But where in all of this is the real Moore? What set of particular tensions drove him to work (and work he did, incessantly) to be an artist, a writer? His interests were manifold: he studied society, religion, politics, music, painting, history, language: but what preoccupied him more than anything was how character may be made or unmade - realized, or left go to waste. In this sense, because of his abiding concern with what may be said to constitute an individual life, how it may be developed, shaped, and understood, he is a moralist. And he is fascinated too with those forces and tendencies, whether inside or outside the personality, which inhibit the development of a life, a character. The achievement of the personal conscience, as Fr Gogarty put it to himself in *The Lake,* is a great achievement, and that novel, along with many others, shows the difficulties inherent in releasing the 'personal conscience' or the 'soul', the 'inner life', all terms he used to describe his central preoccupation, from constraint. Not something to be conjured by powerful images, in Moore's view, this 'soul' is a thing that is wavering, changeable, but insistent. And, he maintains throughout his work, not to listen to the call of instinct, which is the soul seeking its own space in an individual life, is a kind of death. Moore's work is full of deaths and resurrections.

Moore has been spoken of as a kind of feminist, and his first major novel shows us a girl breaking resolutely from a life of dead cliché, fixed opinions, casual indifference. Alice Barton in *A Drama in Muslin* (1886) turns her back on the world of petty privilege and nasty competitiveness that is the world of the Irish landed aristocracy in their decline at the end of the nineteenth century. Moore's picture of this society, the background to his theme of psychological and feminist liberation in this novel, is a devastating one. The landlord class has given itself over to triviality; and a coarse materialism is evident everywhere, particularly in the marriage market which revolves around Dublin Castle. Girls are trained to disport themselves there, quite shamelessly making the best of their physical attributes - and

Moore explicitly connects this crass commoditization of sex with prostitution.

Alice, her mother says, seems to delight in 'holding opinions no-one else does'.[1] She refuses to give in, inside herself, to the prevailing ethos. But there is nothing hysterical about her protest; rather is it a quiet restrained attentiveness to a core of value, of integrity, that Moore makes no attempt to analyse. He suggests it by describing her quality of intent awareness of nature, always a healing force in Moore, and her resolute patience in adapting to an unglamorous life of unpretentious industry as the journalist-wife of the equally quiet, equally hardworking Dr Reed. A quality of grey steadfastness, a secular and commonplace fortitude, is what we find ourselves admiring in Alice Barton. Hers is a quiet but profound rejection of the wild amorality of the landlord society that produced her; and Moore's writing, sombre and controlled, registers a possibility, not quite mounting to affirmation, that the soul, the self, may find a space for itself, even if it is in a shoddy, recently built London suburb, where the trees are dusty and the gardens small.

Esther Waters (1894) moves very close to pessimism. A study of Esther's harsh life as housemaid, single parent, long-suffering wife of an addictive gambler, it is unremitting in its portrayal of human cruelty and indifference. But Esther Waters is never broken down by life. The novel unfolds a relentless series of misfortunes but she survives it all with 'Saxon' steadfastness, courage and self-respect. She retains her dignity and exhibits an utter fidelity to her dominating instinct: her love for her boy Jack.

The novel is very like Zola in the unflinching picture it gives of society's victims: the gamblers, the drunks, the hopeless, the obsessed. Some of the most powerful writing in the book describes the 'baby farmer' Mrs Spires, who takes care of the babies of mothers who are employed as wet nurses by the rich. Mrs Spires does not feed her charges too assiduously (they quickly get ill on the unboiled milk); and indeed she's prepared to kill them for the small consideration of £5. But Moore's pity in this writing does not shift into moral indignation at society's injustices; indeed, it includes Mrs Spires herself in its scope. This is life, he is saying, it is cruel and hard, incredibly so at times, and yet Esther faces up to it, remains resolute, does not become a victim. Nor is her capacity for suffering and sacrifice glorified. As Moore wrote in *The Lake* (1905; revised 1921):

> we cannot sacrifice ourselves all our life long, unless we begin to take pleasure in the immolation of self, and then it is no longer sacrifice.[2]

And here too there is no obsessional fixation on Esther's part, or on Moore's, with suffering; just a steady adjustment to what life presents, an integrity grounded in the simple love for her boy. The writing is immaculately alive to event: the narrative is effectively clear and pure, in that there is no attempt to generalize or draw conclusions about the nature of society. Instead we get crystal-clear sequence. The narrative flows effortlessly around Esther, who remains steadfast and entirely simple. There are moments of great tenderness, as when she looks at her little boy Jack running before her on a January morning:

> They were in the midst of those few days of sunny weather which come in January, deluding us so with their brightness and warmth that we look round for roses and are astonished to see the earth bare of flowers. And these bright afternoons Esther spent entirely with Jackie. At the top of the hill their way led through a narrow passage between a brick wall and a high paling. She had always to carry him through this passage, for the ground there was sloppy and dirty, and the child wanted to stop to watch the pigs through the chinks in the boards. But when they came to the smooth, wide, high roads overlooking the valley, she put him down, and he would run on ahead, crying, 'Time for a walk, mummie, tum along', and his little feet went so quickly beneath his frock that it seemed as if he were on wheels.[3]

The novel concludes with the grown boy, kitted out for life and its dangers, in a scene alive to the vulnerability of young manhood:

> A tall soldier came through the gate. He wore a long red cloak, and a small cap jauntily set on the side of his close-clipped head. Esther uttered a little exclamation, and ran to meet him.[4]

The eye of the painter is there in that detail of the cap, jauntily set. There is a sense of Renoir or Monet, his friends in Paris.

Esther's strength is an inner core of resolve, but the novel does not attempt to explore those instincts of love and duty which keep her sure. They are simple truths, registered profoundly but unanalysed.

In the 1890s Moore was casting about for directions: Wagner, Schopenhauer, aestheticism, all beckoned. But his main objective, and his dilemma as a writer, he summed up in one of his two Wagnerian novels, *Sister Teresa* (1901):

> With words you can tell the exterior facts of life, but you cannot tell the intense yet involuntary life of the soul – that intricate and unceasing life, incomprehensible as an ant heap, and so personal though it is involuntary.[5]

What he was after was a new form for a new content. He wanted his fiction to turn inward, and he wondered how he could develop a style which would convey that 'underlife' or inner life, the soul's own music, that moves and shifts ceaselessly, according to Moore. In an essay in *Cosmopolis* in 1893 he defined this 'underlife' as 'that vague, undefinable yet intensely real life that lies beneath our consciousness, that life which knows, wills, and perceives without help from us'.[6] Therein, he believed, was to be found the core of personality. A style which would try to capture this inner reality should work cumulatively, should be aware of, indeed embody, evanescence; it should present its material in such a way as to *illuminate* (Moore's word) sensation, experiences, insights; so that they become charged with an inner pressure, and outer and inner become reconciled. His own life, his own soul, was, he felt, unresearched, an untilled field. Or to change the image, it was a lake that had to be crossed.

The return to Ireland to take part in the Irish Literary Revival gave him new material, and helped him discover a new form, and a different style, a style for depicting the movements of being, its changing states.

Towards the end of the 1890s Moore began to think that England was becoming drearily masculine. The Boer War he saw as evidence of a new imperialist materialism and inflexibility. In *Ave* (1911), the first volume of *Hail and Farewell*, he describes how he could see the greed for the gold-fields in Pretoria disfiguring the faces of anonymous people in Piccadilly:

'everybody's bearing and appearance suggested to me a repugnant sensual cosmopolitanism.'[7]

The English landscape darkened on him; English poetry, his beloved Shelley's *Prometheus Unbound* even, failed to rouse him out of his disaffection. He became annoyed by the verbal system of the language itself, thinking that English verbs had lost their charge. He described it as 'a woolly language without a verbal system or agreement between the adjectives and nouns'.[8]

All of this, needless to say, tells us more about Moore's state of mind at the time than it does about England or the English language. We recognize, as Moore himself did later (his moods of these years are ironically replayed in *Hail and Farewell* (1911–14)), the inane simplifications of hysteria. Not surprisingly, given this attitude, and the fact that at the time he was engaged in trying to guide Yeats out of the mythological tangle of Fomors and Tuatha Dé Danann he had got himself into in writing *The Shadowy Waters,* one day Cathleen ni Houlihan herself put in an appearance while he was gazing at the Burren. 'A sentimental craving for the country itself', was what he called the emotion that this experience aroused in him, 'a certain pity, at variance with my character, that had seemed to rise out of my heart.'[9] He is describing, not without embarrassment, a sense of *personal* relationship with the country that many Irishmen feel. It is often conveniently defined negatively, by establishing England as an opposite to be hated, a mechanical male brutality rummaging Ireland's feminine compliance, and this is the disturbing process that Moore chronicles for us in *Hail and Farewell.* He had become susceptible.

Life darkened for him, and he found himself in a situation, appalling for a realist, where his moods no longer easily engaged with the patterns of daily life. His underlife had come adrift of the external world. It was a time of psychological and artistic crisis and it was evidently a very disturbing thing for him to hear, on the Hospital Road in Chelsea, a voice coming, not from within, but without, urging him to 'go to Ireland'.[10] However one chooses to regard this (and though Moore makes fun of the whole thing in the aloof irony of *Hail and Farewell,* it is far from certain that this was his attitude at the time), there is no doubt that in returning to Ireland he was trying to be true to an impulse from his own unconscious.

There were other reasons, too, more amenable to rational

evaluation, for his return. He was, with Edward Martyn and W.B. Yeats, a director of the Irish Literary Theatre; he had become convinced of the desirability of reviving the Irish language, and had written and spoken on behalf of the Gaelic League (even threatening to disinherit his brother Maurice's children if they were not brought up in Irish). He was enthralled by Yeats's transcendental idealism, so much at odds, he thought, with the sobriety of the Saxon, which now bored, where it once had called forth his admiration, as in *Esther Waters*. But in the end, he was following his instincts. He had reached a turning point, a crisis, of which his estrangement from England and his eccentric attitude towards the education of his brother's children were symptoms. His life had gone dead on him, psychologically and artistically, and the way out was to leave, to go into exile from his dead life and make a new life for himself in the old place.

The Irish language, which, he wrote to his brother, 'interests me more than anything else', seemed to incorporate, in what he knew, in theory, of its concreteness and lack of abstraction, this new life.[11] Though he was, he thought, too old to learn the language, he formed the idea of assisting the Gaelic Revival by writing stories of Irish life, to be translated into Irish by Tadhg O'Donoghue for publication in the Jesuit periodical, the *New Ireland Review*, which was edited by Fr Tom Finlay. Three of the stories appeared in the journal - the Irish versions of 'The Wedding Gown' ('An Gúna Phósta'), 'Almsgiving' ('An Déirc') and 'The Clerk's Quest' ('Tóir Mhic Uí Dhíomasuigh') - but the editor felt that the subsequent stories, 'Homesickness' and 'The Exile', could not be included because of the increasing bitterness of Moore's attacks on the Irish Catholic clergy. Thus developed the collection *The Untilled Field* (1903).

After a lengthy engagement with late nineteenth century English Catholicism in *Evelyn Innes* (1898) and *Sister Teresa* (1901), Moore, almost as soon as he returned to Ireland, began to formulate the idea that the cultural and emotional stagnation that he found there were attributable to the inflexibility of its religious institutions. Where in England he had imagined Ireland a domain of spiritual freshness and vivid life, he now began to see it as a place petrified by a pious anxiety to keep life orderly and respectable. The priests, in Moore's view, went in for dreary and abstract transcendentalism, shored up by platitude, denying the changeableness that he saw as life's very essence.

Art, Moore argued, remains faithful to the changing quality of life's patterns; it does not simplify, console or dictate. As he wrote his Irish stories he began to rediscover the flexibility of the artist. Like the priests who became the object of his ridicule in 'The Exile' or 'Some Parishioners', he had, on leaving England, been guilty of a kind of inflexibility, the inflexibility of a man with a cause. Now he was beginning to see Ireland as it was, through his writing, which meant detaching himself from those simplicities he had created about Ireland out of his own emotional need. Again, the writing involved a departure from a dead view of life into a fuller, because more lively, version of the way things were. He was going into exile from a false self into a realization of a truer one. Exile, thought of in this way, may be the necessary condition for a writer to be in: it means forsaking the old moulds assumed out of duty, obligation, hysteria or exhaustion, to accommodate the self to the new shapes life continually evolves.

Why, it might be asked, is Moore, in *The Untilled Field* and indeed *The Lake*, so interested in the priests of a Church which he regards as a stranglehold on the spontaneity of life in Ireland? One of the reasons why he can write so well of them, why the play of irony often sharpens into anger, is that he himself knew only too well the attraction, for a mind not self-possessed, of a code of fixed ideas, a cause. There was in Moore (as in Joyce) a good deal of the priest. He wrote well of the comforts of the presbytery, the beeswaxed security of the convent, but he also showed, in the writing he did in Ireland (and subsequently), that life's impulses are constantly escaping the constraints orthodoxy would place upon them. This makes him, as a writer, capable of celebration.

Characteristically, the celebration is often tempered by the sense that the freedom obtained by throwing off the old ways can be a bleak freedom. It is so for Catherine in 'The Exile', who leaves the comfort of the convent for the difficult 'loneliness' of the outside world: she marries a man whom she loves but who doesn't particularly care for her, and who is an ineffectual. Much the finest man in the story is her husband's brother, James, who is in love with her, and because of that goes to America, leaving the farm for the couple. There is no simple message here; the story presents the complex difficulties of life's choices with objectivity and sympathy. Moore does not develop an interior life for James which would allow us to see his decision to leave for America as an inevitable progression of his nature: it is an abrupt story, but also delicate, in that it does not belie the way life transforms one set of situations into another.

Kate Kavanagh, in 'The Wedding Feast', like Catherine, leaves for America, escaping from her arranged marriage to Peter MacShane. She knows 'there's no judging for oneself' in Ireland, and opts for the unpredictability of her own nature, her own odd, aloof freedom, which can, on the morning of crisis, after she has kept her husband of a few hours out of her bedroom, allow her to think that elderflower water is good for the complexion.

To begin with, the stories of *The Untilled Field* were written for a cause, the Gaelic Literary Revival, but gradually, as his understanding of Ireland and his relationship with it complicated, the writing moved from those fixed ideas and illusions. It became a mode of exploring the shifting unpredictability of life, its constant susceptibility to change, and in so doing it grew freer, more accurate, in that it too drew closer to the way things are, thereby acquiring a better, because more humane and flexible, quality of judging.

The story 'Almsgiving', though it does not have Ireland or the clergy for its theme, is all about the change from a set of false ideas to a fuller engagement with an enlarged view of the state of things. At the beginning the narrator meets a blind beggar in a dark passageway and searches his pockets for a penny, but the rain coming on, he walks quickly away. The narrator is oppressed by the thought of the bleak life of the beggar, and he imagines how much fuller it could be. From then on the narrator avoids the blind man's dark place, until one day, on an impulse, he goes back. They talk, and to his amazement, he finds that the object of his sentimental pity has a family, that the children go on holidays to the seaside, and that the blind man has a friend, a policeman, who takes him out on day excursions. The story concludes:

> A soft south wind was blowing, and an instinct as soft and gentle filled my heart, and I went towards some trees. The new leaves were beginning in the high branches. I was sitting where sparrows were building their nests, and very soon I seemed to see farther into life than I had ever seen

> before. 'We're here,' I said, 'for the purpose of learning what life is, and the blind beggar has taught me a great deal, something that I could not have learnt out of a book, a deeper truth than any book contains. . . .' And then I ceased to think, for thinking is a folly when a soft south wind is blowing and an instinct as soft and gentle fills the heart.[12]

There is a Joycean quality in these cadences, in the soft repetitions, but also in the quality of the insight. Gaucheness intrudes, too: all the sermonizing about learning and teaching is heavy-handed, but it in no way invalidates the depth the writing sounds. Moore is celebrating a reawakening to life from the deathly rigour of prejudice and opinion. The narrator thinks the blind man's life a dismal thing, lived out in darkness, but in the end it is he who receives alms: the gift of comprehension of the beggar's life, its variety and richness. The shallowness of the earlier neurotic and obsessed reaction is contrasted with the humanity of the later. The narrator divests himself of the encumbering comfort of 'several coats' of prejudice to discover a more complex understanding. 'Instinct' is the word Moore has for it here, and it is the awakening of Fr Gogarty's instinctual life that is his main preoccupation in *The Lake* (1905).

As he wrote *The Untilled Field* he worked deeper, finding access here and there, but in no easily consistent way, to the buried lives of the people and the country, whose experience he wished to delineate. But it is only in *The Lake* that he overcomes the artistic difficulty of working into the 'underlife' in a completely convincing way. Moore's technique of interior narration, and the fluid style he finds for it, knit Gogarty's mind to the landscape around Lough Carra so intrinsically that its changing colours and shifting moods become an impressionist illumination of the changing quality of Gogarty's own mind.

Caught in a web of Irish frustration, timidity, remorse and self-hate, Gogarty gradually, and with great difficulty, learns to attend to the changing process of life within him, the fluid wisdom of instinct. By hearkening to that, the 'lake in every man's heart',[13] Gogarty comes into possession of himself for the first time.

The Untilled Field shows us how complicated Moore's preoccupation with Ireland was, how it seemed a place of great simplicity and naturalness by comparison with England, but how it was also hampered by prejudices and conventions of its own. The great tyrannizer over life's natural instincts was the Church, the dreary institutionalism of which seemed to inhibit every living nerve from spontaneity. The only way out, in the stories, was exile, with the danger that the exile might leave, only to find himself caught in the webs spun out of his *own* rigidity, his *own* tyranny over his natural self. The mind is good at making traps to catch itself and one of the most effective of these is to imagine an exterior cause as responsible for a personal fault.

The Lake, which, Moore said in the preface to the 1921, greatly revised, edition, belonged 'so strictly' with the stories that his memory included them in the same volume, is all about leaving and what it means, or about what it means to leave responsibly. It concentrates and deepens the concerns of the Irish short stories. The plot is very simple: Fr Gogarty, parish priest of Garranard on the shores of Lough Carra, casts out Nora Glynn, the attractive young schoolmistress who has become pregnant, by speaking against her from the altar. He is a tyrannizer, a judger, over her, but over himself as well. A correspondence develops, first with Fr O'Grady, who looked after Nora when she first came to London; then with Nora herself, during the course of which Gogarty realizes that he has loved her all along and that his public attack on her was powered by his sexual jealousy. He made her the victim of his own affliction. There was a failure of humanity, which, through great distress and serious illness, he comes to recognize. He realizes that his own life has been a dead one, shored by custom. She, with her individuality, her style, wakened him out of his stasis, but as soon as she did he wanted her for himself and no one else. Eventually he decides that the only thing for him to do is to make a complete break with his life in Garranard and go to America. At the end of the book he swims the lake, the book's presiding symbol, leaving his clothes by the shore so that his parishioners will presume him drowned.

Moore finds depth in *The Lake* by making the consciousness of the priest, evolving towards self-knowledge, the central focus of the book. Like the peasants of *The Untilled Field* and like his own parishioners, Gogarty belongs to the landscape around him: born and bred there he knows it intimately, even thinking of writing its history. But unlike his parishioners he feels estranged from it as well; he senses that he has got into a rut and needs to change. Moore, in the novel, makes the landscape a constant reflection of his changing thought, as changeable as the differing colours and atmospheres of the lake. Gogarty entertains a scheme to bridge Lough Carra; but the lake is the pool of his instinctual life, his source, his core, troubled by his relationship with Nora Glynn. Moore's writing creates a unity between exterior and interior; the style itself is adapted to convey Gogarty's vacillations, the tone of his mind. It is fluid, impressionistic, searching in its meditative syntax. Often he does not know what he thinks, and the style re-enacts that hesitant sensitivity, that doubtful wavering between one thought and another.

Through the technical expedient of making the flux of his mind the centre of the novel, the intolerance or the slightly comic sympathy Moore tends to have towards the priests in *The Untilled Field* deepens into a more human understanding in *The Lake*. This is why Moore wrote in the 1921 preface that the novel holds a special place in his affections because of the difficulty overcome in the telling:

> the one vital event in the priest's life befell him before the story opens, and to keep the story in the key in which it was conceived, it was necessary to recount the priest's life during the course of his walk by the shores of the lake, weaving his memories continually, without losing sight, however, of the long, winding, mere-like lake, wooded to its shores, with hills appearing and disappearing into mist and distance. The difficulty overcome is a joy to the artist, for in his conquest over the material he draws nigh to his idea, and in this book mine was the essential rather than the daily life of the priest, and as I read for this edition, I seemed to hear it. The drama passes within the priest's soul; it is tied and untied by the flux and reflux of sentiments, inherent in and proper to his nature, and the weaving of a story out of the soul substance without ever seeking the aid of external circumstance seems to me a little triumph. It may be that all ears are not tuned, or are too indifferent or indolent to listen; it is easier to hear 'Esther Waters' and to watch her struggle for her child's life than to hear the mysterious warble, soft as lake water, that abides in the heart.[14]

Gogarty comes into possession of himself by leaving 'the dead wisdom of codes and formulas, dogmas and opinions'. He seeks in the end what he calls a 'vagrancy of ideas and affections' but it is a wise vagrancy, attentive to 'the law of change which is the law of life'.[15] The swim across the lake which concludes the novel, beginning with the sheer physical delight of a muscular naked body striving against the dark moonlit water, ending in cold, exhaustion and a touch of fear, is, in its complexity, a fitting coda to this intricate novel, which depicts the shifting quality of the human personality in its troubled relations with itself and the world outside. The lake and the untilled fields about it become an image of the complex interaction between the inscrutable impulses of the unconscious and the multitudinous world beyond it which it only comes to know with great difficulty. The 'difficulty overcome', to which Moore refers, is the difficulty of finding a form for this complexity, and this he did by finding a style for Gogarty's 'essential life', his 'soul'.

'The law of change is the law of life,' Gogarty says, but Moore has his priest discover the peculiar and eccentric patterns of his nature, a discovery which frees him from the ready-made opinions of others: 'there is no moral law except one's own conscience . . . the moral obligation of every man is to separate the personal from the impersonal conscience.'[16]

The discovery of personal conscience, Gogarty thinks, frees one to love, love being participation; but participation with life involves a simultaneous recognition of the self and the validity of other lives. What Moore celebrates in *The Lake* is the moral flexibility (not indifference) that Gogarty attains through discovering his own inner self, which involves an encounter with that which is other.

In *Hail and Farewell* Moore's comic vision flows out of a sense of the absurdity of those who, for whatever reason, fail to acknowledge their fluid humanity, their ever-changingness, the difference and indifference of others. Instead they set up static images of themselves with which they make their behaviour comply. The fluid technique of *Hail and Farewell* owes much to Moore's presentation of Gogarty's moral realization in *The Lake*, his technical breakthrough in that novel.

If we compare *Hail and Farewell* with Yeats's *Autobiographies* we may find by contrast Moore's defining qualities. Moore's autobiographical study of his part in the Irish Literary Revival acted as a catalyst to Yeats's own major autobiographical undertakings, which began with *Reveries over Childhood and Youth* (1914). Angered by Moore's churlish treatment of him in *Vale*, the closing line of Yeats's collection *Responsibilities* (1914) comments that he has become a 'post' for passing dogs to defile. Yeats's *Autobiographies* are deeply engaged in self-making, building a character, something strong and unified to stand against the modern tide. Essentially tragic in tone and approach, Yeats makes grand gestures of refusal. Darwin, Huxley, Bastien Le Page, the trio of dread materialists that haunt the *Autobiographies*, are rejected along with the age and the values they are made to embody. Yeats stands against them, proud and lonely, along with William Blake, Henry More the Platonist, Mohini Chatterjee (who maintained that all life was illusion, that men danced on deathless feet), MacGregor Mathers, Madame Blavatsky, Lady Gregory. These are all like-minded friends, who prize wisdom, who seek coherence, and are part of Yeats's mythology; they are Olympians. Moore, however, rejects nothing. When he tells us of his hysterical revulsion against England in the 1890s he does so ironically, so we see the comedy of a mind obsessed by zealotry, by inane and hysterical anger. The Dublin through which he moves is vivid with highly individual personalities, who not only cross Moore's path; they affect him and change him, as indeed Ireland itself does. Yeats sees his life as a stage, on which he plays a predestined part which involves conflict with a force which *almost* overwhelms him. That force - materialism, hatred, abstraction, mechanization - is his opposite. The conflict with the opposite is the energy source that drives the oppositional force-fields of his writing. Yeats creates an heroic engagement with history, time and circumstance, in which his language triumphs by subduing these things to its order.

Moore is different. In *Hail and Farewell* there is no heroic fury, but there is no bitterness either. There are antagonisms, such as Moore's attack on Catholicism; but the account of that episode, including his public announcement of conversion to Protestantism in the *Irish Times*, becomes broadly farcical; and his sense of the ridiculous begins with himself. There is no consistory of like-minded individuals; Moore is a strangely solitary figure in the book, apart from the healing and tender friendship with Stella (Clara Christian) who is always associated with nature, like Nora Glynn in *The Lake*. The people he meets, the friendships he forms, are woven into a narrative that is easy and fluent and which moves with a relaxed and confident mastery.

The narrative is that of one who knows that he can move with confidence any way he wishes through his biography because the core is sure. And that core is Moore's renewed sense of self, a freshness and enlargement of being that came to him through his involvement with Ireland, and out of the patient struggle with his material (himself) since the 1880s. It is very hard to convey that sense of buoyant, brimming life in *Hail and Farewell*, because Moore, showing the nonchalance of mastery, does not explain himself or analyse his motives. The account he gives of himself is comic, as if to say: knowing myself as I do, sure of myself as I am, there is no need any longer to strive by assertion, conflict, anger. There is an invigorating freshness, a quality of continuous surprise as the curiously uneventful yet absorbing narrative unfolds. We come to know Moore in all his phases, and yet, still, there is something hidden. A decorum withholds him from confessional. The style, relaxed and sinuous, interweaves art and life in a tapestry that presents us with a shifting impression of a personality, an illumination of being, as embodied in one writer's text. The following extract describes a meeting between himself, Lady Gregory and Sir Edwin Arnold, author of *The Light of Asia*, in which the ex-Indian civil servant versified Buddhist doctrines. His own reactions interweave with the anecdote; the touch is light but sure:

> The conversation turned on the coloured races, and I remember Sir Edwin's words. The world will not be perfect, he said, until we get the black notes into the gamut. A pretty bit of Telegraphese which pleased Lady Gregory; and when Sir Edwin rose to go she produced a fan and asked him to write his name upon one of the sticks. But she did not ask me to write my name, though at that time I had written not only *A Modern Lover*, but also *A Mummer's Wife*, and I left the house feeling for the first time that the world I lived in was not so profound as I had imagined it to be.[17]

In the following vignette of Synge, the man stands forth, illuminated by telling impressions:

> while Synge perished slowly, Gogarty recovered in the same hospital after an operation for appendicitis. One man's scale drops while another goes up. As I write this line I can see Synge, whom I shall never see again with my physical

> eyes, sitting thick and straight in my armchair, his large, uncouth head, and flat, ashen-coloured face with two brown eyes looking at me, not unsympathetically. A thick stubby growth of hair starts out of a strip of forehead like black twigs out of the head of a broom. I see a ragged moustache, and he sits bolt upright in my chair, his legs crossed, his great country shoe spreading over the carpet.[18]

Moore's later fiction has received very little attention. *The Brook Kerith* (1916), a neglected masterpiece, retells the gospel story. It grew out of Moore's fascination with religion, belief and the history of Christianity. Moore's account of the gospel story is startling indeed. Jesus begins in peace and serenity and preaches a simple gospel of love and understanding. Then, maddened by the obtuseness of his disciples, and their craving for vision and miracles, he turns to hatred of human life, and its capacity for bitterness and anger. The scene in which the disciples try to outdo each other with visions is both funny and terrifying; and illustrates the mind's desire for interpretation, fixed meanings, illusion:

> he looked into their faces, as if he would read their souls, and asked them to look up through the tree tops and tell him what they could see in a certain space of sky. In fear of his mood, and lest he might call them feeble of sight or purblind, his disciples, or many among them, fell to disputing among themselves as to what might be discerned by human eyes in the cloud; till John, thinking to raise himself in the master's sight . . . said that he could see a chariot drawn by seven beasts, each having on its forehead seven horses; the jaws of these beasts, he averred, were like those of monkeys, and in their paws, he said, were fourteen golden candlesticks. Andrew being misled by the colour of the cloud which was yellow, said that the seven beasts were like leopards; whereas Philip declared that the beasts were not leopards, for him they were bears and they began to dispute one with the other, some discerning the Father Almighty in a chariot, describing him to be a man garmented in white - His hair is like wool they said. And seated beside him Matthew saw the Son of Man with an open book on his knees. But these visions, to their great trouble, did not seem to interest Jesus; or not sufficiently for

> their intention; and to the mortification of Peter and Andrew, James and John, he turned to Thaddeus and Aristion and asked them what they saw in the clouds.[19]

Angered by human obtuseness, Jesus begins to preach against the world. The difficult Jesus of the gospels, the one who sets son against father, who brings a sword rather than peace, emerges in writing fuelled by Moore's own disgust at Puritan or Jansenist or nationalist zeal. Such a man, poisoned by obsession, Moore implies, is heading for crucifixion. He has lost the simple instinct for life.

Joseph of Arimathea, whose discipleship Jesus had earlier rejected, and who confused wisdom with intensity, having far too much of the latter, becomes Jesus's saviour. Jesus, according to this narrative, did not die on the cross; we are told that he went into a coma, and that Joseph of Arimathea brought him back to health in his garden. Again the healing power of nature is evident, its ability to recall the instinctual life of the soul, to cleanse it of the mire of prejudice, intensity, opinion and conflict. Jesus grows back into life raking the leaves in Joseph's garden. He returns to the mountains where the Essenes live, as a shepherd, wise in his attentiveness to the ordinary acts of life. He is happy here, above Galilee, living an entirely anonymous life, when Paul arrives. Paul, for whom Christ's death is eternal life, is astonished at the old shepherd's words and thinks he's mad. Jesus asks him, out of pity for his activity and desolation, to stay among the Essenes and seek the self, 'for it behoves every man . . . sooner or later to seek himself; and thyself, Paul, if I read thee rightly, hast long been overlooked by thee which is a fault.'[20] Jesus is urging Paul to the simple acceptance of the 'personal conscience', the innate soul. After his experience in Jerusalem, the anger, the hatred and the crucifixion, Jesus tells Paul he had no thoughts, but gradually, he says:

> thought returned to my desolate mind as the spring returns to these hills; and the next step in my advancement was when I began to understand that we may not think of God as a man who would punish men for doing things they never promised not to do, or recompense them for denying themselves things they never promised to forgo . . . if we would arrive at any reasonable conception of God we must not put a stint upon him. And as I wandered with my sheep

> he became in my senses not without but within the universe, part and parcel, not only of the stars and the earth, but of me, yea, even of my sheep on the hillside. All things are God, Paul: thou art God and I am God, but if I were to say that thou art man and I am God, I should be the madman that thou believest me to be.

This is shocking, as shocking as Joyce's *Ulysses* (which advances very similar ideas in the 'Ithaca' section and elsewhere) but all the more so for being so direct and unambiguous. This is the Godless Christianity of Don Cupitt and the later twentieth century. It is also the core of Moore's vision. Literary history has not rescued this book, one of the great spiritual meditations in twentieth century writing, to put beside T.S. Eliot's *Four Quartets* or Nikos Kazantsakis's *Christ Recrucified.* Subtle, powerful and movingly written, the narrative is constructed so as to align itself with the consciousness of the two principal characters, Joseph of Arimathea and Jesus himself. Men betray the simple truth, but that is 'part and parcel' of the way things are; all the time nature waits to release its powers that will invigorate the self in each and every living thing. Something of this sense, of an abiding energy, not without an element of trouble in it, is conveyed in the description of Lake Galilee as Joseph encounters it afresh after two years' absence, studying in Alexandria, at the beginning of the novel.

> The lake had always seemed to him a sort of sign, symbol or hieroglyphic, in which he read a warning especially, if not wholly, to himself. But the message the lake held out to him had always eluded him, and never more completely than now. At the end of a windless spring evening it came into view a moment sooner than he had expected, and in an altogether different aspect - lower than he had ever seen it in memory or reality - and, he confessed to himself, more beautiful. Like a great harp it lay below him, and his eyes followed the coast-lines widening out in the indenture of the hills: on one side desert, on the other richly cultivated ascents, with villages and one great city.[21]

This is not just description, though that is where it begins. It is a style of narrative, involving the smooth flow of a melodic line, which Moore adapted to relate impressions of the outer world to inner moods and feelings, which latter charge the content, so that details become illuminated with a significance, the significance they carry forward, in the changed state of art, from life itself. Again, here, we see the relaxed assurance of the master, effortlessly evolving the shift and play of life in a form which is lucid, supple and cool.

There are still later works, almost entirely unexplored, except by enthusiasts. His last book, *Aphrodite in Aulis* (1930) is a story of utter simplicity. A family tale, of marriages, careers, business, the story is entirely lacking in novelty or sensation. It is set in ancient Greece in Aulis, just across the coast from Euboea, whence the Greek ships left for Troy 5,000 years before the time in which the action is set. The book is serene and full of life, the work of a writer who has sought the self and its mysterious peace; and found narratives to convey its movements. These narratives are attuned to the chords life sounds in its natural and inevitable recurrences. So that the last story Moore tells is about nothing more than father and daughter, son-in-law, grandchildren; the building of a temple on a hillside; the pet wolf the children keep; the stone fountain in the corner of the courtyard; a young couple crossing the straits of Euripus between Aulis and Euboea.

> when the boat entered a sunny inlet she begged him to say if it were not true that there was no country in the world like Greece. We know of none other, Biote, but in no country did a day dawn more beautiful than the one we are breathing. A fish flopped from the cool depths. To glimpse the world above the wave, said Biote; and the slim dragonflies that flit and hover on gauzy wings, each on his business or pleasure, enjoy the morning as we do.[22]

Written in his seventy-seventh year, *Aphrodite in Aulis* unfolds the life of a trading sea-port in the Greece of the fifth century BC. Completed shortly after he had recovered from an operation, the book is crammed with lustrous and vivid perception.

George Moore made himself a master of the arts of narrative. He learned how to unite external impressions with mood and feeling; and in doing so created a style of writing, a quality of active presence, that celebrates the variousness of the actual. A driven man, he knew in himself the obsessions he mocked in others; nor did he spare himself. His commitment to the art of fiction was total, and he grounded it in a spacious reverence for life itself, that spaciousness that issues in a sense of variety, peace and calm. Preoccupied, like many other twentieth century novelists, with the quest for the self, he is unusual in that this search does not issue in large upheavals of psychic storm and stress. There is illness, suffering - such are the prices to be paid for neglect of the soul, Moore implies - but the mood is melancholy rather than despairing when he contemplates fruitless lives and inanition. His other mood is steady and relaxed, that of a man shorn of all illusions, but temperate, gentle and wise; alive to the ever-changingness of life, ready to accept its transformations; and capable of registering such movements in a narrative form spacious enough to accommodate them.

4

W.B. YEATS

'The wheel where the world is butterfly'

'A sudden blow': Yeats liked surprise, violence, the unpredictable, the irrational.[1] He deliberately tried out unusual thought, and often set himself against everyday life and 'normal' thinking. He hated the common dream. To awaken from that was the object of the artist, as he saw it. The artist should 'seek out reality, leave things that seem'.[2] What is real is not what is there before the eyes, under the sun. What is real is the antithesis of the common, the everyday. History, for Yeats, is illusion, a subhuman accountancy of everyday fact. It was imagining that mattered, in defiance of fate and of actuality.

In 'The Fisherman' Yeats tells us that he began imagining, out of scorn of the Ireland of fact, his fisherman, climbing up to the mountain streams. It is a satisfaction to his mind to contemplate the solitude there. This was his 'vision of reality' even though, he says defiantly, the man was 'but a dream':

> All day I'd looked in the face
> What I had hoped 'twould be
> To write for my own race
> And the reality.[3]

He has not forgotten the nationalist aspirations of his youth, when he had hoped to be like Davis, Mangan and Ferguson, singing to 'sweeten Ireland's wrong',[4] and when he had wished, thinking of the example of William Allingham, to have had songs of his sung, the singers not knowing who the author was. In expressing a desire to write for his race Yeats is wholly in line with a great body of European nineteenth century thought which was concerned with race and racial origin. One of the effects of the French Revolution was to cause the European nation states radically to assess their racial identities and the integrity of their institutions, languages and mythologies.

The modern understanding of the British constitution, as defined by Burke, was a powerful and conservative reaction against the kinds of possibilities in human affairs that the French Revolution embodies. Burke's analysis in the *Reflections upon the Revolution in France,* which pointed to a connection between radicalism and tyranny, was borne out in the Reign of Terror, and in the establishment of a new French Empire with Bonaparte as head, which spread throughout Europe as far as Russia. Germany, in particular, was a country which felt its identity deeply threatened by the Napoleonic invasion and much nineteenth century racial and linguistic theorizing originates in a movement which set out to assert the authenticity of Germanness as a means of resisting the might and power of the imperial and revolutionary French armies. This resistance had racial and linguistic elements, and the theoretical basis for it was worked out in the writings of the philosopher Johann Gottlieb von Fichte, and the ethnologist, Wilhelm von Humboldt, among others.

In Berlin in 1807–8 Johann Gottlieb von Fichte delivered a series of *Addresses to the German Nation* in which he outlines the relationship between language and cultural identity, as he understood it. Fichte is worried that the French victory over Prussia in 1806 will mean the extinction of German culture. In these lectures, delivered in Berlin, an occupied city, we have a full statement of the equation between language and culture which became a cornerstone of German Romantic thinking and of Romanticism generally. This equation also had a very considerable effect on the complex of ideas that evolved into nineteenth century nationalist thinking; and became a strand in European thinking about race. Fichte says:

> language is not an arbitrary means of communication, but breaks forth out of the life of understanding as an immediate force of nature.[5]

The essence of the German people, which is under threat by external oppression and an internal failure to grasp the importance of cultural authenticity, is bound up in the language. The people 'do not form the language; it is the language which forms them.'

Later on in the *Addresses* he argues that there can be no literature nor a culture without political independence for the German race, and that the sign of that independence is the language:

> Just as it is beyond doubt that, whenever a separate language is found, there a separate nation exists, which has the right to take independent charge of its affairs and to govern itself; so one can say, on the other hand, that, where a people has ceased to govern itself, it is equally bound to give up its language and to coalesce with its conquerors, in order that there may be unity and internal peace and complete oblivion of relationships which no longer exist.[6]

Wilhelm von Humboldt, who also emphasized the importance of the integrity of race, formulated a view of the inner form of language in his later writings on the Kawi language of Java, after a lifetime's study of language and its origins. He held that each people has its own world outlook and that that was to be found in the inner form of the language. A people who lose touch with their 'inner form' lack a sense of life. This inner form occasions certain deep attitudes and predispositions, and is the ground or 'spirit' of a nation, 'an involuntary emanation of the mind of a nation'.[7]

What is remarkable about these early nineteenth century German meditations on ethnolinguistics for the historian of Irish literature is the way in which the writings of Davis, Young Ireland, Mangan, Ferguson, on the integrity of nationhood and the importance of indigenous culture, follow the German example. A race is conceived of as a unit, with a spiritual dimension, and one which realizes itself and represents itself in language primarily and in culture generally.

At the end of the century Yeats saw himself as continuing the work of Mangan and Davis. John O'Leary lent him the writings of Young Ireland. He met Maud Gonne, who was a nationalist and an active one, and he came to know Douglas Hyde, whose thinking about the relation between the Irish language and the essential being of the Irish people linked back to Young Ireland and beyond them to the Germans. Yeats admired Hyde's idea that the inner nature of a people was to be found in their language. He did not know Irish, but he studied Irish legends, stories and folktales, the object being to discern, through them, the 'emanation' of the 'nation's mind' of which von Humboldt spoke.

Yeats, in opting for this approach to Irish culture was identifying himself with one of the two main streams in nineteenth century tradition; that to do with Romanticism, the quest for origin, and for the inner forms of meaning. In making this choice he was turning aside from the other tradition, identified with his father, J.B. Yeats: that of positivism, scientific realism and materialism. W.B. Yeats hated what he regarded as the mechanical intellects of Darwin, Huxley and Bastien Le Page, because they preoccupied themselves, in his view, with matter when they should be seeking the spirit; with realism when vision was the only reality; with social organization rather than with the inner structures of a people; and with dissection rather than with wonder. Yeats chose wonder and sought out the lineaments of race and his own version of reality, which is the opposite of what is commonly conceived of as such: 'Seek out reality, leave things that seem.'[8]

Yeats from very early on disliked the kind of dissection of personality he saw in the novels of George Eliot, which he regarded as being just another example of scientific rationalism, as if the essence of a person could be uncovered by mechanical analysis. The underlying passions and moods in a character were more significant to Yeats than the eccentricities of specific aspects of behaviour because they were connected to larger patterns of feeling which derived from the collective racial memory. You did not find out about yourself by self-analysis and introspection, but by studying legend, mythology and language, where the larger passions and dominant patterns of thought were evident. Myth, legend, language revealed the emotional disposition of a people or a nation and put the individual in contact with tradition.

When Yeats describes Samuel Ferguson in his first published piece of criticism, he sees him as being opposed to the commonplace Victorian life of his own time. Ferguson matters because he did what all real poets should do, in Yeats's view – he sought out race, and the dominant emotions of personality. He made his search by disinterring legends, and this activity, in Yeats's view, made him 'real', because he was acting in defiance of the futility and pointlessness of the life around him. At the very beginning of his article, published in *The Irish Fireside* for 9 October 1886,

Yeats sets out his priorities, which were also Ferguson's. There are seven great cycles of legends:

> all differing one from the other as the peoples differed who created them. Every one of these cycles is the voice of some race celebrating itself, embalming for ever what it hated and loved. Back to their legends go, year after year, the poets of the earth, seeking the truth about nature and man, that they may not be lost in a world of mere shadow and dream.[9]

The poets seek the truth, so that they may not be lost in this world, so apparently real, but which is really a dream. When Yeats was living in London in the 1890s, meeting with the poets and writers in what is known as the Rhymers' Club, he admired them because they seemed to have found out the lie of everyday life; which is, that it pretends to be most important. In 'Ego Dominus Tuus', twenty years further on again, he remembers Lionel Johnson and Ernest Dowson, his friends of the 1890s, as men who had 'found life out and were awakening from the dream'. Yeats makes this statement in *Per Amica Silentia Lunae,* a work to which 'Ego Dominus Tuus' is the poetic preface. In the poem he writes of what the poet searches for; and it is clear that his attitude has not changed in essence since his first published essay, that on Ferguson:

> The rhetorician would deceive his neighbours,
> The sentimentalist himself; while art
> Is but a vision of reality.
> What portion of the world can the artist have
> Who has awakened from the common dream
> But dissipation and despair.[10]

This is a harsh statement, but he is thinking of the fates of his friends: Johnson died young, from a fall in a public house; and Dowson, who also died young, was frustrated in love. This was the price they paid for breaking out of the comfort of the everyday into a different kind of reality.

Art rejects the commonsensical and the mechanical world to turn to another order of reality where larger patterns and dominant modes of feeling are discerned. The artist is not interested in self (in Yeats at least) or in self-interest: he seeks the opposite of that, the anti-self, and this, in Yeats, is connected to the emotions of race, of multitude. This is what he says about the anti-self, again from *Per Amica Silentia Lunae*:

> The other self, the anti-self or the antithetical self, as one may choose to name it, comes but to those who are no longer deceived, whose passion is reality.[11]

Literary criticism has perhaps become over-accustomed to the discussion of Yeats's idea of the anti-self, but that should not hide from us the strangeness and the radical quality of the notion. We should not domesticate it as a piece of Yeatsian stock-in-trade. It is central to Yeats's entire pattern of thinking and is linked to his particular and very intriguing ideas about tradition, race and reality.

The anti-self is the opposite of what is given in the everyday, what the ordinary mind takes for reality. It is entirely involved with the mask, in that Yeats thinks that the anti-self comes to inhabit the mask. The idea of the mask helps us to understand what Yeats is attempting to clarify for himself in *Per Amica Silentia Lunae* and throughout his work: the mask is formal, traditional and rigorous, and opposed to the facial expressions and agitations of the moment. It is impersonal:

> all that is personal soon rots: it must be packed in ice or salt. Once when I was in a delirium from pneumonia I dictated a letter to George Moore telling him to eat salt because it was a symbol of eternity; the delirium passed, I had no memory of that letter, but I must have meant what I now mean. If I wrote of personal love or sorrow in free verse, or in any rhythm that left it unchanged, amid all its accidence, I would be full of self-contempt because of my egotism and indiscretion, and foresee the boredom of my reader.[12]

Yeats hated the cult of personality. He thought that by trying for the opposite, the anti-self, the mask, the activity of the poetic will would be roused to full intensity. Metre, rhyme, stanza and period are all attempts to realize a formality in defiance of the incoherence of the everyday. Yeats, as much as any of the great modernists, experienced the disarray and fragmentation of modern life, but his approach to it remained entirely traditional: indeed, the greater the sense of disarray the more strongly traditional and simple his writing became.

What was he after in this seeking of the anti-self and the mask?

He was after unity and passion. Time and again in Yeats's work these words pull our attention towards them. Yeats looked for unity in that he wished to hammer his thoughts into a unified system.[13] In *Per Amica Silentia Lunae* we see him trying to find in the human soul and in what he calls the 'world-soul' the lineaments of a coherent design. He sees the human soul (*anima hominis*) and the world-soul (*anima mundi*) as overlapping: the human mind is constantly drawing upon a collective store of wisdom in a great memory bank. Too great an emphasis upon personality or upon originality deprives the mind of contact with this store:

> It is not permitted to a man who takes up a pen or chisel to seek originality.[14]

Without this contact the mind becomes listless, preoccupied with the passing moment and with objects.

The mask was the symbol of tradition, continuity and unity. Yeats's thought gets even more complex, however. His idea is that there is, over and above and under all, a supreme unity, One, and that all passion, activity, rhythm, thought and energy come from that. The passions, as he calls them, are of great significance, because they bring us into contact with what has come from the central unified One of being from which reality derives. There are, in Yeats's view, certain governing loves and passions for particular times, races and persons, and these are the opposite of what lies before the eyes at any given moment. So that virtue in art, in poetry, lies not in finding yourself, but in calling up that which is the opposite of the self, what the mind has least known and understood:

> By the help of an image
> I call to my own opposite, summon all
> That I have handled least, least looked upon.[15]

If this is done it can only be done with passion, and it leads to contact with the One, which Yeats imagines as a wheel in *Per Amica Silentia Lunae* and in *A Vision*:

> the passions, when we know that they cannot find fulfilment, become vision; and a vision, whether we wake or sleep prolongs its power by rhythm and pattern, the wheel where the world is butterfly.[16]

The wheel where the world is butterfly: the passions bring us to a sense of this, but the passions make us seek the impossible, that which is outside and beyond the scope of the everyday. They do, however, connect with a system, a unity, which Yeats sees as surviving all when time comes to an end:

> When all sequence comes to an end, time comes to an end, and the soul puts on rhythmic or spiritual body or luminous body and contemplates all the events of its memory. . . . That condition is what animates, all the rest is fantasy, and from thence come all the passions and, some have held, the very heat of the body.[17]

Yeats then goes on to quote his poem 'The Moods', first published in 1893:

> Time drops in decay,
> Like a candle burnt out,
> And the mountains and woods
> Have their day, have their day.
> What one, in the rout
> Of the fire-born moods
> Has fallen away?

This poem repeats the idea, already there in prose, that the passions, or the 'moods', carry with them an impetus which comes from some kind of central core of being. Yeats is not thinking here of emotions, in the normal sense of the word, but of passion or mood or something that carries out of the everyday into a connection with the large patterns that make themselves apparent in the lives, not just of individuals, but of nations or races also. In an essay of 1895 on 'The Moods' he wrote: 'It seems to me that these moods are the labourers and messengers of the Ruler of All.'[18] By mood or passion Yeats is thinking of something like the *furor poeticus* or Shakespeare's 'fine frenzy'. He thinks of the poet as someone whose calling is to seek after the inner forms, the inner patterns, to seek out the mathematics and geometry of a system that is hidden to ordinary ways of looking. Instead of looking the poet should gaze: in the gaze, which is half-trance, some indication of the huge memory of the system is given – again, the 'wheel where the world is butterfly'. Time and again he comes back to the idea of the core, a centre, a seminary 'of all things that are born to live and die/According their kynds'

– Spenser's words, quoted in *Per Amica Silentia Lunae*. And his view of the poet is that he or she is committed to creating images that will delineate the activity of the moods or passions moving or dancing to a pattern of geometry or mathematics that lies at the centre of things: 'he is more type than man, more passion than type.'[19] The last thing the poet seeks is individuality or originality. This attitude affects every aspect of Yeats's thought and makes him totally traditional in style, subject matter and language. It also makes him increasingly difficult to understand in a century where personal opinions easily hold sway, in the public acceptance, over traditional knowledge or wisdom.

Yeats wanted to be counted 'one with Davis, Mangan, Ferguson'. In his late essay 'A General Introduction to my Work' he tells us about what he admired in them:

> they were not separated individual men; they spoke or tried to speak out of a people to a people; behind them stretched the generations.[20]

They were not original men, preoccupied with self. They wanted, in Yeats's view, to speak for community and for tradition, and this was what attracted him. This community nationalism merged totally, in Yeats, with his philosophic and highly idealistic notion of the poet as seeker after the glimmerings of the huge system of being itself. He does tell us in the poem where he places himself in the same line as the poets of Young Ireland, Davis and Ferguson, that he is more ambitious than they; he has more to tell:

> Nor may I less be counted one
> With Davis, Mangan, Ferguson,
> Because, to him who ponders well,
> My rhymes more than their rhyming tell
> Of things discovered in the deep,
> Where only body's laid asleep.[21]

Among the things 'discovered' are the 'elemental furies', he says. He has no fully clear notion at this stage (1892) what his aim is but he does see himself as performing a more portentous task than that engaged upon by Davis and just as significant, in his mind, as that to which Parnell gave his life. The task was the renewal of an Irish cultural continuity, a resurrection of a sense of tradition, a reactivation of the old patterns of knowledge and of wisdom. His task was stupendous, because what he was doing was turning aside from all the predominant ideologies of his time in order to reach for a new system of priorities based on Irishness, legend, folklore, saga; and out of that he set out to make an image of Ireland that would have contact with the real Ireland, not the one of everyday, but the ideal one which was part of the entire system of being itself.

Taking his cue from Matthew Arnold's *On the Study of Celtic Literature* (1866) he saw the Irish as passionate, emotional and free of the despotism of fact, but he went further than Arnold to argue that they were antithetical to the modern world, in touch with the anti-self and with the mask, and therefore in touch with the hidden wisdom of Europe. He said that they were capable of understanding the mathematics of being itself, because the traditional mind, the folk-mind, had not altogether disappeared. The Irish, in Yeats's argument, were still in touch with the inner forms of their culture and this made them responsive to life itself:

> When Pearse summoned Cuchulain to his side,
> What stalked through the Post Office? What intellect,
> What calculation, number, measurement, replied?[22]

This extract is from 'The Statues', a very late poem of Yeats's (9 April 1938) which shows how consistent his thought was throughout his life, despite the highly accumulative and synthesizing nature of his mind. He always believed that it was his duty as a poet to strike through to a central core of reality; that that for an Irish person was a specifically Irish task because there was not a way of avoiding the collective memory or soul of which the individual mind or soul was a part; and that to make such a contact with the core was to reach to the inner forms of a race which manifested themselves in language, culture and ways of life. So that to make this kind of contact was indeed to be in touch with life but in a way which avoided the busy-minded concentration on the things of the passing hour, which is the way, Yeats would argue, most people interpret 'liveliness'. When he writes about the tide of life rising in *Samhain* this is the kind of life to which he refers, and it is the opposite of activity and frantic engagement.

Thinking in this manner, it is possible easily to understand why Yeats, when he reflects in his *Autobiographies* on the Irish movement in literature after the fall of Parnell, thought that there was an entirely satisfactory logic in the way that a cultural renaissance should follow a lull in politics. Frantic engagement, the busyness of politics, the poisonous mixture of ambition, hope, idealism, hypocrisy and hatred – all these, in Yeats's view, gave way to the emergence of a different kind of reality, the one connected to the great 'wheel' and to passion, but not passion for an object to be realized in terms which a democratic mass could understand, but for the mathematics of the inner form of reality itself. And this meant not the elevation of personal instinct or private emotion, but the recognition of the governing ideas and types, images rather than individuality.

Yeats made Irish mythological and legendary material his subject matter, as Ferguson had done before him. He honoured the Irish Victorian because, in his view, Ferguson understood the necessity of placing a high value on this material if modern Irish culture was to be a continuation of that which preceded it. This argument is obvious enough, but Yeats introduced a different element into his prospectus for changing the mood and feeling of modern Ireland. His ambition was to write for race and reality, which meant that he wanted to get at the mathematics of the inner forms of the Irish nature, because by doing so he would activate the latent energies of life itself. Holding this attitude, he was totally in line with the thinking on culture amongst the German Romantic poets, philosophers and ethnolinguists of the early nineteenth century. To turn to myth was to turn to the imprints made upon the collective mind of a particular people by the central core, and thereby bring about change. The inner forms, though neglected, remained active. In an introduction to Lady Gregory's *Cuchulain of Muirthemne,* a collection of the material relating to one of the main personae he employed in his phantasmagoria, Yeats writes:

> the Irish stories make us understand why the Greeks call myths the activities of the daemons. The great virtues, the great joys, the great privations come in the myths, and, as it were, take mankind between their naked arms, without putting off their divinity. Poets have taken their themes more often from stories that are all or half mythological, than from history or stories that give one the sensation of history, understanding, as I think, that the imagination which remembers the proportions of life is but a long

> wooing, and that it has to forget them before it becomes the torch and the marriage-bed.[23]

When Yeats speaks here of the proportions of life he is thinking of realistic or lifelike representation of the kind he accused Keats of in 'Ego Dominus Tuus'. The true poet, Yeats is arguing, takes his inspiration from the *types* of great emotion, rather than from personality or realism, and mythology reveals those types or structures. His view of myth is very like that of Lévi-Strauss, who detects in mythology the patterns of relationship and opposition which determine social structure and culture itself. Like Yeats, Lévi-Strauss also thought that particular races and tribes had specific systems of signs by means of which they could be compared with and differentiated from other races and tribes. Both writers took direction from the linguistic and cultural theory that originated in early nineteenth century Germany.

In following through the line of thought above, in which Irish culture is seen to have certain governing traits and characteristics, Yeats had, inevitably, to consider the most appropriate *means* of expression for an Irish cultural system: if there were certain signifieds then there should be a set of preferred signifiers. Such a consideration brings the thinking very quickly to questions of language. It is all very well to say that Irish subject matter is essential in an Irish context, but what of the Irish language itself? Yeats would know from his understanding of the general drift of cultural thinking in Romanticism that it was inadequate for a poet to think of language as a means of communication pure and simple. He would know that Romanticism considered deeply the idea that a language encapsulated a total world-view, a complex of feelings and prejudices, and latencies which involved memory and inherited dispositions. Could there be such a thing as an Irish literary movement in English?

Yeats was entirely sympathetic in principle to Douglas Hyde and to the Gaelic League. He hoped that there would be a literature and, even more significantly, a theatre in Irish. Furthermore, he inspired George Moore who returned to Ireland and threw himself into work which he anticipated would help the Gaelic League. With Lady Gregory and Hyde, Yeats studied the folklore and poetry of Anthony Raftery the nineteenth century Gaelic poet of Mayo and Galway, who became something of a model for the idealized cultural figure that the Irish Literary Revival projected. Raftery was a local poet; he lived among the people; he shared their sorrows and joys; his methods and world-view were entirely traditional; he had the atmosphere of a character who belonged entirely to the landscape and the people; and it seemed as if his poetry translated directly the collective hidden life of an entire community out of an Irish shared memory into the living circumstances of the people among whom he lived. He was seen as the voice of an entire world-view: to Yeats and Lady Gregory he seemed to realize what Davis and before him, the German idealists, advocated about culture. He was also a symbol of opposition to the mainstream of European, English and Anglo-Irish culture, in that his art was practised either in ignorance or in defiance of the centralized cultures of the West; and this would make him, in Yeats's definition, someone for whom the 'common dream' of the inert, modern industrialized culture of the nineteenth century had never exercised any attraction. He became one of the emblems of adversity.

But Raftery's was a language that remained unknown to Yeats. And it would be a very purblind kind of nationalist obsession that would fault him for that. It was a subject about which he had complicated feelings, summed up in the well-known phrase from 'A General Introduction to My Work': 'Gaelic is my national language; but it is not my mother tongue.'[24] It is very difficult, he says, to write in anything other than one's mother tongue. This statement comes at the end of a section in the essay on the subject matter of his work, which began with an account of John O'Leary, the old Fenian, giving him the works of Davis and Young Ireland to read; and which then moved to an account of the particular kind of belief to be found in Irish tradition. He maintains that there is, behind that tradition, a 'great tapestry', in which Christian and pagan interlink, where Christ is still the half-brother of Dionysus, and where someone 'just tonsured by the Druids could learn from the nearest Christian neighbour to sign himself with the cross'.[25]

It is not a useful task to attempt to determine whether Yeats is correct about this or not. What is plain is that he is thinking very much in terms of continuity, that there is such a thing as Irish tradition, that it is very old, that it has certain characteristics, and that he himself is in the tradition. And yet there is the question of the language, which Yeats does not address directly, although he does become entangled with it.

He does tell a story, just before the quotation about English being his mother tongue, and it is an interesting and puzzling one. He recounts how he addressed some Indians and others at a London society some years before, and in the course of the speech attacked English complacency about other cultures. He spoke with hatred of Wordsworth's sonnet in praise of François Dominique Toussaint, 'a Santa Domingo Negro', written in the year when Emmet led his rebellion and was executed. He told the Indians how they were being forced to learn everything, even Sanskrit, through English, and warned that they would end up without any language, ignorant of their own wisdom, and inept in English.

On the one hand, he feels part of a tradition that is older than Christianity. On the other hand, surely the anecdote about Indian language and culture is telling a different story: that there is discontinuity, which causes anger, a sense of futility and uncertainty. Yeats would know that a language conveys a sense of the integrity of a culture. But his mind is defiant and strange. He would also argue that the lack of a native language in Ireland which was also a mother tongue was exactly the situation which should call out of the writer or poet every effort of will of which he was capable in order to *create* a sense of cultural continuity and tradition in spite of and because of its precarious nature.

And besides, there was still a great deal of ancient Ireland to be found, in folklore, songs, stories and in a general habit of mind: 'I have heard the words "tetragrammaton agla" in Doneraile,' he writes, portentously, in the same essay, insisting upon the presence in the Irish 'tapestry' of elements even from cabbalistic thought.

What sort of view did Yeats have of the Irish mind, and how did he see himself as participating in its reactivation in a context where, as he admits, the Irish language is no longer the mother tongue?

He argued that the Irish mind, culture and tradition preserved a contact with very old understandings and knowledge. We have seen that he thought of life as having a central core, which he imagined as a wheel, from which were flung passions, images, types. Individualism, analysis, sentimentality, had nothing to do with these impulses that proceeded from the centre: the poet came close to them by adopting a mask; a play could contact them through masks and through dance; and they observed a mathematics and proportion which constrained an artist, if he was to try to be true to them, to adopt a high degree of formality and to be traditional. Otherwise the artist was left with the personal, which rots. It was Yeats's claim that the Irish had a capacity for this contact: they were mediumistic, oracular and formal, when the times were functional, conversational and slack.

It is a fierce argument, partly galvanized by an intense hatred of England which Yeats never fully overcame.

> Remember all those renowned generations,
> They left their bodies to fatten the wolves,
> They left their homesteads to fatten the foxes,
> Fled to far countries, or sheltered themselves
> In cavern, crevice or hole,
> Defending Ireland's soul.
>
> *Be still, be still what can be said?*
> *My father sang that song,*
> *But time amends all wrong,*
> *All that is finished, let it fade.*
>
> Fail, and that history turns into rubbish,
> All that gaunt past to a trouble of fools;
> Those that come after shall mock at O'Donnell,
> Mock at the memory of both O'Neills,
> Mock Emmet, mock Parnell,
> All the renown that fell.[26]

This is one of the 'Three Marching Songs' as rewritten for his *Last Poems and Two Plays*, published by Cuala Press after his death in 1939. In a manuscript list which he drew up for the order of the poems the songs follow directly on 'Cuchulain Comforted', Yeats's tender poem about the dead Cuchulain, written in strict Dantesque terza rima, showing how the brave Cuchulain meets his opposites, cowards, in death; the songs are then followed by 'In Tara's Halls' in the sequence, where an ancient high king of Ireland prepares himself for death. He is entirely formal, inhuman almost, paying no tribute to God, or making no declarations of love. These poems, in their different ways, open into one of the most devastating and chilling of all of

Yeats's poems, 'The Statues', a piece full of hatred, pride, love of country, glory in heroism and traditional arrogance. He claims in this poem that the Irish have a special mission, to measure the mathematics of being, just as Pythagoras did, or Phidias. He maintains that they have an instinct for remaining in touch with the core, the centre. There is discontinuity; the Irish, like all others in modern times, experience fragmentation, but the poetic argument is that this very fragmentation drives them into an activity of the will that enables them to remain in touch with passion, the 'moods', and with that geometry of being itself that, he claims, Pythagoras and Phidias worked out for Greece. Classical Greece is a powerful symbol for Yeats at this stage: he is arguing for a continuity between Greek culture and Irish culture; the Irish, because they remain true to their own forms and mathematics, stay in touch with the lineaments, the geometry, of being itself, as the Greeks first discovered them for the West:

> Pythagoras planned it. Why did the people stare?
> His numbers, though they moved or seemed to move
> In marble or in bronze, lacked character.[27]

Planned what? It: the thing, the centre, the logos. Yeats is almost saying that Pythagoras, or someone (he shifts his thinking later) planned the order of life; that is why the people stared, but Yeats is testing and exciting his reader: can you see why they stared at these statues that Pythagoras planned the 'it' in? The numbers seemed to move in the figures, so lively were they, but the statues had no character. They were types, numbers, passions, masks, not dissections of opinions or emotions. And those most in touch with passion which is type, young boys and girls in love with love, they knew what was going on in those blank characterless effigies:

> But boys and girls, pale from the imagined love
> Of solitary beds, knew what they were,
> That passion could bring character enough,
> And pressed at midnight in some public place
> Live lips upon a plummet-measured face.

That face in the dark, to which they have climbed, is the mask, that which they have handled least, least looked upon, the thing that is furthest from them, but the thing which, in its formality, represents the inner structure, the mathematics, towards which individuals, in Yeats's view, must direct their will, otherwise they become lost in accidental history, technicality, discussion, futile argument and self-analysis. The boys and girls have no time for these refinements: they want the harsh mathematics of Pythagoras, because that gives their instincts shape.

Yeats always surprises. The next move in the poetic thinking is extremely daring. He changes his mind about Pythagoras. It was an intellect greater than his that tracked down the numbers on which the statues were based. He asserts that the men who chiselled the 'calculations' evident in Greek statuary had an intellectual force so in touch with life itself that it was that force and not military power that enabled the Greeks to defeat the Persians at Salamis:

> No! Greater than Pythagoras, for the men
> That with a mallet or a chisel modelled these
> Calculations that look but casual flesh, put down
> All Asiatic vague immensities,
> And not the banks of oars that swam upon
> The many-headed foam at Salamis.
> Europe put off that form, when Phidias
> Gave women dreams, and dreams their looking-glass.

Europe conquers Asiatic vagueness through the calculations of being, the life-mathematics, evident in the statues.

The next stanza, a most puzzling one, explores an Asiatic vagueness, which Yeats sees as following on from the deliberate exactness of the Greeks:

> One image crossed the many-headed, sat
> Under the tropic shade, grew round and slow,
> No Hamlet thin from eating flies, a fat
> Dreamer of the Middle Ages.

Christianity developed a Buddhistic emptiness. But in the last stanza Yeats returns to Ireland and asserts that Pearse, in the Post Office, when he did what he did, recalled Cuchulain, and in doing this was not just bringing back ancient Ireland, but was also bringing back Greek calculation and measurement. Pearse's gesture was ludicrous, to a commonsense view, but in calling Cuchulain to himself he was taking on the formality of the mask, thereby creating a continuity with the Irish past, despite the failure and disgrace of Irish culture and the fact that fragmentation had taken place. Even the language had all but gone. The Irish had been 'wrecked' by modernization, formlessness and discontinuity, but they had not been content with this situation: they had fought against it with such effort that the discontinuity had, to some extent, been bridged, and modern Ireland, through Pearse and through the energy of will he had embodied, had come into contact with life again in the way that the Greeks had been when they could calculate the measurement of being:

> When Pearse summoned Cuchulain to his side,
> What stalked through the Post Office? What intellect,
> What calculation, number, measurement, replied?
> We Irish, born into that ancient sect
> But thrown upon this filthy modern tide
> And by its formless spawning fury wrecked,
> Cling to our proper dark, that we may trace
> The lineaments of a plummet-measured face.

The prose draft of this stanza reads:

> Where are you now? It's better that you shed the sunburn and become pale-white; did you appear in the Post Office in 1916? Is it true that Pearse called on you by the name of Cuchulain? Certainly we have need of you. The vague flood is as its . . . from all quarters is coming . . . Come back with your Pythagorean numbers.[28]

The Irish can find the mask, which puts them in touch with their inner form, their type. Each nation has its mould, to which it should return, if it is not to lose itself in accident and in traffic with the ordinary and predictable methods of thought. Ireland is like Greece. It is not the same as Greece: its mask, the plummet-measured face, the pattern, will be different, but the Irish, if they continue to make this climb to the 'proper dark' will be like the Greeks in their centrality – the word, it will be remembered, Yeats used in praise of Ferguson.

In *A Vision* (1937) Yeats quotes Hermes as saying:

> 'It is impossible that any single form . . . should come into being which is exactly like a second, if they originate at different points and at times differently situated; the forms change at every moment in each hour of the revolution of [the] celestial circuit . . . thus the type persists unchanged

> but generates at successive moments copies of itself as numerous and different as the revolution of the sphere of heaven; for the sphere of heaven changes as it revolves, but the type neither changes nor revolves.'[29]

This passage lies behind Yeats's thinking in 'Easter 1916', where he speaks of the changing clouds and skies - 'minute by minute they change' - and then speaks of the stone, which is 'in the midst of all'. This stone is the stone of Pearse's heart, and Cuchulain too has a stony face. They are cold but passionate. Individuality conforms to type and finds centrality and freedom. Again in 'The Statues' Pearse and Cuchulain are pulled together. Yeats's language, his rhetoric, is the medium by which they are linked. It performs the tasks of creating the cold and passionate alliance of modern militarist and legendary type, so that, in the argument of the poem, it is not the man Pearse who stood in the Post Office, but Cuchulain, Ireland's inner mathematics. And, in *A Vision*, directly after the passage quoted, Yeats goes on to assert that nations do have inner forms:

> But nations also were sealed at birth with a character derived from the whole.

By 'the whole' here he means the wheel, where Greek and Irish revolve together around a centre.

It would be pointless to debate whether Yeats is right or not in his interpretation of culture, continuity and centrality. This is not the concern. What is intriguing about the writing here is its imaginative power, its rhetorical confidence and its cultural strategy. Yeats is saying, in effect, that the Irish have an instinct for the centre. Even though the Irish are wrecked by modernization, by history and by oppression, they will not be kept under. They climb, like the passion-crazed boys and girls of Pythagorean Greece, up to their 'proper' dark, their own special darkness, seeking the harsh outlines of their ancient nature. There is discontinuity, formlessness, breaking, but Yeats's rhetoric asserts continuity, form, the 'whole'. His answer to the problem of the relationship between language and culture in modern Ireland is a 'doing' rather than an intellectualization. By virtue of the fact, he implies, that any language can be so energetic, can do such things as link Greece, Ireland and the question of the inner forms of life itself, by these evidences you can see that despite the loss of the Irish language and of many Irish ways of life there can be continuity. You can see it in my language, he says, you can experience it as a poetic excitement. Continuity does not depend on contingency. The signs are not good for Ireland, the signs were not good for Pearse in 1916. But to submit to logic and to common sense is to be fragmented, to give in to the inner subsidence of self-doubt. The Irish, he asserts, have the instinct for the centre, and that is their power.

He is a cultural myth-maker and he bases his fictions upon notions of pride and upon the idea that nations or peoples have certain central patterns of behaviour which can be contacted. To contact these patterns involves formality and effort of will, but if they can be contacted then calculation, measurement, authority ensue. This is what the poem 'The Statues' leaves us with. What follows, in the sequence Yeats outlined, is appalling in its audacity. The next poem is 'News for the Delphic Oracle', where Yeats, an Irishman, proceeds to tell the Delphic oracle itself what the afterlife is really like. It is as if he says: this is news for you, oracle, which I am in a position to deliver because I, one of the Irish, have climbed to the proper dark to get in touch with the calculations necessary to authority.

In Porphyry's *Life of Plotinus* there is an account of how Amelius consulted the oracle at Delphi on the slopes of Parnassus to find out what had happened to the soul of Plotinus, the philosopher.

The oracle, as delivered to Amelius, is preserved in Porphyry's *Life,* in verse form. It tells us how Plotinus fought his way through the waves to the place where the Ever Holy live, among them 'stately Pythagoras, and all else that form the choir of Immortal Love'.[30]

Yeats's 'News' is his version of the afterlife, but in saying that one is not saying enough. It is his attempt to envisage an afterlife from an Irish point of view; he wants to be an oracle to modern times, because, as Irishman, though 'wrecked', he can climb to the kind of dark necessary to sponsor this audacious authority. In his 'News' the dead are 'codgers'. Among them are Niamh and Oisin from *The Wanderings of Oisin*. This three-part 'News' of his is a rewriting of the three islands of *The Wanderings of Oisin* and a rewriting too of the old Irish genre of *immram* or voyage tale. So Greek, Gaelic and his own personae and masks are interrelated:

I

There all the golden codgers lay,
There the silver dew,
And the great water sighed for love,
And the wind sighed too.
Man-picker Niamh leant and sighed
By Oisin in the grass;
There sighed amid his choir of love
Tall Pythagoras.
Plotinus came and looked about,
The salt-flakes on his breast,
And having stretched and yawned awhile
Lay sighing like the rest.

The mood is one of lassitude, inertia, hardly of content or joy. He takes up the oracle's description in Porphyry's *Life,* which he described as one of his favourite quotations, one by which he tests people and figures from history, but he changes it entirely. There is an element of mockery here of the whole notion of the supernatural and the afterlife, even an admission, in the tone, that it may all be somewhat boring. These are 'codgers', golden codgers, maybe, but codgers engage in 'cod', foolishness, pedantry. So these are the immortals. This strategy, of boredom, mockery, doubt, is unsettling. The next piece of news opens with the Holy Innocents trying to keep their balance as they ride into the afterlife on dolphins:

II

Straddling each a dolphin's back
And steadied by a fin,
Those Innocents re-live their death,
Their wounds open again.
The ecstatic waters laugh because
Their cries are sweet and strange,
Through their ancestral patterns dance,
And the brute dolphins plunge
Until, in some cliff-sheltered bay
Where wades the choir of love
Proffering its sacred laurel crowns,
They pitch their burdens off.

This piece of news is all activity and flurry: the Holy Innocents, killed by Herod in an attempt to murder Christ, come to the afterlife, where the choir of love wades out to greet them. Pagan and Christian are interlinked, as Yeats argued they continually were in Irish tradition. The grammar of this stanza seems unstable (in the line 'Through their ancestral patterns dance' it is not entirely clear to what 'their' refers: dolphins?; waters?; Innocents?) but the overall idea is clear. Christian martyrs are received into a pattern which predates them. The dolphins, the waters, the Innocents and the choir of love are all part of a prearranged order, a dance, through which they proceed. The poetry tries to convey that order to us. The ecstatic waters laugh at the wounds of the child martyrs of Christian tradition. The view of the afterlife, though it takes its materials from all sorts of sources, is very much an Irish one, Yeats would maintain. It is 'flowing, concrete, phenomenal',[31] natural and supernatural are bound together, and there is an interplay between pagan and Christian.

'Flowing, concrete, phenomenal' – these were the words Yeats used to describe the kind of Druidic attitude he saw behind Irish life and history and which he hoped would replace the faith in technology and mechanization in Europe. These words can be applied to stanza II of 'News' and, with even more appropriateness, to stanza III.

This last piece of 'News' is full of lust and sensuality. Remember, this is the afterlife as Yeats projects it.

III

Slim adolescence that a nymph as stripped,
Peleus on Thetis stares.
Her limbs are delicate as an eyelid,
Love has blinded him with tears;
But Thetis's belly listens.
Down the mountain walls
From where Pan's cavern is
Intolerable music falls.
Foul goat-head, brutal arm appear,
Belly, shoulder, bum,
Flash fishlike; nymphs and satyrs
Copulate in the foam.

Thetis's belly listens to Pan's music. It drives her crazy, while Peleus is lost in an admiring trance. The satyrs and the nymphs pick up the wildness of that music, and act upon it. An energy, a pattern, an impulse, issuing in Pan's intolerable music drives even the dead crazy. Again natural and supernatural interpenetrate.

What conclusion do we draw from this poem? In its sequence in Yeats's *Last Poems* we can see that Yeats has planned it as an Irish version of the afterlife, as what an Irish poet can see who climbs to the proper dark. It is an entirely unsettling piece. There is little obvious coherence between the three sections, and yet, as a poem it has great power. Through all three parts there is a sense of an order predominating; an idea that the dead, too, like the living, go through a pattern in their lives, a dance. Pan's music co-ordinates this activity.

It is a difficult poem to interpret, in that it would be foolhardy to attempt to sum up its message. We are offered three oracular statements, each one very concrete and circumstantial, as well as being shocking and unsettling: boredom, waters laughing at wounds, then bestial orgy. We know how unstable human judgement is, we know human boredom and cruelty, we know that lust is insatiable: all these are presented in the poem as indications of what might be the master-patterns of our time. But Yeats makes no large claims like these. He gives us the images, with disturbing force and clarity, and allows them to work on the imagination and the moral intelligence.

Yeats held that each nation, each culture has its governing passions and types. His theory of the mask revolved round this conviction, because he thought that to reach the governing passions the poetic mind (which he would argue is central in the transmission of any cultural identity) had to opt out of the common and the ordinary and seek the 'image' – that which was handled least, least looked upon: the mask. That was the way to achieve reality and to write for race. In opting for the mask the poetic mind was choosing formality and passion rather than variety and sentiment. In making such a choice a poet like Ferguson became central, in that he put himself in contact with the governing passions and inner forms of Irish culture. Yeats wanted to be that kind of poet – central, authoritative, traditional, Irish.

He acknowledged a radical break in Irish tradition, but he

thought that after the death of Parnell it would be possible to continue the work of Ferguson, Davis and Young Ireland by directing attention to Gaelic Ireland, its legends, mythologies and folklore. Crucial here was his contact with Douglas Hyde, Synge, Lady Gregory:

> John Synge, I and Augusta Gregory, thought
> All that we did, all that we said or sang
> Must come from contact with the soil, from that
> Contact everything Antaeus-like grew strong.[32]

The contact with the soil was the getting down to basics, to the governing patterns or deep structures that underlie Irish life, literature and culture. To make that contact was to overleap the chasm in Irish cultural life that was the consequence of the disappearance of the Irish language as the agreed system of representation in Ireland. But that, to Yeats, would make the task all the more attractive. His entire creative psychology was based on the notion of difficulty: that only that thing which of all things is not impossible but most difficult is what raises the will to full intensity. So to make the jump back, into contact with a culture on the point of death, was the guarantee that what he was doing was right. It is a hopelessly illogical position but he would argue that the only triumph is in persisting in what the 'common dream' would think of as failure. As one of his masters, Blake, said: 'if the fool persist in his foolery he will grow wise.'

What did he achieve? It is all very well to outline the Romantic, idealist, essentialist, cabbalistic elements in Yeats's oppositional, perhaps Nietzschean thought, but what does his poetry offer as a resolution of the problems of continuity and tradition? He offers language. He offers a rhetorical space in which a complex and mature intelligence contemplates what seems to lie at the root of questions of culture. What he sees there is, at bottom, quite simple: he thinks that a culture embodies a nation's basic patterns or characteristics. Art is most authoritative when it concerns itself with these central configurations. Art should be marked by and calculated according to these inner patterns. It should not traffic with the passing hour too much: it should seek the mask. The mask allows the dance, because through the mask the artist is released from individuality into the freedom of the larger patterns and their formality. An Irish writer, if he or she is in touch with the governing passions of

Irish culture, will be like a Greek sculptor at the time of Phidias: he or she will have measurement. But this authority is open to any writer from any race. In Ireland there is a better chance that such a contact may be made *because* she has been wrecked by history; because there is discontinuity, violence, hatred, confusion. If she does not lose herself in panic, argument and despair she may have news for the Delphic oracle. Yeats's audacious imaginings and his rhetorical fury show what may be done in defiance of fate.

5

J.M. SYNGE

'Transfigured realism'

It just happens that I know Irish life best, so I made my methods Irish.

Synge in an interview to the *Evening Mail*, 28 January 1907[1]

Yeats tended to turn his friends into Olympians, in the memorializing rhetoric of his verse or in the gnomic pronouncements of his prose. His enemies got similar but opposite treatment. J.M. Synge was a close friend, as well as someone deeply admired. Yeats described him variously, but the phrase he used in 'Coole Park, 1929', though simple and unaffected, sums up much about the man and the artist: 'That meditative man'.[2] It registers Synge's scholarship, concentration, attentiveness and collectedness. These meditative qualities derive from a very strong interplay, in Synge's temperament, between a powerful subjectivity, an ability to absorb and concentrate variousness; and objectivity, a readiness in the spirit to encounter things other than itself. This interaction, between self and that which is different from it, is one of the dynamics that gives Synge's work its energy and vitality, and its composure. In a notebook of 1908 he wrote:

> The artistic value of any work of art is measured by its *uniqueness.* Its human value is given largely by its intensity and its richness, for if it is rich it is many-sided or universal, and, for this reason, sane - another word for wholesome - since all insanities are due to a one-sided excitement.[3]

The balance required is one between 'uniqueness' and 'humanity', between the subjective and the objective. Such an interaction is needed, Synge insists, if insanity is to be avoided.

On this matter he completely knew what he was talking about. His early prose writings tell us of his struggle to balance self with history, subject with object. The relation between his own inner being and the external world was a baffling and frightening one. In his 'Autobiography' he says that 'while the thoughts and deeds of a lifetime are impersonal and concrete - might have been done by anyone - art is the expression of the essential or abstract beauty of the person,'[4] which as a formulation does not take us very far. But Synge, it is clear, is at this point working *against* history, saying in effect that life's vapid accidents are of little interest; what matters is some ideal or abstract form. These phrases were written towards the start of his autobiographical writings (although the dating of these documents is, it is recognized, a problem) and as such seem to show a Synge who is feeling his way and who is uncomfortable with the multifariousness of reality. He refers often to the image of the symphony, to indicate his hope that life has such a form; whereby each individual action and event can be translated into a complete and satisfying order.[5]

History and external reality trouble him because he has experienced terrifying situations where there existed no secure relation between these and the subjective self. There is a particular kind of incident, which surfaces again and again in Synge, whether in his dramatic writings, his prose or his autobiographical meditations, and that is the situation where he loses himself in fog, cannot distinguish the exact features of the objects around him, and has an experience of grotesque dislocation. One such incident took place in the Dublin mountains in his late teens, when he was out collecting specimens of moths, flowers, butterflies and such like, satisfying his interest in natural history:

> One evening when I was collecting on the brow of a long valley in County Wicklow wreaths of white mist began to rise from the narrow bogs beside the river. Before it was quite dark I looked around the edge of the field and saw two immense luminous eyes looking at me from the base of the valley. I dropped my net and caught hold of a gate in front of me. Behind the eyes there rose a black sinister forehead. I was fascinated. For a moment the eyes seemed to consume my personality, then the whole valley became filled with a pageant of movement and colour, and the opposite hillside covered itself with ancient doorways and spires and high

> turrets. I did not know where or when I was existing. At last someone spoke in the lane behind me – it was a man going home – and I came back to myself. . . . I recognized in a moment what had caused the apparition – two clearings in a wood lined with white mist divided again by a few trees which formed the eyeballs. For many days afterwards I could not look on these fields even in daylight without terror.[6]

The Wordsworthian phrasing in the last sentence (echoing 'for many days, my brain/Worked with a dim and undetermined sense/Of unknown modes of being'[7]) indicates that Synge is associating these experiences with the transformations in perspective that art brings about. Though it is terrifying, this experience is exciting, and in some sense liberating. Reality, the thing out there, is moved out of its fixedness and acquires a disquieting strangeness. Synge goes out of himself in this process, and is drawn back by the sound of a voice; again something that repeats itself frequently in his writings, and a pattern also found in Wordsworth.

Synge tells us he was a collector, and of his interest in natural history, but a scientific, orderly attitude to nature and to history may be overturned by a freakish occurrence, such as the one he describes. This leads to a one-sided excitement, a loss of composure.

In a notebook written between 1896 and 1898 Synge tells us that he obtained a book by Charles Darwin when he was about 14. It opened at a passage in which Darwin asks how the similarity between a man's hand and a bird's or a bat's wing may be explained, except by evolution. Synge describes his reaction:

> I flung the book aside and rushed out into the open air – it was summer and we were in the country – the sky seemed to have lost its blue and the grass its green. I lay down and writhed in an agony of doubt.[8]

Darwin's insights into the connections between nature and man over huge historical periods unsettled Synge's consciousness as they unsettled many minds used to assuming that man had a natural ascendancy over the rest of nature and of matter. Darwin's theories pointed to a kinship between man, beast and matter itself that distorted given attitudes and perspectives, literally so in Synge's case - the sky and the grass seem to lose their colours - but there are many more instances: Tennyson, Arnold, Rimbaud, to name but a few. Synge tells us that some weeks after this episode he regained his 'composure', but that this was 'the beginning' of a new phase of understanding forced upon him by the 'charm' that he feels now sundering him from his parents and friends. The story is easily told, but it is difficult for Synge to convey the horror and the fascination of this awakening to the terror and strangeness of nature and of man. In a notebook written in 1908 he says, summing up what he has attempted to do in his plays and topographical works, that he has 'tried to give humanity and this mysterious external world'.[9] His discovery of Darwin and his related experiences of dislocation, compelled him, as an artist, to concentrate upon the strangeness of nature and reality. He was convinced that poetry and art should collaborate with reality in some way or other (otherwise it would lack the necessary edge and saltiness), but how could this be managed if reality, nature and history were 'mysterious'?

'All art is a collaboration,'[10] he wrote in the preface to *The Playboy of the Western World*, at which point he is thinking of the collaboration between artist and the material out of which art is made: stray phrases, stories and so on. He tells us that while he was writing *The Shadow of the Glen* he listened through a chink in the floorboards to the conversations below and got more help from that than 'any learning' could have given. This episode raises the complex matter of Synge's obsession with language, but for the moment what is registered here is Synge's ability to *pay attention*. He concentrates, listens, attends, and does so in reverence and openness: this attentiveness is related to art, to writing. It is an outgoing of the spirit to the encounter with variousness and variation:

> In all healthy movements of art, variations from the ordinary types of manhood are made interesting for the ordinary man. . . . Besides this art, however, founded on the variations which are a condition and effort of all vigorous life, there is another art - sometimes confounded with it - founded on the freak of nature.[11]

Variation, departure from the fixed stereotype, is what attracts him, but freakishness repels. Insanity, mania, follow on from freakishness, which is one-sided and extreme. Such a lack of balance may, to some extent, be countered by a discipline of attentiveness to the detail of actuality. This process may be seen at work in an episode in 'Glencree' from *In Wicklow and West Kerry and Connemara,* written in 1907:

> I remember being in the heather one clear Sunday morning in the early autumn when the bracken had just turned. All the people of the district were at Mass in a chapel a few miles away, so the valleys were empty, and there was nothing to be heard but the buzzing of a few late bees and the autumn song of thrushes. The sky was covered with white radiant clouds, with soft outlines, broken in a few places by lines of blue sky of wonderful delicacy and clearness. In a little while I heard a step on a path beneath me, and a tramp came wandering round the bottom of the hill. There was a spring below where I was lying, and when he reached it he looked round to see if anyone was watching him. I was hidden by the ferns, so he knelt down beside the water, where there was a pool among the stones, pulled his shirt over his head, and began washing it in the spring. After a little he seemed satisfied, and began wringing the water out of it, and wandered on towards the village, picking blackberries from the hedge.[12]

The waywardness of the tramp, the fact that he is outside the usual sets of conventions (he, like the narrator, is not at church), are all registered in the story, which attends to describing the scene with the utmost clarity. The events that unfold in the writing, though matter-of-fact, are, in another sense, charged with strangeness. The tramp intrudes upon the drowsy peacefulness, the vacancy even, of the opening sentences, as the narrating consciousness re-enacts the lull and relaxation of the quiet moment in the woods. Then comes the shocking detail of the act of stripping, followed by the disturbing recollection that the tramp put the wet shirt back on, before he goes off, picking blackberries. There is no interpretation in the paragraph itself: the scene is given in its luminousness. The following paragraph, which was not included in the 1910 edition of the works which Synge oversaw, does offer a gloss, saying that this man 'seemed to have lifted himself also into the mood of the sky',[13] which suggests that Synge perceived a relation between the man, the setting and the observing consciousness. A balance is struck, wherein the external world is presented, in all its variations and complexity, while at the same time there is, in the prose, in the way the images unfold, a sense of a framing consciousness, an awareness ready to go out to that which is external to itself, and interact with it, ponder it, register it completely. This readiness to involve the mind with that which is different from it is Synge's meditative attentiveness, his, to use a phrase from an unpublished manuscript, 'transfigured realism':

> Transfigured realism simply asserts objective existence as separate from and independent of subjective existence. But it asserts neither that any one mode of this existence is in reality that which it seems, nor that the connexions among its modes are objectively what they seem.[14]

'Transfigured realism' is a method, an artistic discipline, which simultaneously allows to history and the external world their own distinctness, while at the same time retaining a sense of the uniqueness of the observing consciousness, or the self. Slippage either way is a loss of 'composure', such as happened when he first encountered Darwin's disturbing question, where the external world assumed a horrific and radical strangeness. But that loss, that terror, also conveyed, to the youthful Synge, that the 'connexions' between the mode of existence, between, for example, a man's hand and a bat's wing, are 'not what they seem'. Their true 'connexions' may only be discerned through science, philosophy, or, for the artist, in 'transfigured realism' which allows the actual strangeness inhering in the apparent relations between events to emerge. Synge's method is to break the film of familiarity to reveal the reality in any situation, always, he implies, a complex matter. He structures and shapes his writing in such a way as to allow this inner reality, hidden to the 'ordinary' eye, to emerge. His writing seeks to change our method of looking, of apprehension, and a powerful instrument in accomplishing this is his language, but that consideration will be kept to the close of the chapter.

The story of Yeats's meeting with Synge in Paris and of the advice he claimed to have given to the younger man, that he should go to Aran and give expression to a life which had not been expressed before is well known.[15] There can be little doubt that Synge's periods on the islands were the making of him as an artist. His experience there totally altered his artistic outlook, in that it sharpened for him, made emphatic, the difference between his own customary life (of free-thinking, relatively comfortable aesthete/writer/photographer), and the life he found off the west coast of Ireland.

Towards the end of the first section of *The Aran Islands* he recounts the dream experience he had one night, which sums up the profound excitement the place generated in him. He dreams that he is walking among buildings, with an 'intense light' on them. He hears the music of a stringed instrument which comes closer to him, quickening all the time, until it begins to move in his own 'nerves and blood'. He feels the urge to dance, to join with this dream music. To yield he knows means to be caught up in a terrible agony, so he holds his knees with his hands. But he cannot resist; he is swept away into the music and the dance until all sense of his own individual self is gone. Then, with a shock the delight turns to agony and he struggles to free himself. With a burst of frenzy, totally out of control, he breaks back to normal consciousness:

> I dragged myself trembling to the window of the cottage and looked out. The moon was glittering across the sky, and there was no sound anywhere on the island.[16]

Synge is describing an experience in which the power of the attractiveness of this world, so different to him, becomes so great as to lead, almost, to the dissolution of the self. He is drawn into the collective, the alluring totality in which individual variation is cancelled. But with an effort of will he pulls back, asserts his difference from that ultimate surrender, and returns to variation: he himself varies from the collective, and it has manifold variations in itself. The moment that concludes the episode, when he looks out of the window at the moon on the sea, with all its implications of change, re-establishes variation, difference, the activity of transfigured realism, which measures these separations and holds them up for the mind. The story of this dream is nothing less than a description of the making of Synge the artist.

In part three of *The Aran Islands,* when we come to the episode recounting the threshing of the rye and the making of the straw ropes, Synge weaves a powerful and sinewy arrangement of episodes which shows a confident and subtle mastery, aware of the interactions between the different stories and episodes and the relations between their modes and his narrating consciousness.

Just before this description of the threshing and the rope-making, Synge is lost once more, on a cold foggy September night. He cannot feel his own body, he says, and seems to exist 'merely' in his 'perception of the waves and the crying birds'.[17] Once again, Synge's mind has moved out to engage with the objectivity of the world, and once again it is potentially extreme and dangerous. Two grey shadows appear; they are the islanders, going home: 'I spoke to them and heard their voices.' Variation re-establishes itself, and he comes back to his own self, but now in the company of others. Then follows the description of the threshing, full of light, warmth, colour and activity. Here are human beings in a community of variation and difference; this is not a collective:

> A few days ago when I was visiting a cottage where there are the most beautiful children on the island, the eldest daughter, a girl of about fourteen, went and sat down on a heap of straw by the door. A ray of sunlight fell on her and on a portion of the rye.[18]

In wet weather the rope-twisting is done indoors, with the person twisting receding out of the door on to the lane and into the field beyond. All the cottages in the village do this work, so that the laneway 'has a curious look, and one has to pick one's steps through a maze of twisting ropes that pass from the dark doorways on either side into the fields.'[19]

He has created a style in which the life of the islands, in all its severity, intermingles with his own impressions. The method is disciplined attentiveness, a meditative transfiguring realism that gives its due value to the objective and subjective impulses.

The imagination of island people, and of those he met on the roads in Wicklow, West Kerry and Connemara, he found 'rich and living'. Fed by that, encouraged by its vitality, he felt able to give, in his plays and prose works, this 'reality' back again, in translated or transfigured form. 'Reality', he wrote in the *Playboy* preface, is the root of all poetry, and he was drawn to what was 'superb and wild' in it, what would shift the ordinary focus and move the audience, by offering them something different from the sombre fatalism of Zola, or the sickly joy of 'musical comedy'.[20]

The relations between things in the objective world are not always what they seem, he wrote in his gloss upon the concept of 'transfigured realism'. Reality is full of surprising shocks, and the artist who wants to base his or her fictions on life should find a way of accommodating these thrusts of being, giving them a live and supple shape. But first of all they must be noticed, so the basic discipline is meditative attentiveness. In 'In West Kerry', published in 1907, he describes how, on the journey to Dublin from the south-west, the station platforms are thronged with people, saying farewell to their sons or daughters leaving to take the emigrant ship from Queenstown to America. The old men and women 'wait with anguish'; one old woman makes a wild rush after the train when it moves off. Then the mood shifts, things are hardly ever predictable.

> Two young men had got into our compartment for a few stations only, and they looked on with the greatest satisfaction.
>
> 'Ah,' said one of them, 'we do have great sport every Friday and Saturday, seeing the old women howling in the stations.'[21]

This is deadly accurate, funny and very moving at one and the same time. In the *Playboy* preface, as well as saying that reality is the root of all poetry, Synge adds that the writer, in a culture where the imagination is rich and living, can transmit that reality in a comprehensive form; one that will comprehend the swift transitions that take place in actuality, as in the train compartment he shared with the two young men who enjoyed the tragic show every Friday and Saturday.

As Mary King has pointed out, there is something haunting about the opening of *The Well of the Saints* (first performed in 1905):

> MARY DOUL. What place are we now, Martin Doul?
> MARTIN DOUL. Passing the gap.[22]

The 'gap' is there on stage, in 'a low loose wall' at the back, signalling the various gaps that are to be explored theatrically and psychologically: for example that between subjective and objective views of the world. The two blind people, Mary and Martin, through the saint's cure, must experience the shock of objectivity when they face the fact that the illusions with which they have mutually sustained each other, claiming, in their darkness, that they are beautiful and desirable, are based only on the stories they have constructed. But there is also the gap between Molly Byrne's good looks (she is a 'fine looking girl with fair hair') and her harsh and shallow worldly wisdom. There is the gap between Martin's capacity to love, his readiness to throw himself completely into rhapsody for Molly's sake, and his weather-beaten physique, with a 'head . . . as bald as an old turnip you'd see rolling around in the muck'. There is the gap between blindness and vision, and there is the gap between the life of the village the Douls came upon, and the larger life beyond, to which Martin is continuously drawn. To Molly Byrne, whom he tries to entice away with him, he says:

> Let you come now, I'm saying, to the lands of Iveragh and the Reeks of Cork, where you won't set down the width of your two feet and not be crushing fine flowers, and making sweet smells in the air.
>
> MOLLY BYRNE. . . . Leave me go, Martin Doul.
>
> MARTIN DOUL. Let you not be fooling. Come along now the little path through the trees.[23]

The 'little path through the trees' is the way through to the larger, more expansive world that awaits, in Martin's visionary rhapsody; it is a world which is absent, it is a 'gap', but like the gap on the stage, which is an absence, it is there for us in Martin's talk: an absent presence. Molly Byrne's pleas to be left alone are the cries of anxiety and fear roused by the terrifying paradox embodied in what Martin says: come with me, into the gap, the illusion, which is made real by virtue of my speech. The audience can watch this interplay in the gap between their own lives and the enactions and speech that are taking place on stage. Synge's power of concentration acquires dramatic charge and presence in the way he draws together the relations between different, even contradictory elements in a situation, so that the theatrical energy is focused, intent, simple and concentrated. Yet he is also alive to the continuous activity of variation as between the different points of view of the protagonists, and the variations and shifts each character may discover in his or her own changing points of view. There are gaps between illusion and reality, blindness and vision; and there are gaps between the ordinary valuations placed on each of these terms and the new ones the play unfolds; but, more searchingly perhaps, Synge explores the discontinuities inherent in actuality (as in the train compartment in the south-west), and puts them on stage. This is where his troublesome, disruptive energy comes from: it is a capacity for recognizing difference and continuous variation, while giving them an apparently reckless but totally coherent shape. Hence Joyce's admiration, Moore's praise and Beckett's acknowledged debt.

In *Riders to the Sea,* first performed in 1904, all is fated. There seems to be no variation whatsoever. Maurya's family is doomed to follow the fate of so many on the islands as Synge knew them. As Maurya herself says, in a phrase that is almost grotesquely comic, 'there does be a power of young men floating around in the sea.'[24]

The stage is set with the appurtenances of death: some 'new boards' stand by the wall when the play opens, brought for the funeral of the drowned Michael, once his body is found. The boards are used, however, for Bartley's funeral, the last of Maurya's menfolk. In the play everything is known, familiar, inescapable. As has been pointed out,[25] the psychological geography of the play is continuously brought to the forefront of attention. The sea is bad by 'the white rocks', there's 'a great roaring in the west',[26] which will get worse when the tide turns. Cathleen hears someone 'passing the big stones'. Bartley is going to the fair to sell the mare, against Maurya's wishes, who knows he is going to be killed like all the rest. She does not see him when he goes out, so she goes down to the 'spring well' to give him a hunk of the newly made bread and to break the 'dark word'. This reality, the reality of the mind-set of the characters on the stage, is powerfully objectified. Each place or thing ('Give her the stick, Nora, or maybe she'll slip on *the big stones*' (my italics)) has its own definite article, creating a contour of consciousness, for the audience, in which this reality is strongly demonstrated through incessant naming. This world, beyond the cottage, outside the world of the stage, is objectively registered in the text spoken by the actors; it is known, to the characters, and luminously familiar; but it is also a dangerous place, fraught with the continuous reality of death. The relation between the sea and the islanders, between the forces of nature and the supernatural, are inscrutable, for all the familiarity of the contours of the island. No one knows what will happen to anyone when they pass the threshold, out of the warmth of the kitchen, where bread is baked, but where the materials for a coffin also stand ready. For the kitchen, with its comforting, life-giving fire is no haven from the unknown relations between the forces of the world beyond. We recall again Synge's 'transfigured realism', where the object is clearly set apart from the subject, but where the relations between the different elements in the objective mode are not always what they seem. Here, in *Riders to the Sea*, they are inscrutable and terrifying. It is certain that Maurya's men are doomed. She knows this, and must accept it.

This powerfully registered and fearfully present objective world is there in the fact that the characters name it. The audience do not *see* the white rocks, the big slippery stones, the spring well, or Bartley's mad ride down to the sea. They are, like the 'gap' in *The Well of the Saints*, an absent presence, in the unique way theatre can bring absence into play.

The outside world does come in, of course, in its effects: Bartley's body is carried into the kitchen in exactly the way Patch was brought in when Bartley was a baby lying on Maurya's two knees. The same thing happens again and again. Death repeats itself in exactly the same way each time. Maurya describes Patch being brought in:

> I seen two women, and three women, and four women coming in, and they crossing themselves and not saying a word. I looked out then, and there were men coming after them, and they holding a thing in the half of a red sail, and water dripping out of it - it was a dry day, Nora - and leaving a track to the door.

As soon as she says this the same thing begins to happen again: women come in, crossing themselves; they are followed by men carrying a body. Nora looks out, and says:

> They're carrying a thing among them, and there's water dripping out of it and leaving a track by the big stones.[27]

The nature of the relations between 'things' in the objective world is baffling and mysterious - a person may become 'a thing' - but the inevitability of doom is clear. All fall prey to victimage. And yet the action does not stop at this point; the play moves again, and this move takes it into greatness, the quality that called forth the praise of Herbert Grierson, who rated it with Greek tragedy. The next move is a subjective one, Maurya's turn away from the overpowering objectivity of things to the variation possible in the human psyche, which can imagine an acceptance of even total loss:

> They've all gone now, and there isn't anything more the sea can do to me. . . . I'll have no call now to be up crying and praying when the wind breaks from the south.[28]

This move towards a strange buoyant freedom, a release from striving and from hope, creates an extraordinary surge of energy at the close of the play. It is, almost, a victory. Death here unveils 'the mountain-range of being'[29] to quote Martin Heidegger, in the sombre and glorious freedom of Maurya's speech, at once resigned, relaxed and totally alive to the reality that has unveiled itself. The polar opposite of Senecan futility, it reaches into a confident freedom, which allows things their reality, but which holds its own arena as well: it is a steady 'composure' (Synge's own word recording his recovery from the shock of Darwin) all the more assured because of the volume of suffering it speaks from. This speech is a departure from the fixed and inescapable fate embodied in the world beyond the kitchen, where the geography is haunted by a doom that is unalterable. In this language Maurya breaks out of the deathly recurrence presented dramatically in the play: she narrates a death only for the same thing to happen again on stage. This sequence, where an action is doubly presented, underlines the terror of objective reality, only to have it absorbed into the comprehensiveness of Maurya's vision. The effect is one whereby what we see on stage is charged with the intensity of concentrated awareness: we really look at what is happening, attend to what is being said.

The ear, Adrienne Rich has said,[30] can be cleansed to a severer form of listening. This rigour is Synge's discipline, which inspired Yeats and Beckett, amongst many others. Ann Saddlemyer, in particular, has shown the process of this discipline: her editorial work on the plays and the letters revealed a Synge who worked and reworked this material with a fierce and unremitting self-criticism. In *The Playboy of the Western World,* first performed in 1907, levels of significance play into one another, to create a most complex web of interaction between story and deed, subjectivity and objectivity, and dramatic action and audience response. Synge himself said as much in a letter to the *Irish Times* in the middle of the *Playboy* controversy. P.D. Kenny ('Pat' was his pen name) had reviewed the play for the newspaper favourably, and said that its realistic environment was 'more a psychological revelation than a dramatic process', which, as criticism, is, to some extent, aware of Synge's dramatic method and his theatrical preoccupations. In the letter Synge wrote: 'There are, it may be hinted, several sides to "The Playboy". "Pat", I am glad to notice, has seen some of them in his own way. There may be still others if anyone cares to look for them.'[31]

In *Riders to the Sea* the objective reality of stones, sea and the island itself is powerfully present by virtue of the fact that it is continually called to mind in the text's naming of these locations, indeed presences. That reality, baffling but inescapable, then invades the stage in the form of Bartley's carried body, so the gap between the kitchen where children are fed and nurtured and the harshness of the life beyond is made physically present to us on the stage. It is less odd to speak of a 'gap' being present, if we recall the 'actual' gap in *The Well of the Saints.* In *The Playboy* there is, as Pegeen Mike has to admit, 'a great gap between a gallous story and a dirty deed', and that gap is the space in which the dramatic action takes place. Like *Riders to the Sea,* the play reaches its climax by physically confronting the audience with the gap: a man who was supposed to be dead confronts his own son, and would-be killer, in utter rage and with the extremest violence.

The first part of the play is a celebration of the power of language not just to name, but to fashion reality, to play with it creatively. Christy Mahon, the 'play-boy', is a Christ figure. Reborn by virtue of the narrative he finds such an accommodating audience for in Mayo, he becomes attractive, vital, energetic. At the opening of Act II, he is in fine spirits. There is 'brilliant morning light', on this Easter of the body. Christy is 'bright and cheerful', cleaning Pegeen's boots. He looks into the looking-glass and he notices that he has changed. He seems handsome, and he predicts that his skin will acquire a new lustre, the freshness and vitality of the hero, the man of the hour. He has always had an intimation he was like this, in reality:

> Didn't I know rightly I was handsome, though it was the divil's own mirror we had beyond, would twist a squint

> across an angel's brow; and I'll be a growing fine from this day, the way I'll have a soft lovely skin on me and won't be the like of the clumsy young fellows do be ploughing all times in the dung.[32]

This transformation has come about through the power of his story, which he tells with increasing vigour each time he recites it. The villagers delight in this tale of ferocity, so different from their ordinary lives. Pegeen Mike is courted by the playboy in language which has all the space and humour of Connacht folk song intermixed with the elaborate and impassioned rhetoric of Petrarch's sonnets to Laura, which Synge studied and translated:

> If the mitred bishops seen you that time, they'd be the like of the holy prophets, I'm thinking, do be straining the bars of paradise to lay eyes on the Lady Helen of Troy, and she abroad, pacing back and forward, with a nosegay in her golden shawl.[33]

This bravura performance links the strangeness of folk song with the Italian renaissance, as well as referring to antiquity. Christy's linguistic energy has expanded to such an extent that he can now effortlessly make these transitions, just as, physically, he can overcome all obstacles: he has won everything there was to be won at the races earlier in this, the third Act. But climactic and gorgeous courtship is darkened for the audience by their knowledge that Old Mahon is not dead, that he has been around for some time. At the beginning of this Act Synge has presented us with the first of the many shocks to be administered before the end of the play, shocks that register the gap between what is said and the actual situation. Philly and Jimmy have come back from the wake; slightly drunk. Jimmy, answering Philly's slightly malicious prediction that Christy will run out of luck and will eventually be caught, says: 'his father should be rotten by now.' As he says this Old Mahon passes by the window, 'slowly'. Philly's and Jimmy's conversation goes on to discuss what might happen if someone with 'a long spade' down in Kerry were to dig up the two halves of Old Mahon's skull:

> JIMMY. They'd say it was an old Dane, maybe, was drowned in the flood. (*Old Mahon comes in and sits down near door listening.*)[34]

Reality, in the form of the old man, is now on stage, a visual counterpoint to and farcical interrogation of the storytelling and invention that proceeds, all to do with deaths, bones, skeletons:

> Did you ever hear tell of the skulls they have in the city of Dublin, ranged out like blue jugs in a cabin at Connaught?

Philly responds to Jimmy's sepulchral inventions by telling of a skeleton he used to assemble, as a young lad, with 'thighs as long as your arm', at which point Old Mahon stands up to show them his own cracked skull, asking them to tell him 'where and when was another the like of it':

> PHILLY. Glory be to God! And who hit you at all?
> MAHON. (*triumphantly*). It was my own boy hit me. Would you believe that?

Mahon is 'triumphant' because of the outrageousness of what has happened; he exults in it. He, too, like Christy, has an audience, and his storytelling abilities contest with Christy's in this Act. But the core of the dramatic tension is that he is the visible refutation and evidence of Christy's act, grown heroic in the telling, a tension expressed at this point in the contrast between Old Mahon's presence on stage and Philly's and Jimmy's talk about skeletons, bones and old Danes. The effect is broadly comic here, but in the course of this Act the farce becomes savage.

Mahon tries to assert his old authority over his son, threatening to 'skelp' him if he does not come along with him. Pegeen Mike mocks the playboy, who now turns vicious again. He goes for his father and lays him out. The villagers seize him now and treat him as a criminal, not a hero. They tie him up, Pegeen tries to burn him with a sod of turf, and Christy bites at Shawn Keogh's leg. Old Mahon comes in, to be killed a third time, 'on all fours'. Son and father confront each other on their knees, before Old Mahon unties Christy. The objective reality of the story the villagers have collaborated in with Christy is now before them, and it is entirely different from the heroic narration of it. It is brutish, violent and unpredictable, because Christy himself has changed, objectively, by virtue of that story; he now assumes authority over the father: 'I'll see you from this day stewing my oatmeal and mashing my spuds,' a transformation Old Mahon strangely accepts, and says: '(*With a broad smile*) I am crazy again.'[35] Mayo remains static ('We'll have peace now for our drinks'), while the playboy and his father are off out into the world of difference, change; that objective world beyond the imagining of the villagers where the relations between things are not what they seem.

In *The Playboy* the objective world, in the form of the playboy himself, invades a static situation and transforms it. He, too, is transformed, because his energy finds a context in which to work: to develop his self-image he needs a mirror. He discovers himself as a subject in the receptive listening of the Mayo people and in so doing increases the vitality of his presence, overcoming all obstacles in the objective world, even his own father at the close. He is transfigured as is his reality.

As Synge himself said, there are many sides to this play. It is a comic meditation on the transformative power of the imagination as it moves between stasis and activity; it is an objective exploration of the *relationship between* passivity and action; and it is a criticism and celebration of the human capacity for storytelling. Christy's storytelling makes a difference, to himself and to the Mayo people: change takes place in him and in Pegeen Mike. Although the objective would challenge him, in the form of the old man, he is able to change that relationship itself by the end of the action. The weight and power of objectivity is lightened. The audience know, with Pegeen, that there is a great 'gap' between a gallous story and a dirty deed; but they see Christy and his father passing through it, as Pegeen Mike cannot.

Christy Mahon, Synge's great storyteller, is a master of variation, as well as, eventually, 'all fights'.[36] *Deirdre of the Sorrows*, first performed in 1910, returns us to the tragic world of *Riders to the Sea*, where inevitability is once again the master. Deirdre is locked in a story she cannot remake, despite her efforts to do so. 'Saga people', Synge was worried after he had completed the first draft of the play, might loosen his 'grip',[37] but the saga of *Longas Mac nUislenn* appealed because in it was already scripted a fate for Deirdre from which she cannot escape:

> DEIRDRE. (*without hope*). There's little power in oaths to stop what's coming, and little power in what I'd do, Lavarcham, to change the story of Conchubor and Naisi and the things old men foretold.[38]

The iron sadness of this tale, one of the oldest in Irish literature, drew Synge because of its challenge. How could he make a story working out to a preordained end theatrically interesting? It was the antithesis of *The Playboy*, where the field of potential opens up totally in the gap Christy goes through with his father at the close. Here everything is closing down, right from the start. There is no otherworld to interfere with the action, as in Yeats; nor are there the diversions of social conscience or humanism, as in Ibsen. It is a play which concentrates, with iron rigour, on human weakness, inconsistency and unhappiness. Maurya, in *Riders to the Sea*, faced into reality scoured of fear, strangely liberated in being stripped of all hope. Here hope waxes and wanes, but at the back of it all, at the back of Deirdre's mind, there is the knowledge that activity is futile and useless, a knowledge she shares with Conchubor:

> The like of us have a store of knowledge that's a weight and terror; it's for that we do choose only the like of yourself that are young and glad only.[39]

Conchubor is wrong about Deirdre; she too has this 'store of knowledge', about fatality. But where is the dramatic interest of the play? Did Synge succeed in re-creating a 'transfigured realism' with this story?

The play concentrates upon the 'weight and terror' of a situation in which people are doomed, no matter what they do. The fact of death is presented, as well as the mercilessness of age and the inconsistency of love. These are objective facts and they exist, independent of our subjective wishes about them, one way or another. There is nothing to be done about them. This tale, like Darwin's interpretation of nature and history, indicates that there can be no ascendancy over the reality of existence. It is out there, unknown and terrifying, and may invade at any moment. Deirdre's escape from Ireland, her courtship of Naisi, the loyalty she exacts from his brothers, are all deferrals of the ultimate confrontation with death, and she knows it. So that it is with a kind of relief she faces the grave in the third Act. She pulls the curtains in the hut Conchubor has given them on their return to Emain, to find the grave he has prepared for the Sons of Usna. Deirdre says: 'It's a grave, Naisi, that is wide and deep.'[40] Synge totally avoids any trace of romanticism in regard to this situation. Instead of consolatory or brave talk of being united in death, there are harsh questions, and deep divisions between the lovers. Synge tormented himself with the writing of this Act and remained unsatisfied, but he was trying to turn the tragedy right into the bleakest realization possible: that men and women die, honourable in one breath, frantic and disgraced in the next. The drama faces the objective reality of death, and the prospect that the relations between the different attitudes to this reality are fluid and changing, right up to the last silence. Deirdre asks Naisi if she were to die first, would he find another to take her place. Naisi replies, and Synge makes every word count:

> It's little I know, saving only that it's a hard and bitter thing leaving the earth, and a worse and harder thing leaving yourself alone and desolate to be making lamentation on its face always.

He moves from his own terror and sadness at death to a pity for her whom he thinks will remain after him. How could anyone stand being alone and desolate making lamentation for very long? She says that he is making 'strange and distant talk', to which he replies:

> There's nothing, surely, the like of a new grave of open earth for putting a great space between two friends that love.[41]

The grave is the final gap, the final absence. That, for Synge the playwright, is that. Not a trace of the consolatory intimation of an otherworld enters. The drama concentrates on the actuality of death; the terms remain completely human, and focus on its inevitability.

Deirdre of the Sorrows moves steadily to present that which the action defers from the outset: the deaths of Deirdre and the Sons of Usna. He did not use the version of the story in the *Book of Leinster*, followed by Geoffrey Keating's *Forus Feasa ar Eirinn*, where Deirdre survives Naisi and is kept as Conchubor's mistress for a time, until she smashes her brains out by throwing herself out of a chariot against a rock.[42] Synge's purpose is single and monochrome: the drama must move to the actuality of death. There are fissures and divisions as the action approaches this 'weight and terror', particularly between Deirdre and Naisi, which shock in that they reveal very little commonality of feeling between them as they face the catastrophe. All identities are, to one degree or another, fictions, Synge is implying. All love is, to some extent, fictional, an invention. The vision, in its bleak but steady, composed scepticism, its composure, is akin to that of Samuel Beckett:

> I read of Galway, Mayo, Aranmore,
> And men with kelp along a wintry shore.
> Then I remembered that that 'I' was I,
> And I'd a filthy job - to waste and die.[43]

The naked utterance of this late poem stands in stark contrast to the language of the plays, with their use of what has been called 'dialect'. There has been much debate about the sources which Synge drew upon, and heated discussion of the authenticity of Synge's language, St John Ervine claiming, for example, that he was a 'faker of peasant speech'. Declan Kiberd has shown that some of his most striking phrases he took from actual letters from friends he had made on Aran.[44] Nora's 'No man at all can be living for ever' in *Riders to the Sea* is a direct translation from a letter to Synge by Martin McDonough of Inishmaan written in 1902: '(Ní) féidir le aon nduine a bheith beo go deo.' The simple fact about Synge's Hiberno-English speech in the plays is that it is an English written as if it were a translation from the Irish, so that the hidden language of modern Ireland beats behind Synge's rhythm and syntax. He was struck by Douglas Hyde's *Love Songs of Connacht,* in particular by the literal prose translations Hyde gave at the foot of each page. These prose versions, which mirrored the Irish syntax faithfully, were a grounding commentary on the original Irish text on the left-hand side of the page, and the verse translations, on the right.[45] This curious English of Hyde's was a half-way house between Irish and English verse - it went into the gap between the two cultures and civilizations. An example of this would be Hyde's literal version of 'Mala Néifin' ('The Brow of Nefin'), one of Synge's own favourites, which he remembered when writing Christy's love-speeches to Pegeen:

> If I were to be on the brow of Nefin and my hundred loves by my side, it is pleasantly we would sleep together like the little bird on the bough. It is your melodious wordy little mouth that increased my pain, and a quiet sleep I cannot [get] until I shall die, alas![46]

This language is clumsy and thin compared to the drive and pulse of Synge, but it is clear that the absent Gaelic haunts Synge's syntax. If we take the speech (already quoted in this chapter) which Christy makes to himself before the mirror at the beginning of Act II of *The Playboy*, and translate it into Irish, it is clear how immediately present the Irish is in Synge's English. This is the speech beginning 'Didn't I know rightly I was handsome', previously quoted:

> Nárbh fhios agam go cruinn go rabhas dathúil cé gurbh é scathán an diabhail féin do bhi againn thall, a chasfadh claonamharc thar éadan aingil; agus is mé a bheidh ag éiri galánta ón lá seo amach, sa tslí go mbeidh cneas tláith álainn orm, agus ni bhead cosúil leis na buachaillí tuatacha a bhíonn i gconaí ag saothrú talún agus aoíligh.

No claims are made for this translation. Synge's poetic language is much more energetic than the Irish here, but it is clear that Synge, while writing English, had continually in his inner ear, the grammar and syntactical impetus of Irish. He writes English as if it carried Irish inside it. But the Irish is absent of course; Synge writes English, but an English alive to the absence of Irish, an absence so intense that it is almost a presence. Synge's dramatic language goes into the gap between the two languages to become an absent presence, a 'thing which is not'[47] to logic or objectivity, but which exists objectively, on the page, in the theatre. Synge's language is the means by which he achieves his 'transfigured realism'. It exists objectively, separate from our subjective or orthodox views about language. It is different, and stands apart from the normal usages of English by its deliberate and thoughtful strangeness, and in so doing it affirms its objectivity. But the set of relations between its terms, its grammar in other words, while it does follow something like the system of English, is also made strange by the closeness of another grammar, another set of relations, that of Irish.

Synge's language is a field of play that operates between two languages, two sets of attitudes, two constructions of the world, two grammars. In this field things are not what they seem, ever, but stand out clearly, in their oddness and immediate reality to create a 'transfigured realism' whose method is a language that goes into the gap between Irish and English. It does so with concentration, circumspection and readiness to observe all the differentiations and variations of being. His theatrical method *is*

Irish as he said it was in the interview given to the *Evening Mail* which is the epigraph to this chapter; it is the Irish language itself.

6

JAMES JOYCE

'He rests. He has travelled'[1]

Simon Dedalus, modelled upon James Joyce's father, John Joyce, was one of those Corkmen who enjoyed life. He kept 'the ball rolling anyhow' as he tells Stephen in *A Portrait*; and he and his pals, including the plaintively named 'poor little good-hearted Johnny Keevers of the Tantiles',[2] enjoyed themselves in Cork city, and 'were none the worse of it either'.

Stephen, all too aware in *A Portrait* that he is 'sundered' from his father and his world, is less self-conscious, more accommodating, in *Stephen Hero*. There we are told that Stephen persuades his mother and his father to read Ibsen. His mother rises to this challenge; Simon Dedalus, however, does not do so well, or so it appears at first glance. He has a down to earth approach to literature, and seeks to relate the Norwegian's themes to his own experience:

> Following the custom of certain old-fashioned people who can never understand why their patronage or judgements should put men of letters into a rage he chose his play from the title. A metaphor is a vice that attracts the dull mind by reason of its aptness and repels the too serious mind by reason of its falsity and danger so that, after all, there is something to be said, nothing voluminous perhaps, but at least a word of concession for that class of society which in literature as in everything else goes always with its four feet on the ground. Mr. Dedalus, anyhow, suspected that *A Doll's House* would be a triviality in the manner of *Little Lord Fauntleroy* and, as he had never been even unofficially a member of that international society which collects and examines psychical phenomena, he decided that *Ghosts* would probably be some uninteresting story about a

> haunted house. He chose the *League of Youth* in which he hoped to find the reminiscences of like-minded roysterers.[3]

Needless to say, he is disappointed. There is a sense in which Joyce, here, in his concession to the four-footed attitude to literature and to life, has acknowledged two central aspects of his own approach to writing: that there is a great deal to be said for the sane, normal, everyday cast of mind in relation to art; and there is something to be wary of in metaphor. A simple, literal-minded approach has a lot to be said for it, not least because it is the sort of attitude shared by a great many people. There is, he is suggesting, comically, something false and dangerous in metaphor, in the attitude of mind which will call a thing something else, calling Ireland 'Dark Rosaleen' for example, or the Church 'Mother' Church. The corollary of this distrust is the virtue of calling a spade a spade.

Simon Dedalus 'kept the ball rolling anyhow', which is what a storyteller does. Narrative is the movement of the 'ball' along a line, its movement shifting as it encounters different things along its path, deflecting its impetus in response to fresh directions and impacts. In some respects we can adopt this 'rolling ball' as a model for Joyce's narrative strategy, one distrustful of metaphor, open to chance. There is a danger, in this model, of reducing Joyce's narrative voice to a dreary exercise in Newtonian physics, whereas his stories are densely wrought and wonderfully implicated. The point worth stressing here is that whatever the complex and manifold elaboration of signs, the essential impetus in Joyce is along a path or trajectory of movement, an activity of consciousness amongst things, a peripatetic multifaceted mirroring of things in time by a moving presence.

Take the extraordinarily charged simplicity of the narrative line in *Dubliners*; as it moves through differing scenes the awareness of the unfolding consciousness is so intensely alive it seems to miss nothing. In 'Clay', for instance, the narrative line seems to be recording a series of tense situations, but the incidents are presented in a luminous and steady progression which evolves rhythmically in a prose meticulously alive to the shock and impressions registered *by* Maria, as she moves through these experiences, and *for* us, as we read:

> [Joe] was very nice with her. He told her all that went on in his office, repeating for her a smart answer which he had

> made to the manager. Maria did not understand why Joe laughed so much over the answer he had made, but she said that the manager must have been a very overbearing person to deal with. Joe said he wasn't so bad when you knew how to take him, and he was a decent sort so long as you didn't rub him up the wrong way. . . . Nobody could find the nutcrackers, and Joe was nearly getting cross over it and asked how did they expect Maria to crack nuts without a nutcracker.[4]

And so on. 'Scrupulous meanness'[5] is the phrase Joyce used to describe this style, but while there is a holding back from intervention, from commentary, there is also, in the writing, a quality of openness to the movement of impression and shifts of feeling. This 'openness' needed restraint, a quality of reserve and attentiveness he described as 'classicism' in *Stephen Hero*.

An openness to things is essentially the same quality of attention as he described, comically, as Simon Dedalus's 'four-footed' approach to literature and to life. Things are as they are; go to them direct; don't interpret, moralize, or vaporize them by metaphor. But as Patrick Kavanagh knew, some means must be found of disentangling the immediacy and significance of a thing, a scene, a mood, a look, from the variousness of 'defining circumstances'.[6] If this cannot be done then there is a danger of 'spiritual anarchy', as Joyce described it in *Stephen Hero*, an indiscriminate democracy of impressions, such as we find in William Burroughs; or, as Joyce saw it, in the Romantic temper.

The Romantic temper is 'an insecure, unsatisfied, impatient temper which sees no fit abode here for its ideals and chooses therefore to behold them under insensible figures':[7] A.E.'s formless spiritual essences in *Ulysses*. The classical temper, 'ever mindful of limitations, chooses rather to bend upon these present things and so to work upon them and fashion them that the quick intelligence may go beyond them to their meaning which is still unuttered.'

That last phrase: '*their meaning which is still unuttered*', should be underlined, because Joyce is insistent that the classical temper, patient, intent, and intensely aware, looks to present things, seeks to reveal them as they are, but without pretending to reveal their secrets. He is not, in other words, a gnostic, seeking an alchemical revelation in the here and now. The here and now must be clung to, as Stephen reminds himself in the exposition on Shakespeare in the National Library, not transformed into something else. It is miraculous enough as it is. Joyce's classicism, then, literal, patient, aware, is a circumspect and reverential moving towards things, to leave them as they are, but to hold them up in the formal revelation which writing is; an elevation, an epiphany of what is.

The classical temper, because it bends the mind to phenomena, runs the risk of materialism; Romanticism runs the risk of disappearing into the vapours of moods and essences. Yeats, as Richard Ellmann has indicated, acted as a kind of Virgil to Joyce's Dante; he was mentor *and* warning. But it would be wrong to say that Yeats stood in, for Joyce, as an example of the Romantic temper. In *Stephen Hero* we are told that Stephen reads avidly Yeats's arcane stories 'The Tables of the Law' and 'The Adoration of the Magi', that he knows them by heart. But this study does not mean that Stephen is attracted to the alchemicana of Owen Aherne.

In 'The Tables of the Law' we find that Michael Robartes, whilst attracted to the sensuous surrender to ghostly intimations, presences, stands against them, while Aherne does not. The spirits in the private temple Aherne has devoted to his own worship speak to their supplicant, and ask him to mingle with them:

> 'let your heart mingle with our hearts, which are wrought of Divine Ecstasy, and your body with our bodies, which are wrought of Divine Intellect.' And at that cry I understood that the Order of the Alchemical Rose was not of this earth, and that it was still seeking over this earth for whatever souls it could gather within its glittering net; and when all the faces turned towards me, and I saw the wild eyes and the unshaken eyelids, I was full of terror . . . so that all I held dear, all that bound me to spiritual and social order, would be burnt up, and my soul left naked and shivering among the winds that blow from beyond this world and from beyond the stars.[8]

Joyce's dialogue between the 'hic' (Aherne) and 'ille' (Robartes) is just as intense as Yeats's; but he inclined more toward the 'hic', whereas Yeats tended towards the 'ille'. In doing so Joyce ran the risk of materialism, just as Yeats had risked becoming involved too much in the rose whorls of the order of the alchemical rose. Both Yeats and Joyce escaped the traps the intellect had set for them by continuous movement, by the espousal of an uncertainty principle, and by remaining attentive to the integrity of things as they are, which calls for 'continual affirmation'.[9] Joyce's style of processional awareness is the syllogism by means of which he moves from the world of things to the world of writing, which affirms only what is, and is scrupulously careful to do no more than this. The 'meaning remains unuttered', and because there are no loutish attempts at explication, at the giving away of secrets, a 'sane and joyful spirit *issues forth*' (my italics).[10]

Issuing forth, venturing forth, movement, travel, change: these different words attempt to register the central, abiding impulse in Joyce's work, that of a continuous going out (an *aisling* in the old meaning of the term, implying a venturing forth from fixedness), a probe into the variousness of things and their impact upon the consciousness which ventures forth.

In the discussions of aesthetics that form part of the atmosphere and mood of *Stephen Hero* and *A Portrait,* Thomas Aquinas is drawn in. It is not the intention here to provide yet another summation of this discussion and its relationship to Joyce's epiphanic method; rather it seems appropriate to emphasize in this context the processional, mobile aspect of the way in which the discourse moves.

Stephen wants to grasp the 'act itself of intellection', or of aesthetic 'apprehension', the other word he uses. He dismisses, in his discourse with Lynch, the idea that aesthetic apprehension and delight are linked to some utilitarian or moral function or object. He puts forward the notion that it is the *relations* between aspects of the thing itself and the stages of aesthetic apprehension that are significant. The model he is trying to propose is *relative*; in other words, the elements of the model (integrity, harmony and radiance) are in relation to each other and to the mind which perceives them. These elements move in relation to each other, continually; we move and change in relation to them. So, we speak correctly when we say that something beautiful *moves* us; this movement, this moving experience, is a shifting set of relations whereby the act of cognition, intellection, apprehension, is achieved; but the thing that moves us is there before us. It is still; its meaning never completely uttered. It is other to us, and so the movement of intellection begins yet again, a process quite different from the 'kinetic' effect whereby we are *motivated* to some kind of utilitarian action.

'Are you laughing in your sleeve?' Lynch asks Stephen, who replies that Aquinas, as a poet, might have understood him more completely. There follows then an apparent digression, but by now Joyce is not wasting any words, and we can assume that this departure from the line of enquiry is intended as part of the rhythmic evolution of the argument. He mentions Aquinas's hymn *Pange lingua gloriosi*, but, he says:

> there is no hymn that can be put beside that mournful and majestic processional song, the *Vexilla Regis* of Venantius Fortunatus.[11]

Lynch begins to sing it, then: 'They turned into Lower Mount Street.' Stephen's method is processional and peripatetic. As significant as the ideas developed (and they are developed, not concluded) is the physical movement of Stephen and Lynch through the Dublin streets, and the encounters they have with various people and events: a long dray laden with old iron; the stupid youth Donovan who has read the 'ultra-profound' Lessing; a basket on the head of a butcher's boy. Stephen's intellection is creating a relationship between these things that is joyful and serene and entirely simple. Joyce's art shows us this process at work, and makes it a 'processional' which is both 'fortunate' and moving.

In 'The Wandering Rocks' section of *Ulysses*, Stephen is comfortably disposed of by the Englishman, Haines, who, 'pinching his chin thoughtfully with thumb and forefinger' reflects that his companion of the early morning must have an *idée fixe*: 'Such persons always have,' he confidently asserts. Haines has just been informed by Buck Mulligan that he's missed Dedalus on *Hamlet* in the National Library, something the Englishman seems not to regret, as Shakespeare, he intones, is the happy hunting ground of unbalanced minds.[12]

The last thing Stephen has about *Hamlet*, or about anything else for that matter, is an *idée fixe*. On the contrary, he is all too aware of the 'ineluctable modality of the visible', the materiality of matter, its 'out there-ness', through which he proceeds.

The account of Shakespeare which Stephen gives in the 'Scylla and Charybdis' episode is one in which life and art interact. He goes to great trouble to present to his auditors, George Russell,

R.I. Best, John Eglinton and Buck Mulligan, as much circumstantial detail about Elizabethan London (local colour as he calls it) as he can work in. We see Shakespeare leaving his house in Silver Street, the flag is up on the playhouse, the bear Sackerson growls in the pit, Drake's sailors chew their sausages as they stare up at the apron stage. Shakespeare, in Stephen's story, is playing the ghost of Hamlet's father; he speaks the name Hamlet, to his son, who is not his son, his own son, whom he called Hamnet, having died. Ann Hathaway, Hamnet's mother, is the guilty queen.

It is all a tangle, and Stephen has no fixed theory. He hates what he's doing, and is panic-stricken at times, but he wants to drive home to himself and to others that art and life interpenetrate: art is not an ideal creation of 'formless spiritual essences' as A.E. insists, because such a notion is absurd and, to some degree, revolting. Stephen wants to convey his view that Shakespeare moved through his life converting this experience into the moving relations between the different elements of his art. This readiness to encounter change and difference, and yet remain steady and resolute, without surrendering to spiritual anarchy, is the strength and fortitude of the classical temper, which is focused by the calm application of the will. Our bodies change, all changes, but nevertheless there is continuity of some kind. Ordinary common sense tells us so:

> As we . . . weave or unweave our bodies . . . from day to day, their molecules shuttled to and fro, so does the artist weave and unweave his image. As the mole on my right breast is where it was when I was born, though all my body has been woven of new stuff time after time, so through the ghost of the unquiet father the image of the unliving son looks forth . . . that which I was is that which I am and that which in possibility I may come to be. So in the future, the sister of the past, I may see myself as I sit there now but my reflection from that which then I shall be.[13]

These scholastic manoeuvres are saying only the obvious, but not the obvious which is the 'hell of hells' described in the discussion of classicism in *Stephen Hero*: here the philosophizing is a technique for separating thought from meaning. Stephen is bending his attention to language in order to emphasize the following: that it is a process of discovery as it unrolls its signification; that identity is, to some extent, built up by means of language; and that identity nevertheless is something, out there, that can be spoken of.

The challenge to the artist, for Shakespeare, is: how extensive can the linguistic operation be, how extensive can the self be, that it may incorporate - as much as possible? Everything? Dedalus's daring, panic-stricken thought, unsure though it is, goes for *everything*. Just as all being is reflected in the weaving and unweaving of the molecules in one body, so all life may be reflected in the negotiations of the imagination. These are high claims that Stephen makes, and Joyce is putting himself to the test in weaving these totalizing insights into the fabric of his text. He is attempting in his own writing what Stephen claims Shakespeare accomplished in his. Stephen sees him, in his mind's eye, in a rosery of Fetter Lane, that of Gerard the herbalist, thinking of his woman as she betrays him:

> he walks, greyedauburn. An azured harebell like her veins. Lids of Juno's eyes, violets. He walks. One life is all. One body. Do. But do. Afar in a reek of lust and squalor, hands are laid on whiteness.[14]

One life is all life, potentially. Inner and outer interrelate, are the same, in Stephen's thought, which conjunction is Joyce's objective. Shakespeare's art ventured forth to accomplish the widest possible range of encounters; and in doing so he was searching the fullest extent of his own potential:

> He found in the world without as actual what was in his world within as possible. . . . Every life is many days, day after day. We walk through ourselves, meeting robbers, ghosts, giants, old men, young men, wives, widows, brothers-in-love. But always meeting ourselves.[15]

The thing, the event, the person other than us is there before us, in its difference; but it is also a part of us, once recognized as different and separate. If there is a reconciliation between subjective and objective there must needs have been/be a sundering. Or, put bluntly and simply, because Joyce's aesthetic is basically entirely straightforward, there is a self, an observing consciousness; and there is that which is observed. The approach to the other is simple. Consciousness moves to apprehend the thing, 'the Ding hvad in idself id est,'[16] which is the 'true inwardness of reality', an inwardness whose meaning can never be uttered, because such utterance is loutishness.

Haines and Mulligan, one an Arnoldian Celtophile, the other a pseudo-classicist, have no difficulty whatever in assigning meanings and interpretations. Mulligan, especially, devours things, just as he enjoys himself hugely in sentimentality and good fellowship. When he and Haines assign to Stephen an *idée fixe* they are in the thickly carpeted Bewley's coffee shop, and Mulligan, while he 'explains' Stephen's obsessional personality, avidly watches the scones coming. This is the core *he* wants to get his teeth into. Haines asks Mulligan if Dedalus writes anything for the literary movement:

> Buck Mulligan slit a steaming scone in two and plastered butter over its smoking pith. He bit off a soft piece hungrily. – Ten years, he said, chewing and laughing. He is going to write something in ten years.[17]

Joyce's moral contempt is strongly in evidence, his hatred for the confident indifference of the apparently fortunate. He is here a Dante subtly accusing Gogarty/Mulligan of greed, sloth and calumny. But this picture changes, the scene moves, aptly enough in an episode with the title 'Wandering Rocks', were it not the case that this mobile, shifting quality, an awareness of the variousness of the impacts life makes, is Joyce's basic vision:

> Elijah, skiff, light crumpled throwaway, sailed eastward by flanks of ships and trawlers, amid an archipelago of corks, beyond new Wapping street past Benson's ferry, and by the threemasted schooner *Rosevean* from Bridgwater with bricks.

The river, the little throwaway leaflet, the docks, then the ship we heard mysteriously sounding at the end of 'Telemachus', all of these put the stifling moral indifference in Bewley's into perspective. Life is one; and it is bigger than envy and hatred. It includes trade, people, prophets, wine, fish, as well as Mulligan's unholy communion with its 'smoking pith'. Mulligan's pseudo-classicism is part of and contained within the classical temper of this small vignette, which moves to include, patiently and serenely, things as they are, without converting them into metaphor or allegory. The simplicity of the method gives the ship a curiously mysterious quality, the mystery and joyfulness of ordinary life, as it happens; correcting implicitly Mulligan's false analysis of Stephen, that he lacks the 'joy of creation' because he has been infected by visions of hell. It is Mulligan who is in hell, the hell of the obvious: the scone does 'smoke' after all. It is brimstone.

That is the terrible food Mulligan eats in Bewley's. We should notice, however, that this is not allegory, nor is it metaphor; it is an implication the narrative gathers through attentiveness to things as they are, signalling the presence of a serene and watchful patience in the author, a composure, a classic reserve and balance. These qualities are those Joyce embodies in Leopold Bloom, the good man Stephen is to encounter as he moves through the day of 16 June 1904.

These are the two moving foci of attentiveness in *Ulysses*, each a core of being which opens inwards, to a 'tenebrosity of the interior'[18] as it is called in 'The Oxen of the Sun', a space as extensive and manifold as the interstellar space evoked, later, in 'Ithaca', when Bloom and Stephen look at the stars. These two 'tenebrosities' interact and interchange from 'The Oxen of the Sun' onwards, and that episode researches English, in all its variousness, across its diachronic (which is to say historical) development, in order to mobilize the linguistic potential required for the delineation of this interaction, or, rather, series of interactions. Joyce admires and delights in the organic development of English, its capacity to absorb different linguistic influences; its steadiness, which sponsors its accumulative power; and its precision, which is balanced by its flexibility. But Joyce's linguistic bravura in this episode, stirring as it is in itself, has a purpose. The rehearsal of the history of English, which parallels the process of parturition, is preparing language (and us) for the birth of a new way of looking at the most ordinary and normal thing in the world: two men meet; the older one is considerate towards the younger. That such a thing is so ordinary, Joyce is striving to get us to realize, should not blind us to its miraculousness. His intention is to move us; that is, to move the reader from the sloth of ready-made opinion and indifferent passivity. Hence his exploration of English, revealing to us the amazing interiority and range of the thing we take for granted. It is, in my view, churlish to argue, as some have done, including T.S. Eliot, that this is some kind of attack on English. It is, on the contrary, an assessment and description of its innate and natal power. And what it gives birth to is a new way of looking at human contact. He is like Spenser in this, or Blake, or Giordano Bruno.

These two foci of human 'tenebrosity', Stephen and Bloom, interact with each other most energetically in the underworld of the 'Circe' episode. This chapter brings to a surface, the surface of sequential writing, the vast phenomenology of the unconscious mind. In this psychodrama everything speaks, everything has English, and things can become other things; they can change shapes as easily as they can change names. It is an arbitrary world where anything can have a speaking part, and where the concept follows the meaning, signified depends on signifier, to use Saussure's terms. A fluid universe, it prefigures *Finnegans Wake* of course, but it is also absolutely tied into the impetus of narrative discovery, of travelling, that animates *Ulysses.* Joyce is striving to register, in as open a way as he possibly can, as wide a divergence of matter as his form can accommodate without degenerating into the spiritual anarchy or materialism he knew to be the danger of the classical temper. Stephen and Bloom, here revealed as two tenebrosities, amidst a wild panorama of other interiorities, are two controlling foci to the episode. They shift and change, Bloom becomes a womanly man, Stephen meets the dead, there is terror and deformity; but those two, while they move from who they are, come back to themselves. But they do move; they venture to encounter that in themselves most distinct from that which they began with, only to find themselves all the time. They dilate to contract back to a normal span, to normality itself. They venture out to what is different from them, but the episode shows that the contents of the human mind, while bewilderingly various, are 'all too human', all too recognizable. The familiarity of the scenes shown in 'Circe' (we all have nightmares, bad dreams, fears) should not blind us to the fact that what is revealed embodies human pain, suffering and humiliation. But Joyce's use of this expansive form of arbitrariness allows him to register this inner confusion in a mood of unsentimental observance, of steady and patient appraisal, lightened by a resigned awareness of the predictability of the unconscious. Bloom and Stephen do not 'unite' at some unconscious deep level. They share the human mind, with its unconscious, and the writing draws our attention to the extent of that space wherein these two have plenty of scope for interaction.

Any life extends itself by encountering that which is different, thereby making it more itself. That which is most different is *someone else*, not the horrors of nightmare, or the ghosts of the past.

> What went forth to the ends of the world to traverse not itself. God, the sun, Shakespeare, a commercial traveller, having itself traversed in reality itself, becomes that self. Wait a moment. Wait a second. Damn that fellow's noise in the street. Self which in itself was ineluctably preconditioned to become.[19]

Stephen asserts this in the teeth of the mockery launched at him by Lynch's (speaking) cap:

> Bah! It is because it is. Woman's reason. Jewgreek is greekjew. Extremes meet. Death is the highest form of life. Bah!

But despite the vehemence of Lynch's cap this is a perversion of what Stephen is asserting and Joyce is trying to write out. Extremes meet, but that does not mean they give up that which they themselves are in themselves. The meeting confirms the validity of the going forth and the impetus behind it, which is self and only self. Stephen and Bloom are two separate foci all the more so for their meeting and interacting. They move towards each other to be themselves as they always were, but Joyce's writing stresses the delight of this mutual outgoing, or 'outflinging', as he has it in 'The Oxen of the Sun', a word linked to the 'outgoingness' of 'aisling' in Irish.[20] They are to each other as the fundamental and dominant in the parallel fifths Stephen is striking on the piano in the brothel, surrounded by this writing: 'the greatest possible ellipse. Consistent with. The ultimate return.'[21]

'Eumeas' and 'Ithaca' take the two tired travellers home, traversing various discourses as they proceed. Nothing much happens at 7 Eccles Street, home of Molly and Bloom, where adultery has been committed that day. Bloom gives Stephen cocoa, they chat, they part. As they come out into the night Joyce's prose opens up to them in their ordinariness, sundered yet together, two men on the small turning globe, in Dublin in 1904. The writing reaches out to encompass the interstellar spaces, cold yet vital with the remote energy of being. Giordano

Bruno, the Bruno of *De la causa, principio, et uno,*[22] who sought his divinity in the world of matter, lies behind the heroic *furor* of Bloom and Stephen going out together, in their separateness, from 7 Eccles Street: heroic *furor,* because the Neoplatonic phenomenologist, Bruno, thought that the aim of rhetoric and of thought was to rouse the apprehension to the full intensity of admiration. The world of matter, all the stars and the worlds they contained, were instinct with life to Bruno; all space was being, and being contained all space. So when Bloom and Stephen meet there is a 'trepidation'[23] (to use a word of John Donne's) of the stars. These effects are created by Joyce, imitating Bruno, by letting the language, English, run through the 'Zodiack of his own wit',[24] his liveliest awareness; an English that has been researched in 'The Oxen of the Sun', tested to exhaustion in 'Eumeas', and put to the harshest execution in the cold interrogation of 'Ithaca'. Now he describes their going forth:

> What spectacle confronted them when they, first the host, then the guest, emerged silently, doubly dark, from obscurity by a passage from the rere of the house into the penumbra of the garden?
>
> The heaven tree of stars hung with humid night blue fruit.
>
> With what meditations did Bloom accompany his demonstration to his companion of various constellations?
>
> Meditation of evolution exceedingly vaster: of the moon invisible in incipient lunation, approaching perigee: of the infinite lattiginous scintillating uncondensed milky way, discernible by daylight by an observer placed at the lower end of a cylindrical vertical shaft 5000 ft deep sunk from the surface towards the centre of the earth: of Sirius (alpha in Canis Major) 10 light years (57,000,000,000,000 miles) distant and in volume 900 times the dimension of our planet: of Arcturus: of the precession of the equinoxes: of Orion with belt and sextuple over theta and nebula in which 100 of our solar systems could be contained: of moribund and of nascent new stars such as Nova in 1901: of our system plunging towards the constellation of Hercules: of the parallax or parallactic drift of so called fixed stars, in reality ever-moving from immeasurably remote eons to infinitely remote futures in comparison with which the years,

> threescore and ten, of allotted human life formed a parenthesis of infinitesimal brevity.[25]

And yet the systolic meditation of this one's diastole which immediately follows plunges into the infinity of life in this world, raising a contemplative admiration of the equally ordinary, equally extraordinary mysteries of geology, organic life and molecular division and reunification.

There is, in a sense, no *point* to this kind of writing, other than the stirring up of the mind from sloth to see, so that we may not be like the 'dim-eyed mole' in Bruno's *De la causa, principio, et uno,* who, 'the moment he feels upon him the open air of heaven, rushes to dig himself back into the ground', desiring to remain hidden in his 'native darkness'.[26] In Oxford in 1583, when Bruno discoursed of the rotation of the earth, of the vastness of space, of the life inhering therein, which moved and breathed as a great being, they thought he was mad. George Abbott, later Archbishop of Canterbury, recorded: 'in truth it was his own head which rather did run round, and his braines did not stand still.'[27]

Bloom, wearily, goes to bed: 'He rests. He has travelled' with all and everyone. 'Ithaca' ends with the writing drawing back from Bloom as he lies in bed beside Molly, in inverted position 'At rest relatively to themselves and to each other. In motion being each and both carried westward, forward and rereward respectively, by the proper perpetual motion of the earth through everchanging tracks of neverchanging space.'[28]

The writing acknowledges the earth's movement, and withdraws, as Bloom's conscious mind recedes as he falls into sleep, so that the reader glimpses, in the full stop located centre page at the end of the episode, the earth rotating in interstellar space, a tiny spot, containing Molly, Bloom, Stephen, all of Dublin, the world itself, indeed the entirety of being because one life is all. Then the perspective moves again, because from this remoteness which is charged with Joycean tenderness, we track back into a completely new voice, a new reality in terms of the book's voices: Molly Bloom herself; Gaea-Tellus; the earth; infinity; Penelope, who weaves and unweaves the molecular entirety of being. The time, according to Joyce himself in the system he outlined to Frank Budgen, is no-time, infinity, signified by the figure 8 lying on its side (∞), and celebrating Molly's birthday, 8 September. Her monologue is in eight sentences. Joyce wrote to Budgen:

> It begins and ends with the female word *yes*. It turns like the huge earth ball slowly surely and evenly round and round spinning, its four cardinal points being the female breasts, arse, womb and cunt.[29]

Continuous feminine movement is what concludes *Ulysses*. The male voices are gone; the female voice, 'perfectly sane' to use Joyce's phrase from the letter to Budgen, moves amidst its experience, shifting our perspectives on much that we have encountered in the course of the reading that has been our day in Dublin in 1904.

Richard Ellmann, in a haunting passage in *Ulysses on the Liffey*, speaks of the identity of the archetypal figure whose body the entire book limns. This being, this moving actuality and spirit, which includes Bloom, Stephen and Molly, as well as everything else in Dublin, Ellmann, by analogy with Blake's Albion, calls Hibernion. 'One day', he writes, 'he will be Finnegan.'[30]

The *Wake*'s weltering narratives continuously revolve around a central story, which is never fully told, because in a sense there is no need to. It is the old story, of a father who did something wrong; of a wife whom he betrays but who defends him; and the dissensions between the offspring. The 'matter' of the *Wake*, like matter itself, is 'a troublous and periloose'; it is loose and troublesome, not to mention perilous. But it is the ordinary stuff of all human history. A story tale: 'Ah ho! Say no more about it! I'm sorry! I saw. I'm sorry! I'm sorry to say I saw!'[31]

What is 'seen' is withheld, the meaning, as Joyce had put it in *Stephen Hero*, remains 'unuttered'. Too strenuous an assault on meaning, too presumptuous an assurance that it can be uttered betrays one into the obvious hell of Mulligan and Haines, eating that 'smoking' scone. What matters is the approach towards the meaning, the matter; bearing in mind that matter is 'periloose'. The approach is one of tentative outreaching, travellings towards the object, the story, creating a language which, though continuously and steadily attentive to the 'matter', nevertheless circles around it, listening, watching, hearing the voices talking about it, which themselves derive from it. 'It' is Finnegan, HCE, ALP, Shem, Shaun, the whole 'collideorscope', a network of interactivity, constantly moving. Even the pronouns, those atomic constituents of language, intimately connected to point of view, vantage, position, shift and move about:

> We have to had them whether we'll like it or not. They'll have to have us now then we're here on their spot.

We're here, others were here before us. We're on their spot. They have to tolerate that.

> Scant hope theirs or ours to escape life's high carnage of semperidentity by subsisting peasemeal upon variables. Bloody certainly have we got to see to it ere smellful demise surprends us on this concrete that down the gullies of the eras we may catch ourselves looking forward to what will in no time be starting you larrikins on the postface in the multimirror megaron of returningties, whirled without end to end.[32]

The pronominal position moves from 'we/them' to 'you', which links to the matter of identity or 'semperidentity' that the passage explores. It would be tempting to assume that in the *Wake* we have the postmodernist, relativist text *par excellence*; nothing fixed, nothing sure, all ludic play. But this would controvert the body of the argument advanced here so far, that Joyce held to the conviction that there *is* self, that there *is*, by corollary, that which is different from self; and that each is more fully itself by virtue of that difference. Which is not to say that these entities can be lightly spoken of; the interaction between Stephen and Bloom, or that between Bloom and Gertie McDowell, is mysterious though quite ordinary. But interaction there is, just as life and art interact, which means there is a difference. That is something everyone knows, which to Joyce was a significant consideration, because the four-footed approach to things, avoiding the seductions of metaphor, has dignity.

Joyce suggests that 'semperidentity' is something we cannot escape, 'by subsisting peasemeal upon variables'. A 'pease' meal of variables (such as Lenehan's in 'Two Gallants', where he turns aside from his 'semperidentity' by contemplating how pleasant life might be if he could find the right girl with a bit of the ready as he eats a dish of grocer's peas with vinegar) distracts from things as they are. But again things as they are do not comprise a bleak mechanical arrangement of objective data: things as they are incline to us, as we move towards them. We look forward, given the steady temper of the sane and ordinary man or woman, to what will in no time 'be staring you'. It (undefined) will be 'staring you'. The we moves to you in the writing, drawing the reader into a stare at the 'multimirror' of the *Wake* itself, confronting it confronting me/you/him/her/we/ye/they. Life's 'high carnage of semperidentity' is 'bloody' certain, not just because all die, but also because you merge with me, and him and her. All life is one, being is one, but it separates and recoheres continuously. This Heraclitean double movement is what animates the *Wake*'s 'joyful creation'. It is closer to Yeats than one would at first think. And it also relates to Shakespeare. Shakespeare travelled forth to find himself; he held the mirror up to nature to see himself the more clearly. Joyce himself does not obtrude: his temperament is too classical, too steady for that. And yet we can sense him everywhere, as we do in every word he wrote. Qualities of reverence, patience, ordinariness abound. We sense the 'quick' of him, his *haecceitas,* to use a word that Gerard Manley Hopkins would have used. But he is there, all in all. Because so much else is there he seems to be absent. He went out to encounter that which was different from him. That travelling, an ardour of the spirit, means he rests with that which is not him, the world, his, not which he has created, which created him. In the *Wake* he has disappeared; language speaks, not Joyce; but his voice is everywhere.

7

JOYCE CARY

'Wondering at difference'

Change is terrifying. There is the kind of personality which longs for change and welcomes disruption, but change, real change, tends to produce fear and panic. Change and the shock that accompanies it may be good for you, but whether it is or not depends on your ability to cope with change and to absorb the shock of it.

When Joyce Cary went up to Oxford in 1909 he had undergone, in his own life, a great many changes. His childhood had been a happy one, but there had been a great deal of disruption as well as contentment. His mother, whom he loved greatly, died in 1898 when he was 8. An unpublished essay in the Cary papers in the Bodleian library, Oxford, tells how, soon after his mother's death when staying with relatives in Cookham Dean, he got lost in the woods near the house. Terrified, he is appalled at the sudden noise, the hooting and blaring of the local hunt as it erupts into his already panic-stricken isolation.[1]

The death of his mother, a Joyce from Omagh (Cary attributed his imaginative and reflective qualities to this, the Irish side in his make-up[2]) was a personal disruption in a childhood which had as its backdrop the decline of the Anglo-Irish Ascendancy, of which the Carys of Inishowen had been very much a part. The Cary family were granted lands in 1613 seized from the rebel Cahir O'Doherty. By the time Cary's father married Charlotte Joyce the family fortunes were in a parlous state, and, unable to pay the mortgage or service their debts, they had to move into rented accommodation. Financial ruin was accompanied by increasing social conflict between landed class and tenantry, tensions powerfully evoked in Cary's *Castle Corner*. Cary spent most of his childhood in London because his father had to work as a civil engineer to earn his living, but the family was also becoming embittered by the social changes in Irish society and welcomed the detachment London seemed to offer. Nevertheless, the young Joyce Cary's summers in Inishowen, with his relations there, Carys and Joyces, were magical times, when he felt deeply at home; and Cromwell House, his uncle's home in London, became an Irish version of an Ascendancy house in Gunnersby. There was prep school; then Clifton College public school, which he left at 17, going to France in 1906 and intending to become an artist. In 1907 he began to study art at Edinburgh College of Art, before going up to Oxford to read jurisprudence. He also hoped, however, to become a writer.

Not long after he arrived he was invited out to the home of H.A. Pritchard, a philosophy tutor at Trinity College, who had also attended Clifton. Pritchard, a practitioner of philosophical chop-logic, demolished Cary in the course of the polite afternoon-tea chat. The subject was painting. Cary prided himself on his discernment and his appreciation of the newest developments in painting. However, Pritchard, who 'had a high reputation as a destroyer', lured him into making large and confident pronouncements about art so that he could take him to pieces. Nearly fifty years later, in an article in *The Sunday Times,* Cary reproduced the dialogue:

PRITCHARD. Ah, you don't think much of so-and-so as a painter!

CARY. (*Relieved at this choice of subject, so nice and easy. He had been alarmed in case Pritchard might start on philosophy.*) Good heavens, no. Did you see his Academy stuff this year - Highland Sunset? Awful colour, like mud and glue, awful texture, like limestone, no composition.

PRITCHARD. Why do you think they made him an R.A.?

CARY. They would, he's just their style.[3]

Pritchard goes on to ask if people think so-and-so is good, and why. Cary says that people like to be told what to think, by the Academy, whereas real artists are starving in their garrets. Cary asserts that he knows what's good from 'looking at a lot of pictures - in a special way. You sort of expose yourself to pictures.' But then Pritchard says that surely the people in the Academy know how to look at pictures in a special way as well, and if that is so, then aesthetic judgement can only be a matter of opinion. Exit Cary weeping.

This episode made a deep impression on him. Only once again, at Oxford, did he raise the question of aesthetic judgement. He asked a man who took a double first what he thought the difference was between Beethoven's Ninth Symphony and a music-hall song and the answers he got, he says, were just as poor as those he tried to fend off Pritchard with: 'depth', 'richness of conception' were the terms he was offered.[4] Cary knew the importance of aesthetic judgement, and was aware that this loose and impressionistic way of trying to come to terms with the difficulties involved was useless. The question Pritchard raised dogged him all his life, but by his own account it was not until he was out in the 'wilds of Africa', in the colonial service, that he started on the beginnings of an answer. The problem at that stage crystallized into a deep and challenging question: 'What and how did I know?' The shock, administered in 1909, had initiated the change that, over a long period of time, would turn him into a writer. The title he gave to the account of this event in *The Sunday Times* was 'A Slight Case of Demolition'. Time and time again he was to demolish his own constructions and 'dig up his foundations' (as he put it in *The Case for African Freedom*[5]) in order to make a 'coherent whole'.

Making and building are crucial activities in Cary's conception of the world; he is wary of his reflective side and distrustful of philosophizing. Freedom was the freedom of the imagination engaged with actual life. It was necessary (and not just for philosophy tutors) to clear the site, so that the derelict ruins of prejudice and fixed opinion could be swept aside to allow for vitality and renewal. And yet Cary is no unthinking modernist. He has a very strong conservative streak in him, which, allied to his faith in imaginative freedom, creates all sorts of tensions which his creative work seeks to explore and comprehend. In the essay 'Speaking for Myself' he writes of these tensions and gives them a specifically Anglo-Irish focus.

> They say that tensions make the artist and writer. That is certainly true of the Anglo-Irish writers, and my childhood would have been full of tensions.
>
> Ireland was still a battle ground. My own family had been almost ruined by the rent strike, and my grandfather had

> died of a broken-heart. . . . Even as a small child, therefore, I knew something of real tragedy: the tragedy of social conflict in which personal quality counts for nothing; where a man is ruined not because he has done any wrong, but because he represents a class or race.[6]

This rent strike led to Gladstone's Land Act of 1882, when arrears of rent were wiped out. The Carys, being good landlords, were owed a good deal of money, so this enactment by a liberal government ruined them.

What strikes us in reading Cary's accounts of his childhood, fictional or otherwise, is how the family, in its different surroundings, contrived to create a secure and happy atmosphere. The essay on Cromwell House in Gunnersby reveals an extended Irish family in London, with a one-eyed retainer, Barney McGonegal:

> He had, I dare say, after thirty years close study, as deep a knowledge of my uncle [Tristram] as any man can have of another, and treated him, with what, to an Englishman would have seemed like the rudest frankness. He would question his orders, and criticize his judgement, on anything from the care of dogs to the management of a mushroom bed. But what to an Englishman would have seemed like insubordination was, in fact, the mark of a relationship profounder than any personal loyalty. To Barney, my uncle was the master, and masters had their place of appointment by Heaven. On the other hand, Barney had *his* place also, a place of responsibility and dignity. And as with any Prime Minister to an autocrat, it was his duty to criticize, to state his own point of view, to propose the right policy, even if it was to be rejected, and to remind my uncle of past failures, if the reminder could lead to wisdom.[7]

Despite the upheaval brought about by their social decline, the family in Cromwell House retained a continuity with the past and a vitality that allowed for all kinds of different and highly individual behaviour. Cary describes, for example, how he and his brother would build an aerial railway, by means of a contraption of cord running down the stairs from the top landing to a picture rail, along which they would send various projectiles. They would be allowed to do this for a whole morning, sometimes, despite the crashes as objects fell down the stairs.

The instability and disruption to a settled existence continued into Cary's adult life. After he got married he spent years in the colonial service in Nigeria away from his wife Trudy, who lived with her parents; and even after 1920, when he resigned his post on the strength of selling some stories to *The New Yorker*, they were not really securely settled in their house at 12 Parks Road in Oxford for many years. On occasions the family had to split up while they rented the house to make money. Trudy and the children would go home to her people, while Cary would go to Ireland to stay with relatives in Castledawson and elsewhere.

A house, a family, security - these were things which Cary knew from his experience as a dispossessed Anglo-Irish landlord and as a struggling writer, had to be created by effort of will and by vigour of imagination. Women, in his work, are those to whom this duty most often falls. The house, not just the Big House, but the suburban villa in Oxford, the mud cabin in Inishowen, or the little enclosure a frightened girl will make for her child in the African wilderness in *Castle Corner*, are symbols of order, peace and love in Cary, as in many writers. But for Irish and Anglo-Irish writers the symbol carries a particularly powerful charge in that dispossession was an experience which was visited on the Irish by the Anglo-Irish and the British, and then upon the Anglo-Irish by the British and the Irish.

The dispossession that the Anglo-Irish experienced throughout the nineteenth century, as the series of reforms that began with Catholic Emancipation rendered their position more and more fragile, led them to embrace the services, whether military, civil or colonial. Apart from the fact that many of them, deprived of much of their income from the land, had to earn a living, they were drawn to the services because of the collective support system offered by a regiment or an administrative hierarchy. The Empire provided a house and a home for Cary and for many other Anglo-Irish scions of impoverished families. It should be stressed that Cary, like many of his class and background, totally believed in the Empire. It gave structure and an order which protected freedom. Freedom, to Cary, only mattered if it was freedom for something rather than from something. He distrusted the kind of liberty that functions as permissiveness.

In Nigeria he worked hard at becoming a writer, painstakingly going over draft after draft of various novels. This creative activity had a practical objective: he wanted to have a home with Trudy and his children and he hoped writing would be a way of paying for it; but linked to this was Cary's ambition to find out what he knew and how. After he settled back in Oxford he set himself to write day after day in order to bring his world (his own house of people) into being. It took him until 1932 to publish his first novel, *Aissa Saved,* by which time he was 44.

Castle Corner (1938) was to have been the first novel of a trilogy that would deal with the fortunes of the Corner family from the 1890s up to the end of the first quarter of the twentieth century. Reflecting his taste for obvious, even comically clumsy puns, the Corner trilogy was to be about the changes that take place when a civilization turns a 'corner'. The corner turned is the change from Victorian certainty to the challenging and frightening upheaval of modern democratic materialist life. This trilogy was not completed because Cary was disappointed in the critical response to the first novel, and he also felt that he had not made a 'coherent whole' of the varied material. In a preface written in 1952 he says:

> I had to ask myself if anyone would notice that the book had any general meaning; if in fact, it did mean anything; if the contrast of different characters, though all making their lives, seeking fulfilment of one kind or another, did not result in that very neutral tint which we find in the events of real life. For life, as it occurs, has not meaning.[8]

He is, with hindsight, writing himself into a considerable disillusionment with the book.

The novel is, despite Cary's unease when he wrote this preface, a hugely impressive work, a flawed one perhaps, in that it does not drive forward with an irresistible narrative impulse, but it is possessed of a breathtaking range and scope, and a fiery quality of awareness of people and things. The novel attempts an extraordinarily complete depiction of the 1890s in Ireland, Europe and Africa: the Land War in Ireland; emigration; agrarian violence; the Rabelaisian hilarity of the kitchen servants in Castle Corner; a dinner party aboard a merchant-trading ship on the River Niger; tribal wars; comical attempts at making maps in the African bush; Methodism in England; the rise of the Labour movement; the new capitalism looking to Africa; mock-Tudor country mansions; perverted sex. His ambition was Tolstoiean, one of the writers he admired most. At this stage he has yet to find a technique to integrate such diverse elements into a satisfactory form, but it still makes compelling reading, because of the scale of the task he has undertaken, and the quality of awareness he brings to it.

Cary's method as a writer, from the start, was unusual, if not unique. He worked on several novels at a time, just as a painter will move from canvas to canvas. He did not write his novels straight through from beginning to end; he built them up, constructed them, bit by bit, working from the end to the start, then to the middle, then to climax, and so on. This method, a kind of literary pointilism, gives his writing a curious sense of *presence*, of life unfolding in the moment of apprehension; and it owes something, perhaps, to the concept of 'epiphany' in Joyce, a writer whom he greatly admired and with whom he felt some familial affinity on his Joyce side.

Some impression of Cary's sweep in *Castle Corner*, of the shock of change, of his ability to depict the pressure of event on character, and of his sense of the awesome differences in life, may be conveyed by looking at a few instances from the second quarter of the novel. Benskin, an imperialist and a new capitalist, is explaining to young Cleeve Corner how the Empire brings 'peace, prosperity and free institutions' wherever it goes. What Benskin is looking for, and what he is trying to inspire Cleeve to, is imagination, effort, idealism: 'he talked about Rhodes, Kitchener, Lugard; and Cleeve saw contemporary history in a new light, which fascinated him. His boy's mind loved the pattern, the clue.'

Cary is hinting that the reader should pick the clue up as well. The imperial spirit appeals to the idealistic imagination while Benskin can exploit it for monetary gain. Cleeve is excited because he spots a connection: 'You think Africa is Ireland over again?' Benskin replies:

> 'And America. Except that the Americans wiped out the original inhabitants.' Cleeve stood smiling with the expression of one who looks at a neat diagram solving a problem. 'Do you think we ought to have wiped out the Irish?' he asked. Benskin was shocked. 'No, no, that kind of

> conquest is bad, even economically. Rhodes is a Home Ruler, for instance, and in South Africa ---' 'A Home Ruler.' Cleeve was still more interested. He adjusted this new pattern of which he had taken hold.[9]

This writing is alive to historical tensions. Cleeve, from Inishowen, thinks of himself as not Irish; Benskin's introduction of the notion of Home Rule intrigues him. The Empire may accommodate Home Rule; the pattern may embrace all. Benskin is clever and manipulative, Cleeve obtuse and easily worked upon, just as later in the same day his feelings will be exploited in a different way.

This conversation is taking place at Castle Corner in Inishowen. Cleeve's uncle, John Chase, is back from the petty sessions at Dunvil (Moville) where he is magistrate. While Benskin and Cleeve talk, the drinking proceeds, and John Chase accepts a bet to drive his tandem to Dunvil and back again in twenty minutes. The talk of Africa goes on, but then Cleeve goes upstairs to the bookroom to get a view of the drive to Dunvil and back:

> The bookroom window, a little dormer in the roof, looked over the drive to the high road. Cleeve threw open the dirty casement, and turned his eyes towards the afternoon sun behind Knockeen. The road, vanishing up the hill a mile away to the left was bare; but two carts were drawing into gates, and the drivers, who had jumped down, could be seen dragging furiously at their heads and beating their legs. A boy on a wall was whirling his arms like flails.
>
> Suddenly the tandem flashed into sight, it was more brilliant in miniature. The strong slanting light glittered upon it like the ray from a microscope. It raced up the hill; a minute golden horn flashed in the hand of the minute Darcy, black-coated on the back seat.
>
> He raised it to his lips once then took it away again. The tandem vanished over the hill; and down through the soft air floated the three gay notes of the horn, left behind.
>
> Cleeve stood breathless. He could not express his delight at the completeness, the beauty, the humour of the thing which would have made him laugh if it had not been for the exciting beauty.

> He could feel somebody pressing behind him in the narrow dormer.[10]

This 'somebody' is Bridget Foy, whom he then proceeds to seduce, in the time-honoured manner of the young buck of the Anglo-Irish household. Her comment, when the struggle and the implorings are over, is: 'And that's all for what ye'd put my soul in hell'!![11] Bridget becomes pregnant; and the Corner line ramifies into Catholicism. The son is called Finian, invoking the Fenians, a revolutionary secret society, antecedents to the IRA.

The scene shifts to Nigeria where a Corner relative, Cocky Jarvis, is face to face with the limits to Empire. Jarvis, the courageous man of action, the imperialist, is at the frontier. All energy, boldness and resolution, he is driven by the 'master faith of the age; the idea of the struggle for existence'. Clumsily perhaps, Cary is raising the question of the nature of Jarvis's energy: has he handed his individuality over to some form of collective notion, a faith in impulse? Is he as much entrapped by passion as Cleeve is? Is he transgressing on Africa in just the way Cleeve has done with Bridget? Africa is Ireland all over again.

At the frontier maps need to be drawn, and Jarvis loves filling in the blanks except that the Africans have no idea what he is saying when he asks for the names of places. The interpreter shouts:

> 'This white man wants to know the name of your river': No one answered from the huts but the soldier, in an extremity of horror, licked his dry lips and said 'Gell sah', Gell meaning in Laka, a stream. Jarvis politely thanked his orderly and wrote down, in a beautiful script, 'Gell River,' that was to say, 'Stream River'. . . . Villagers did not always understand what a strange white man meant by pointing to the earth and making a sound like a dog's bark. They answered sometimes, 'I don't know', or simply, 'dirt, grass.' Thus one saw on Jarvis's map such places as Town Town, River River, Idontknow Village, Begyourpardon Rock.[12]

Later on, war breaks out. The Daji slave traders from the north come and destroy the Laka settlements. Bandy, Felix Corner's woman, finds herself in the bush, with the dead and half-dead lying around. The Daji slavers make dogs of those they defeat by cutting off their hands and feet. If their victims are lucky, they die; if not they are tortured by the highly strung Fulani, to whom cruelty is a delight. Bandy, surrounded by mutilated bodies, suckles two children - one, Azai, aged 10, has not bled to death because his hands are not completely severed; the other is a baby, Osho. As the days pass in the bush Bandy builds a small house for herself and her charges:

> In three days Bandy had formed a household which was in miniature the household of a Laka native; with cooking hut, sleeping hut, yam store, waterpots, a heap of firewood; and she herself like chief and junior wives in one, commanded, bustled, scolded like the head wife, provided and cooked like a minor humble wife, gossiped and chattered like a daughter, from morning till night.[13]

Bandy makes a home for herself and exhibits a capacity to survive, but her survival is quite different from Jarvis's 'master faith'. This instinct is creative, sympathetic, human and full of love.

The power of the sequence sketched here lies in its sweep and its desire to bring different things into a coherent whole. Different creative possibilities for different individuals and situations are juxtaposed. Bandy's mothering, creative instinct is compared and contrasted with Jarvis's idealism; his survivalism is rebuked by her resilience. The violence and cruelty of African exploitation of African is linked to Benskin's avid capitalism and his exploitation of Cleeve, who in turn exploits Bridget, who exploits him, in that she now has a hold over the young master which she will use. We get a sense of Cary's intelligence trying to hold this entire period in his mind, even fleetingly, like the thin notes from the tiny bugle that fade away.

Cary wished his work to display the means through which the human spirit expressed itself in his time, for good and for ill, by seizing whatever opportunities it could for gaining freedom to construct the world in its image. But Cary was an artist, not a philosopher, so he sought to locate his sense of his time in specific instances, specific places, specific people. In *Castle Corner* he wanted to show the Empire at a crucial phase of its development (or decline) but the elements, the Irish Land War, Nigeria and England undergoing social change, lack an effective unifying emotion. However, it is clear that he is after the integration of difference, which may be viewed as a characteristically Irish objective, or responsibility. Differences are reconciled by undergoing mutual and mutually responsive change.

In *A House of Children* (1941), the most beautiful of all his novels, the integration of difference surfaces again and again. It is there in the episode in which young Evelyn, deep sea bathing with his father in Lough Foyle, sees a whale. His father tells him 'he's ocean bathing too', and it is this phrase which excites the boy. 'I felt the magnificence of sharing bathing places with a whale.'[14]

This quality of integration is there too in the haunting scene right at the beginning of the novel when Evelyn gets lost in the back lanes of Dunvil:

> The lane was full of rocks, smoothed out like scones, and there were piles of fish-boxes against the walls. Oars and masts stood against the doors. . . . High up against [the] sky, strung from wall top to wall top, several ropes supported the cut-off wings and rumps of skates, which dropped brown blood on the smooth, grey rocks. There was a strong smell of bad fish, tar and salt. I was lost and despairing. . . . Suddenly I saw a dirty ragged little girl stooping down with her eye against the bottom of the door. I stopped crying and stared at her. . . . She looked up at me through the black strings of her hair and said in a hoarse, cracked voice: 'Want to look – its old Sandy.'

He does look. Inside there is a small yard and a large drunk man is chasing two barefoot girls and swearing at them. They are laughing at him and dodging him in the sunlight. The little girl tells Evelyn that Sandy will break their necks when he catches them. She has a hoarse rough voice and Evelyn is so close to her he can feel it vibrating in her thin body. The writing, full of intense, alert attention to the specific moment, continues:

> I felt an intense curiosity in her, not as a girl, but as a being, a person. Perhaps this was the first time that I realised another person. . . . I don't remember a word of [the] talk, only that it was essentially fond. . . . I remember my keen sense of this other person; a sense neither sympathy nor curiosity nor wonder; but containing all three in something greater than any, an indescribable feeling of difference and community in one. It was, I suppose, as if one blade of grass

> should touch another and feel it and think: 'It is not me, but it is very close to me.'[15]

Separateness gives way to intimacy and each requires the other. Individuals are individuals. They must be such to express themselves freely and in doing so they will often be in conflict; nations, too, and states will have different aspirations to freedom. But experience shows that contact is possible: entity can speak to entity, alienation need not be the final word. That, always in Cary, is love, in which the artist is involved, and, crucially in social arrangements, women.

The artist is someone who tries to make differences clear, but shows a means whereby they can be integrated, in art. In the preface to *Castle Corner* Cary said 'life as it occurs, has no meaning'. The differences in life are playing themselves off against each other, endlessly. But in storytelling, in artistry, the differences are brought into some form, some shape, and in doing so they become more pronounced and more exciting.

A House of Children concludes with a production of Shakespeare's *The Tempest,* organized by the aptly named bohemian tutor, Freeman. Evelyn is entranced with the creative activity and energy of the play performance. He has seen the play in rehearsals, and been bored, but now, on stage, the experience is different. Antonio curses the boatswain: 'Hang, cur, hang, you whoreson, insolent noise-maker,' and these words thrill him. He feels the impact of them 'like a real insult', they give him a shock 'of delight and anxiety'. He looks to see how this insult is taken and when the boatswain pays no attention he feels 'deep admiration and a sense of discovery. That's the right way to behave, I felt.'[16]

The play teaches him the power of words, and the feeling for words arouses an awareness of the things themselves:

> Of his bones are coral made; it was a chord of strings, a sextet, each singing quietly in the ear of my soul; not only with music but with souls of their own. A tune of lonely spirits, the sober and upright bone with his bass voice and rather austere character at one end, and the glimmering sea treasure, living jewel, rolling its merman's song at the other. . . . Now I was wondering at difference and the mysterious character of things. When I looked at the cliffs and clouds . . . I was trying to realise their private selves: as

> a savage touches some strange object, seeking to know, through his fingers, its separate quality. So an African chief, a great religious head in his own country, asked to handle my signet ring because he had never seen gold, and dandling it in his palm, he looked not at the ring, but in the air with half-closed eyes. . . . He handed back the ring with a puzzled and doubtful glance, saying only 'Abin mamaki,' a thing of wonder, that is to say [a] prayer for enlightenment, but so common in Africa, that it has ceased to have any force. It is used every day by thousands, in face of motors, planes, condenser engines, railway tickets, stainless knives; but it invokes no enlightenment. It expresses only the sense of man's apartness from things, which is also the acknowledgement of his community with everything.[17]

Not me, but like me, this was the reaction to the little girl who showed him the secret interior through the hole in the door. Not me but like me; this was the meaning of *The Tempest*, and the reason for Evelyn's excitement at the thought of a whale sharing the same ocean as he. Evelyn's story as he narrates it in *A House of Children* relates likeness and difference throughout the novel, where a sense of belonging to a whole world, the magical world of Inishowen holidays, is conveyed, along with a feeling of the strange uniqueness of it all. Storytelling makes the familiar strange; it marks the differences by drawing them together.

In an article for *Harper's Magazine* in 1950 entitled 'The Way a Novel Gets Written', Cary said he began 'not with an idea for a book, but with a character in a situation'.[18] The comment about character is significant. In a piece entitled 'The Duty of Love and the Duty of Reason' he writes:

> If there is any love, any kindness anywhere in people it is in the being of the world. And as love cannot be conceived without someone to feel that love, this being is a personal being. Thus the world has personality, and that personality has goodness, has love, as a characteristic.[19]

Character belongs to the personality of the world; this implies that character is not just simply a collection of learned behavioural tricks, but that, in Cary's view, it originates in being itself. Each character will wish to achieve as much freedom for itself as it can, and so one of the traits of virtuous character is unremitting effort and striving, very much in the Protestant tradition of self-realization, from Spenser through to Milton, Blake, Lawrence and Orwell. Felix Corner, idling away his time on the banks of the Niger, playing with the children, going native, has given up this impulse towards greater freedom, greater self-realization; instead he has chosen the mud-shallows of licence - quite a different thing. He is free *from*, not *for*.

In the Gulley Jimson trilogy Cary places the depiction of character in action at the centre of his concern. Each of the three main participants in the series of interrelated events which the trilogy explores is given a novel: Sara Monday, in *Herself Surprised* (1941), Tom Wilcher in *To be a Pilgrim* (1942), and Gulley Jimson in *The Horse's Mouth* (1944).

The differences in point of view which each presents are reconciled in that they are allowed to stand alongside each other, so the reader is invited into the arena of judgement to participate in the creative process of imagining, feeling and judging.

Sara Monday in *Herself Surprised* continually surprises herself in what she does. Always open to fresh experience, she does not have a moral code. She responds to life, and like Bandy and Bridget Foy in *Castle Corner* she wants to protect her son and her men.

Tom Wilcher in *To be a Pilgrim*, a very Protestant novel, is on a pilgrimage of self-discovery, which involves him, comically, in exposing himself to young women whenever he gets the opportunity. Like D.H. Lawrence or indeed Gulley Jimson in these novels he wants to shake things up a bit. But to Gulley he is entirely conventional, stuck in a rut, a species well known to Jimson and for which he has a name: *Blackcoatius Begoggledus Ferocissimouse*. Nevertheless, timid and black-coated though he may be, Tom delivers a strong and proud paean to England at the end of the novel. She is:

> the pilgrim and the scapegoat of the world. Which flings its sins upon her as the old world heaped its sins upon the friars. Her lot is that of all courage, all enterprise; to be hated and abused by the parasites . . . perhaps to be honest, I should say that she is a bit of a Protestant and therefore a bit of an anarchist.[20]

He goes on to say that England is apt to find herself in 'new lodgings at short notice; with new aspects from the windows of

[the] spirit'. Cary, as is evident from this, and from other writings, loved England deeply and was sincere in his ideal of service:

> People think of me as a writer but my years in the African Service, given to that England of my youthful imagination, are richer to my memory than any of my books.[21]

Gulley Jimson would be totally unimpressed by these sombre sentiments. Gulley, who speaks from the horse's mouth, looks for the essence of any situation, or person or thing. William Blake is Gulley's master spirit who held the following visionary truth:

> And every space smaller than a globule of man's blood opens into eternity of which this vegetable earth is but a shadow.[22]

Blake believed that the imagination of man was the actuality of Jesus Christ in the human, the real. For Gulley, too, 'everything that lives is holy'; and he makes no differentiation between good and evil. Like Blake he holds that contraries are essential to progression. Progression becomes movement, flexibility, keeping the eyes open for everything that happens. Art is the embodiment of this continuous process of discovery. Everything surprises and delights Jimson, and he has no time for despair or fixed views or obsessive hatred.

Coker, the barmaid at the Eagle and Child, the pub where Gulley drinks, is 'about five foot high and three foot broad. Face like a mule, except the eyes, which are small and dark. Methylated.' Coker's trouble is Willy, her young man, 'a ware house clerk shaped like a soda-water bottle. Face like a fist. All eyes and beak. Bass in the choir. Glider club. Sporty boy.' Willy has taken up with a blonde and Coker is furious. Gulley's advice to her is to move on:

> There's plenty of it, waiting to say how do you do, and it smells nicer. . . . I like you Cokey . . . I could feel for you Cokey if I had time. And I don't like to see Blondie getting on your mind, poisoning your springs. The worse she is, the worse for you. Well, I tell you, there's some fellows I daren't even remember their names, or I'd get ulcers on the brain. You take a straight tip from the stable, Cokey, if you must hate, hate the government or the people or the sea or

> men, but don't hate an individual person. Who's done you a real injury. Next thing you know he'll be getting into your beer like prussic acid; and blotting out your eyes like a cataract and screaming in your ears like a brain tumour and boiling round your heart like melted lead and ramping through your guts like cancer. And a nice fool you'd look if he knew. It would make him laugh till his teeth dropped out; from old age.[23]

Gulley's 'tip' from the horse's mouth is to keep moving and to leave the obsessed and the righteous to themselves. Imagination delights in movement and energy, and has no morality. Gulley and Coker visit the collector Hickson to try to raise some money out of him. Jimson doesn't really wish to go but he's dragooned by Coker. On the mantelpiece in the waiting room are some Japanese miniatures, netsukes:

> I showed her the Japanese netsukes on the mantelpiece, real old ones. Carved all over with wrinkles on the soles of their feet. 'Magnify them fifty times and they'd be monuments. It's chunky work. And yet look at the detail.' 'Too foreign looking for me.' 'That's why Hickson likes 'em. He hasn't got any imagination either.' 'Well, what are they for?' 'Imagination.' 'I pity the girl who has to dust this room.' 'So do I if she hasn't any more imagination than you have.' Coker said nothing. She was preening herself for Hickson, pulling down her coat, looking down the backs of her stockings to see if the seams were straight. Admiring them. Real silk. Coker was very particular about her stockings. For eternity is in love with the productions of time.[24]

As Gulley is thinking of Blake and Coker's seamed stockings he is putting some of the netsukes into his pocket to sell them later; only the best ones which Hickson was incapable of appreciating anyway.

Despite Jimson's comment, Coker has imagination; she looks down at her seams, she wants to make an impact, she wants to express herself. That is the way she is. Eternity is different. The introduction of the Blake quotation in Gulley's narrative has a powerful effect: Gulley sees Coker, in her femaleness, as a kind of miniature against the vastness of eternity; she and eternity are seen in a vital parallelism. The excitement of this apprehension and the energetic freedom it carries impel Gulley to steal the netsukes in a *characteristic* moment of personal freedom. Morality is set aside in the intensity of the moment when the difference between mortality, sex, life, art and the vastness of eternity is perceived in a flash of energetic insight.

All through Gulley's story we get this kind of charge, this electric awareness. In Elsinore, a doss house where Gulley and a couple of cronies make a meal of fish and chips reheated in sizzling lard, the writing has a vividly felt celebratory charge.

> So I got my billy on the red and in two minutes the fish began to curl and smoke blue, and the chips shone like bars of gold in champagne.[25]

These images are not isolated colourful effects but part and parcel of the technique that Cary has adopted, whereby Gulley's narrative conveys his character, the pulse of his personality in its difference from us, and in its difference from the conventions which we tend to impose on the concept of character. Gulley is an anarchist in love with energy. He's a thief, he beats up women and he kills Sara Monday. Obsessed with Hitler, he has certain things in common with him. He admires Hitler because he sees him as an artist like himself, who shapes reality, thereby expressing himself, and puts the blue of Hitler's eyes into the whale's eyes which he paints into his last great mural, *The Creation*.

In the second trilogy, which revolves around the career of Chester Nimmo, an artist in the sphere of politics, Cary explores the nature of power in modern society. These novels, *Prisoners of Grace* (1952), *Except the Lord* (1953) and *Not Honour More* (1955) use the same technique of manifold characterization that give complexity and authority to the Jimson trilogy.

Prisoner of Grace is Nina's novel. Through her sympathy and humanity she is destroyed by two very pushy men and eventually killed by one of them. *Except the Lord* is Chester Nimmo's book, in which he tells the story of his early political development, and how he met Nina, his future wife, as a young girl who asked him to read to her one day when he visited the local big house. Nimmo's book is a bleak account of the misery of working-class life in Devon in the 1870s and 1880s; and shows how such a life drives a man who has ambition and human feeling to political agitation, cruelty and revolution. *Not Honour More* is Jim

Latter's story. He is a Fascist who hates the 'talky' boys and clever dicks. He was put in charge of security in the Devon area during the emergency of the General Strike:

> Why did old England take the strike so quietly? Because they hadn't time for anything else. Because they didn't think evil - not at first. Because they're always ready to believe, 'These chaps may be fools - but they mean well.' Because they hadn't got around to saying, 'What we need is a real clean-up of the whole gang, right and left - of all these bugs in the wallpaper' - before the talky boys saw it coming - saw the red light.[26]

Cary makes Latter attractive; we admire his dash, brisk honesty and his loyalty to his men. He was in the African service and loved his 'Luga pagans', who are more honest than all the talky boys in the offices. He has imagination and character. But so do Chester Nimmo and Nina. Between the political opportunist Nimmo and the Fascist Latter, Nina is destroyed. She is a prisoner of her own grace, her capacity to love. Latter kills her 'because of the rottenness. Because of the corruption. Because all loyalty was a laugh and there was no more trust . . . Because of the grabbers and tapeworms who are sucking the soul out of England.' But Cary allows us to sympathize with how Latter can think that.

As in the Jimson trilogy Cary shows us three different personalities side by side. The art consists in creating plural narratives whereby different interpretations of reality are juxtaposed. The reader's understanding is tested out on three different planes in both trilogies, so that fixed ideas are challenged and moved. Reality is presented in a complex and manifold manner; differences between perceptions are not edited or suppressed: they are emphasized and pronounced.

This method of manifold arrangement, of simultaneity of differing awarenesses, is conducted on a large scale in the two trilogies, where the narrative planes interact to create an inclusive quality of insight; where changing perceptions are all accommodated structurally by virtue of the different voices that engage our attention.

But throughout the fiction, this manipulation of material in order to present the difference inherent in people, things or events in juxtaposition, operates all the time. The whale shares the sea with Evelyn; the cliffs and the sea are different from the words we give them; Africa and Ireland are sharply differentiated; yet fiction, art, imagination, is a striving to bring this variousness into 'community', the word Cary uses for this activity in *A House of Children*. The seams of Coker's stockings make eternity happy, and lead to the triumphal excess and elation of an act of theft. There are, Cary was aware, dangers in the collisions between different perceptions: Nina dies as two planes of reality, different from hers, drive against each other. Cary's art seeks to go beyond the morality of the commonplace and of convention, to accommodate a quality of awareness where each separate reality can be given sanction, while at the same time the need for community, from which separateness comes, is not lost sight of. Deeply aware of the actuality of evil, Cary's writing does not moralize. Each of his ventures into narrative breaks down pre-existing sets of understanding to allow for the actuality of situations and of people. The attentiveness and discipline of this art comes out of the rigour by which he sets contrasting and apparently inconsequential events side by side, to comment on each other, as in *Castle Corner*, but also in the fact that while we read, say, Nina's story in *Prisoner of Grace* her reality enfolds us, until we break the spell by listening to Latter's harsh but honourable assertions. The writing remains alive to the insistence of what is, which fidelity corroborates his own feeling that the Joyce side of him was more significant for his art than the Cary side; and which led him to claim an ancestral affinity with another Joyce, James.

8

FRANCIS STUART

'We are all one flesh'

Francis Stuart is a student of waiting. In *Memorial* (1973) he has his narrator, Fintan Sugrue, imagine himself being brought before the examiners in some last-day end of term examination in the Grand Aula. The examiners (one of them to be a woman, he notes) ask him on what subject he would wish to answer questions:

> there would be only one on which to base a claim of a not totally wasted lifetime. I would say, with a certain quiet confidence: Set me a paper on waiting.[1]

Time and again he returns to this theme in his fiction. In *Blacklist, Section H* (1971) he examines how time changes its feel in prison. The prisoner becomes immediately subject to the authority of others; so he must wait, long hours, in blankness, fear, anticipation. There is a sense in which a prisoner is 'inside' this (he is 'inside time'), an experience explored by Ken Smith in his book about Wormwood Scrubs *Inside Time* (1989), written about the period he was poet in residence there.[2] The prisoner inhabits the interior aspect of the confident and lustrous externality of society, business, politics, the arts. He (or she) is in there, quelled into silence and muteness, waiting for the cell to open.

Stuart has studied the watchfulness and agitation of those who wait. In *The Pillar of Cloud* (1948) there is a scene in which Dominic Malone, imprisoned in a French-occupied German town immediately after the war, observes the characteristic behaviour of the jailers:

> An hour or two after the evening meal of soup and slices of bread there was again the jingle of keys and the moment of

> almost intolerable expectation before the opening of the door. The policeman and a French boy of fifteen or sixteen . . . stood in the doorway. The boy came slowly into the cellar, looking around him, throwing that casual French glance around the room that is so different from the close German scrutiny. The boy strolled about the cellar, never actually letting his slightly prominent eyes rest on the faces of the two prisoners, and tapped the small suitcase that Halka had brought with clean clothes to Dominic with his foot. The policeman told Dominic to open it.[3]

The two jailers order Malone and his fellow prisoner to strip the cell of all luxuries and this at a moment when Malone is half-expecting to be released. The policeman comes down to the cellar a second time, alone, and orders him out. His cellmate asks the policeman if Malone is to be freed but the policeman does not answer. Climbing the steps Malone experiences a 'blindness and deafness to outer things' and he hardly takes in the words of the policeman, who is so nonchalant about something which Malone feels intensely, when he says that he is free. In all intensity, Malone thinks, 'one dies a little', a relationship which Stuart explores throughout his writings.

This mood of fearful anticipation, which waiting breeds, is an atmosphere dispersed across the entire range and detail of Stuart's fiction. He is a writer versed in tension, schooled in doubt, expert in suffering, yet never quite lacking in hope. This fear gives a sombre colour to his writing and links him, in the emotional aura it creates, with another stoic of waiting: his friend Samuel Beckett. The atmosphere of watchful doubt, and never fully extinguished faith, gives a strange and unique edge to Stuart's comedy, and comic writer Stuart undoubtedly is, although his humour is, to say the least, unusual.

His watchfulness, based not on some kind of greed of the curious eye, but on appraisal of the things of time, by someone who has known what it is to be bereft of them through being 'inside time', gives a highly charged immediacy to the way in which the writing registers the shock of actuality. Even a minor detail, like the way in which Stuart describes Malone's encounter with a petty official in the 'Good Samaritan' offices at the beginning of *The Pillar of Cloud* has this intense quality.

> 'Let me see, what was the name?'

> 'Malone.'
>
> He scuttled after the official, whose very back seemed to radiate irritation and suspicion.[4]

It is that detail of the back that does it: like those writers that elicit his deepest response - Kafka, Mandelstam, Dostoevsky - Stuart is intensely conscious of the vulnerability of the individual to officialdom and the confident transactors of power, business and money.

His writing is an analysis of the varying atmospheres of waiting. It explores the condition of the victim and his or her suffering, because to be a victim is to wait and to suffer. His fictions are based on his experiences and they are experiments in a kind of autobiographical writing, but the self that these novels unfold is no variation on an 'egotistical sublime'; rather do they explore the ridicule and mockery to which the personality is subjected, and its utter and pathetic dependence on exterior facts. A symbol that surfaces frequently is that of the telephone call, made from a phone-box or from home, on which all kinds of hope ride. The dialling of the digits, bringing, hopefully, the voice of the loved one closer, as the electrical impulses traverse the gulf to someone else's private space, becomes an action fraught with doubt and hope. The self issues its probe of longing, for love and comfort.

> So many digits to dial, each one bringing her a degree nearer! Threads that formed a fragile net cast with a series of clicks against the muted background roar to fall around her.[5]

Stuart's fictional selves are in search of 'reality', a word with a special and tragic resonance for him, as for Yeats. The self in a Stuart fiction is exposed on a small ledge over a fuming abyss; in the rock there is, with luck, a cleft, where some warmth and peace can be found. All the time there is the waiting, which is a preparation for the acceptance of reality. Reality, in this understanding, is the opposite of what is normally accepted as such: the world of money, power, moral codes and uniformity. Literature and art are the means by which the manifold illusion is stripped bare and the imagination gains contact with that which nourishes it and which informs the evolution of life itself. In *Faillandia* (1985) one of the contributors to the journal, which gives its title to the novel, writes of an 'inner evolution' that has taken place in the past few decades of this century as a counterbalance to the widespread fear and anguish:

> Our sensibilities have evolved over the years, astonishingly in the last few decades, both weaving strong threads between us and the past and thrusting explorative antennae into the open spaces whence the unexpected is coming. Perhaps this inner evolution is linked to the increasing threat of exterior doom. This age has created fear and a kind of subconscious anguish formerly undreamed of. It is also seeing a literature arise whose counter-dreams and subconscious energies extend the horizon to a point where even the worst horrors can be encompassed.

In the next phase of the argument the correspondent, in a daring stroke, links these 'explorative antennae' to the branches of the Vine, which is Christ, and in turn he links this to the self, the 'I':

> The roots of this literature are in the past and its shoots in the future. 'I am the Vine and you are the branches'. Here is one of those sentences that reverberates inside the nerve cells, by-passing the rational and intellectual filters. It is the language that the writer giving expression to new concepts has to use. How and in what sense this 'I' is made flesh and dramatised in fiction depends on the temperament and personal experience of the writers in question.[6]

Stuart gives expression here to one of his deepest intuitions, and one which is indeed difficult to hold firmly in the rational mind: there is a link, he would insist, between the individual psyche and the person of Christ (not me but Christ in me) when the psyche is intent on a totally involved response to being, as distinct from the standard presumptuous transactions we make with it. The self, in this mode, is in touch with the structure of matter; or to put it another way, is in a condition of emanation from a collective unconscious. It is, then, single (the Vine) but also ramifying into diversity. The self, in its Christ-mode, is in a state of 'collectedness', of gathered inwardness, waiting for the contact with 'that Person, faithful and true, supreme and ruthless Arbiter who alone distinguishes the real from the hallucinatory . . . The Chief of a High Consistory of Dead Masters'.

Stuart is intent on exploring relationships, obviously relationships between men and women, but also between quite heterogeneous areas of experience and emotion. One of his aims, as he explains in *The Abandoned Snail Shell* (1987), is to discover a model of reality which will do more than 'save the appearances', but one which will provide a means of integrating different perceptions of reality into some kind of coherence: 'The closer a model associates observed phenomena with each other, the more valid it is.'[7] The more the branches are shown to be branches of a single Vine the more powerful and effective the fiction which links them is. And he argues persuasively to convince us that it is fiction and art which give us these integrating models of reality, where disparate phenomena interact, or commune, with each other. A sentence from biology, as in the following extract from *Memorial,* is 'given flesh': 'The same code of triplets of bases is used to define the proteins in all organisms; we're all one flesh.'[8]

The narrative interjects this sentence at a moment of tenderness and entire sympathy. Herra, the young girl with whom Fintan Sugrue, the novelist-protagonist, is in love, has shown him her wrists, now healed, but he can see the slashes which sometimes, she tells him, suppurate. Sugrue, the novelist of *Memorial,* has been waiting for years for something to happen; his waiting has been a kind of intent prayer. Now Herra has come, wounded by her terrible sensitivity to physical suffering, especially the suffering inflicted on animals (she has cuttings about coursing which she carries around with her so that she will not lose sight of its fierce cruelty) and he and she share a sympathetic communion, they become one flesh, scandalous though that is to the world of confident moral judgement and condemnation. The waiting has borne fruit.

In Stuart waiting is a kind of prayer. The victim, the prisoner, the sufferer, looks forward to the moment when the external facts will correspond to internal desire; when there will be a leap of energy to connect two (or more) apparently separate events or perceptions. Prayer is one means the imagination employs for probing reality: it seeks an inward apprehension of reality and is related to the process of waiting. In the 'Selections from a Berlin Diary' he writes:

> Prayer is a very mysterious activity and not at all the simple matter the superficial meaning of the word suggests.

> Intense prayer is a close communion in which a kind of conception of life takes place and brings about the later outward results.[9]

This statement is deeply unsettling. It is unusual to find a writer taking prayer so seriously and indeed giving it the highest priority as an active and creative agent in life. He links it to the writing process itself, saying, also in the Berlin Diary, that 'writing is a kind of communion as well as creation.' Conception, communion, creation, prayer, waiting (because prayer, real prayer, arises from the concentration of desire waiting produces) – all these are related in Stuart's concept of the activity to which the artist commits himself. But it is a difficult concatenation to grasp intellectually; one needs the eventful depictions of fiction to illustrate how prayer arises from waiting and how the imagination may be considered seriously as a means of probing beneath the surface of reality.

In *The Pillar of Cloud*, in a chapter entitled 'The Coloured Ball', Petrov has lost faith in humanity, and has opted for ease. He is transfixed by a vision of what he calls 'The Beast', his image for the violence, torture and cruelty evident in the modern world: 'I have simply given up believing, being patient, waiting.'[10] Lisette, the young girl who is dying of tuberculosis, will not accept this lethargy of despair:

> that is wrong. It is just when we can't bear the waiting and patience any longer that we must wait on. . . . I know that it is the time after the waiting has become hopeless that is the right time; then, if ever, something will happen. It is always so, always.[11]

And then she tells how she first came to this understanding. It was in Lodz, at a fairground. As a child, in front of a hurdy-gurdy stall, Lisette watches a big wheel turn and prizes being won. On the stall was a big, coloured ball. She craves it and longs for it, but has no money for a ticket. She prays, to St Thérèse of Lisieux, at one in her mind with her sister Halka, whom she loves: 'The words of the prayer were a formula in which her tense willing and longing found secret utterance.' For hours she stands, praying, waiting. Eventually the stall-owner gives her a free ticket, the wheel turns, and she wins. She goes home through the fairground, the ball pressed to her heart, 'burning her, burning into her as though it had been the great red sun that had lately set.'

It is not that as readers we believe this fiction: Stuart (and Lisette in the novel) offers the story as an example of how actual fact may, under certain circumstances, coincide with intense desire. Too easily, the fiction is vividly conveying, do we think of reality as a set of laws and fixities, one of which is chance; whereas it is conceivable (it is conceivable because it can be imagined) that reality 'may turn out to be the opposite of what the word still implies - solidity - in popular thought'.[12] Stuart invites us to consider Lisette's prayer as an opening and deepening of consciousness, whereby imagination is bodied forth in the actual; her mind and exterior time become one because although they may be separate branches they belong to a single Vine. The waiting is the schooling of the personality for a changed state of apprehension: 'All things work together for good for the artist who can wait.'[13]

Francis Stuart is obsessed by gambling: the wager is an act of instinctive faith that the conditions will be right, that the accidents will fall into a coherent series of happy alignments whereby the chosen horse will fly past the winning post. In *Pigeon Irish* (1932) and throughout his work, he conveys the thrill of the gamble where the excitement mounts to such a pitch that the beat of the heart can be felt along the arms as the observer raises the field glasses to watch the horses spread out against the green, and the distant white of the flag:

> I saw the white flag go up. I held the glasses to my eyes with my elbows against my chest, and through the length of my arms I felt the echo of my heart-beat.[14]

To go back to the image from the gospels, gambling is an activity which presents the possibility that the different branches of the Vine may be connected as an immediate opportunity and a challenge fraught with risk. Everything becomes significant: the look of the leaves, the face of the jockey, the way someone greets you. Each tiny aspect of behaviour may provide an indication of the path to be taken to the secret outcome. George Moore, in *Esther Waters*, also wrote of the addiction to gambling, but in that novel this obsessive, almost alchemical reading of signs in order to pick the winner is pathetic. Stuart narrates his gambling scenes in a way which imbues them with an atmosphere of theological danger and Kierkegaardian trembling. His gamblers, despite failures and bitter disappointment, keep the faith (*We Have Kept the Faith* was the title of his first volume, a book of poems, published in 1923); they hope always to evoke from the obdurate 'solidity' of the rock of fixed actuality a flow of awareness, a blessing of cash. The absence of 'liquidity', of 'cash flow', is a problem for gamblers; but their way of solving it is to throw their energy against the rock. They keep faith that they may be able to read the signs in order to unite their choice with the actual fact yet to emerge. A kind of predictive magic is involved, or 'detached prayer': 'a prayer in which you saw what happened was good, and it was not a prayer for the shaping of events so much as for the understanding of them.'[15]

Gamblers must know how to watch, wait and pray: they need to learn how to pay attention to the signals being transmitted continuously. The gamblers' act of faith is, essentially, manifest in action: they put their money where their mouths are and test their instincts.

Stuart's fictional heroes are often gamblers and characteristically obsessed by conjunctions, confluences, links other than those of the causal chain:

> He was learning that life developed in the manner of all natural phenomena: through static periods followed by a state of confluent events; and after the time of waiting, the permit came the same morning as the telegram from Iseult.[16]

Causality belongs to the reasonable world of conventional understanding; Stuart continually attempts to depict a fictional 'model of reality' where characters, events, historical periods, may have links other than those of cause and effect:

> Jung . . . believed that there are events whose connection is other than cause and effect. They are associated not by one triggered by the other but by (A) their similarity and (B) their coinciding.[17]

In *The Abandoned Snail Shell,* from which the above extract comes, he suggests that there is a great deal of uncertainty about the inner world of the human being, and the outer world of infinite space, and characteristically links the two:

> There is growing evidence of an 'uncertainty principle' that infiltrates between observer and observed, a cloud whose origin seems generated by our deeper selves. It is quite a long time ago that the astronomer Eddington declared: 'The stuff of the universe is mind stuff.'

If the stuff of being is mind stuff, does this then mean that all there is is subjectivity? For Stuart, no, because the inward self (which all real writing, in his view, seeks to chart) connects with all the past, and indeed Christ himself. The self is the Vine; Christ's activities in the gospels have the 'impact of reality':

> let's take the Gospels. What we want to know is do they reflect reality, which is a better way of putting it than asking, are they true? Because the right question is the one that involves not just the upper mental surfaces in the answer. The worthwhile answers are in tune with the deeper emotional and imaginative pulsations. Reasoning can't distinguish true from false except on fairly extraneous levels. Do you never feel inside you . . . a series of nerve cells, some sort of fine chain, linking you with reality? I think, if we haven't broken it, we're aware of something like consciousness, transforming the vibrations into what can just, at the last link, enter the mind as thought. What I'm getting at is that the Gospels, transmitted to us by this route, do have the impact of reality.[18]

This passage is amongst the most crucial in all of Stuart's writings: it transmits, beautifully and elegantly, the central core of vision. It stresses the value of fiction as a mode of understanding reality; it suggests a unity between the interior self, the psyche, and external fact; it conveys, simply, the notion of a coherence in life which involves past and present; and it intimates that the person of Christ is a way of representing that incredible coherence to the human mind. It opens up, too, for the reader, the sense that the impact this kind of reality may have is affective, intuitive and more complete because more integrated than what we accept as the 'given' model. The impact that this reality can have is one which initiates change by attempting to activate wholeness. Stuart's aim as a writer was to create fictions which would have this kind of impact; they should grow out of an evolution of the personality, an unfolding of its potential, to become more integrated, more Christ-like. Such a fiction will then revolve upon the subjectivity of the author, so the various aspects of his personality, including those normally repressed for the sake of moral or psychological hygiene, will be seen to be a part of a unified consciousness. H, noticing some patterns in the grain of the wood in the furniture of his room in the Pyrenees, reflects: 'Like that must be the process that records a writer's inner growth in the spiral-like pattern of his work.'

Perhaps only writers like Thomas Kinsella and the Gaelic poet Nuala ní Dhomhnaill in contemporary Irish writing have such an intensity of preoccupation with the inner lineation of the self, as Stuart has displayed throughout his work. It is revealing too to consider that Kinsella and ní Dhomhnaill, like Stuart, look to Jung as a guide in these inward journeys.

In *Psychology and Alchemy* Jung speaks of the *nigredo*, an alchemical term to describe the mood of doubt, pain and inner anguish that marks the initial stages of waiting for the transformation that the alchemist hopes will occur. The *nigredo* is a state

> either present from the beginning as a quality of the *prima materia*, the chaos . . ., or else produced by the separation of the elements.[19]

The mood of the greatest part of Stuart's fiction is dark; a sombre grey light is often evident. It is interesting to note that the alchemists associated a bleakness of mood with the confrontation with the primary material, with chaos; and that it was also associated with separation or fragmentation. Stuart is one of those novelists, in this century, who chose to confront chaos and alienation, both of which have been publicly evident on a massive and intense scale. But he has chosen to confront these awesome facts of the modern condition in his fiction, not with an heroic mastery or a wailing grief, but with an intent and vulnerable self, as (and he is quite explicit always with the parallel) Christ did in his own nightmare-ridden time in an out of the way part of the Roman Empire.

Christ embodies the suffering aspect of the human personality, the force that confronts chaos and fragmentation and the repressive contrivances reason invents to keep the tensions bottled up. Christ, in Stuart, is the radical, the complete revolutionary. As in Blake he breaks the 'mind-forged manacles' to free the spirit, which is the self. He suffers because the message he imparts is not a palliative; he says you must change your life, you must suffer, otherwise you will not be free:

> individual well being . . . without which society, despite its prized ornaments, is sick, comes from within. Psychic health depends on liberation from assumptions imposed from outside. . . . The Agony in Gethsemane and the crucifixion . . . shattered any idea that Jesus . . . was a . . . confirmation of the fundamental laws and guide lines laid down by the Theocratic community of Judaea.[20]

On the night Christ was betrayed, according to St John's gospel, he said at the Last Supper:

> I am the true Vine and my Father is the vinedresser. Every branch in me that bears no fruit he cuts away, and every branch that does bear fruit he prunes to make it bear even more. . . . Make your home in me, as I make mine in you.

He promises them pruning, the sharp edge of pain and bitterness. And this from someone who has sought out all the wrong kind of company. In the conversation over lunch between Father Mellowes and Ezra Arrigho in *Redemption* (1950), Arrigho, a fictional self of Stuart's, outlines his understanding of the force of Christ's vision of reality and its revolutionary nature:

> He liked anyone who let themselves be carried away . . . better be carried away . . . and become a prodigal or a lost sheep than not be carried away at all, that seems to have been his point of view. And like you, Father, He sought the mad, the possessed, and the sick and dying, they being in a sense nearest Him and most likely not to be appalled and scandalized by the extravagance of what He was going to do and be at the end, when His hour came. Anything to get away from the calculators, the adders-up and subtractors, the moralists for whom the ordinary fleshly communion was already a little suspect and for whom therefore what He meant to offer would be an outrage.[21]

Because what Christ had to offer was a communion over, above and through the flesh. He was saying that he was in them, in the disciples; and that their deepest selves knew him there. To follow him meant giving not less than everything; yet even the disciples themselves could not stay with him for one hour in Gethsemane. To run from suffering is understandable, because suffering exposes the cracks in the smooth edifice society puts up front, and the last thing sane orderly people wish to do is explore the cracks. Stuart faces into suffering, pain, guilt; he explores the faults in the edifice and makes them, in his fiction, 'tiny' (a favourite word that occurs over and over again) dwelling places for warmth, fraternity and communion.

In *Blacklist, Section H,* H finds, in Kafka, certain sentences which, though he cannot fully grasp what they intimate, nevertheless fascinate him. They speak of suffering and exposure and the relation between these and growth:

> We too must suffer all the suffering round us . . . we have one way of growing and this leads us through anguish. . . . There is no room for justice in this context, but neither is there any room for fear of suffering or for the interpretation of suffering as a merit.[22]

Suffering is what is inevitable if Christ is to be followed; and, to Stuart's way of thinking, there can be no unfolding of the self, no 'way of growing' without accepting, in some part at least, the alienation and isolation he went through. The remarkable thing is that Stuart adopted this theology as his fictional method from the start. His male characters are Christ-selves, probes and sensings in order to discover what can be revealed through a fictional world devoted to the examination of suffering, isolation, pain, futility, failure, sickness and death. Stuart's Gethsemane is to be located in his representations of the Irish Civil War; the Curragh internment camp; war-time Berlin; French-occupied Germany; the sad repressive Ireland of the 1950s; the Northern Ireland of the troubles; and other places as well. He seeks out, in his imagination, as he had done in his life, those places where human suffering is intense, in the hope of perceiving an inner core of truth which will have, for a mind tired of the vapid comforts of mass-illusion and entertainment, the impact of reality. In *Pigeon Irish* a phrase a priest uses, during a drunken respite from a situation plunging into chaos, strikes home into the mind of the hero, Frank Allen:

> 'A deeper fidelity' still echoed in my mind. That was it. That was all that was important. I began to see it, too. But

> hardly anyone understood that. Brigid understood it. And I thought of the pigeon Joe had released, brought down, wounded, bleeding to death; of the ruins of Rafearta Church, with the sunlight pouring into it, and the lake dark through the trees; of the wound on Catherine's finger, of St. Catherine of Siena.

Brigid is Allen's wife; Catherine the daughter of a friend, who is devoted to St Catherine.

> Now I began to see a continuity, an inevitable link between all these things. They were all fitting into each other in my mind and in my heart. They were all part of that deep fidelity. A steadfastness that suffering and time could not weaken, that showed itself through suffering, that expressed its faith and love through suffering.[23]

These paragraphs are perhaps overwritten, but the urgency to link suffering with continuity and coherence is plain. At the core of the Christ-self is a wholeness which unites the branches, however diverse they appear at first. The closer a model associates observed phenomena with each other, the more valid it is. 'Everything that lives is holy,' Blake wrote, meaning, among other things, that all that lives is, to the eye purged of the ready-made formulae for seeing, integrated:

> What is now needed is, I believe, a bridge over the man-made divisions and a return to a more uniform concept, one in keeping with the homogeneous overall molecular reality. A seamless garment rather than a watch is an illuminating metaphor for all that exists.[24]

Stuart's texts are fabrications, textures, which attempt to connect the different elements on the fabric. Pain comes when what longs to cohere, to be whole, to be healed, is set apart: 'the man-made divisions', the 'mind-forged manacles'.

Consider Herra in *Memorial*, the girl to whom the novelist/protagonist reads the Kafka extract quoted earlier from *Blacklist, Section H*. She immediately recognizes its relevance to her condition. A girl, little more than a child, distracted by suffering, particularly suffering inflicted on animals, she tells Sugrue of how she waited, in agony of spirit, for the return of her cat, Lazarella. Sugrue reflects:

> I knew the utterly solitary place where you'd been; it is where the theme of a novel is engendered, but also where the thoughts of suicide can be encountered. . . .
>
> Chased or strayed to a distant garden in a part of the suburbs that neither you nor she knew, thrown scraps by whoever happened to glimpse the bedraggled exhausted creature, or somewhere else unimaginable: you had to try to imagine it, to try to share at least in thought the agony. Rubbish dumps, ditches, drains, scrappily dug graves; holes in the ground.[25]

This intensity of sympathy brings the separate phenomena (Herra, Sugrue, the fiction, Stuart, the reader, the animal world) closer together. The acknowledgement of the suffering, the apartness, the rending, brings communion; where there was indifference there is now a possibility of confluence:

> Nothing can be sole or whole
> That has not been rent.[26]

This is what Crazy Jane says in W.B. Yeats. This wholeness brings about a different atmosphere. The grey mood, the separateness of the elements is still evident of course, but there is a warmth, a glow of faith, 'a deeper fidelity'. Or, to put it another way: 'Knowledge is all-knowing, understanding, forgiving; it takes up no position, sets no store by form. It has compassion with the abyss - it *is* the abyss' (Thomas Mann).[27]

In the quotation from Kafka, cited in *Blacklist, Section H* and *Memorial,* there is a phrase, left out till now, in which Kafka says, 'we have not all one body': hence the pain. But through knowledge, and the kind of understanding Stuart's fiction seeks to awaken, there may be a sympathy, a communion: 'We are all one flesh.' Such a realization can only come out of suffering, which is something easily said, but much less easily grasped as a felt reality. But, Stuart continually reminds us, only suffering can prepare the mind and the body for real communion, because pain, isolation, dread may strip the mind of all the divisions and manacles that it creates and society needs. Then it is possible that a kind of changed seeing emerges, a form of apprehension of others, which is radically attuned to things as they are in themselves:

So each abandoned snail-shell strewn
Among those blotched dock-leaves might seem
In the pure ray shed by the loss
Of all man-measured value, like
Some priceless pearl-enamelled toy
Cushioned on green silk under glass.

This extract, from David Gascoyne's *Night Thoughts,* Stuart uses as epigraph and text for *The Abandoned Snail Shell.* The 'pure ray' is the pure ray shed by radical apprehension of 'real presence', if such a phrase may be cited without blasphemy. This pure ray emanates from the *loss* of all 'man-measured value', by the leaving of the norms, conventions, understandings which buttress social living and the forms of human intercourse. This loss is a kind of death; *is* death, *is* the abyss: 'He who loses his life shall gain it.'

I have said already that Stuart's search is for the inner dimensions of the self, wherein may be found the Christ-self. Hence his fictions are experiments in autobiography, of a kind. But, as he has said in *Faillandia,* how this 'I' is made flesh and dramatized in fiction, depends on the 'temperament and personal experience' of the writer. Some, like Robert Lowell perhaps, or John Berryman, open the personal wounds and bear witness to the terror of a stigmatized self. Others, like Stuart, and to my mind these are much rarer, much fewer in number, bear witness to the suffering and rending pain in order to come to some apprehension of the Christ-self; the old self, the 'I', the known 'I', what St Paul calls in The Epistle to the Romans the 'old man', goes and he is replaced by a new man, a different self, a changed self, capable of communion.[28] This changed self has nothing to do with the ego, save that it is a transformation of it. In this sense does Stuart believe in the resurrection, as a miracle that can take place *in life*: where else do miracles happen but in the world of time, space and matter? The new man who may begin to have an intimation of what it is to look upon matter and time 'in the pure ray shed by the loss of all man-measured value', begins to be capable of communion, fraternity; he is marked by faith; and, in Stuart, he seeks out the company of certain women, women like those who were around Christ, in particular Mary Magdalene. Sugrue, in *Memorial,* would like his question on waiting to be set by Mary Magdalene, who knows the subject 'inside out'.[29] Even a slight phrase, like the last, which is lit with Stuart's peculiar verbal humour (the Magdalene, like a prisoner, knows about the waiting from 'inside'), shows the degree of attentiveness he brings to his fictional realizations.

In *Pigeon Irish*, an early and over-Romantic novel, which nevertheless Yeats praised for its 'cold exciting strangeness',[30] there is an attempt to envision life in a manner bereft of all 'man-measured value' in the interspliced narrative about the carrier pigeons, who speak the 'pigeon Irish' of the title. The three pigeons carry messages between war-torn Europe and Ireland, because normal communications break down. In a strange and moving passage, one of the pigeons, returning to Ireland, sees the blurred 'thin stain' of the coastline. Stuart tries to get the reader to look at Ireland in a new and estranging way, from what it might be like to see from a perspective devoid of 'man-made value'. It is an attempt, as all such can only be, but the writing is powerful in its venturous departure from a fixed reliable vantage to a precarious, even, possibly, ludicrous one:

> Through the long centuries, down through countless bird generations, like a sea-wave thrusting up a river against the down-flowing ripples, a memory stirred in her. Shivering against each ripple, absorbing it, thrust on by the tide behind. Failing at last until at that moment of being turned, of falling backwards into the river's flowing, another wave comes, catching it up, remoulding it out of water, thrusting on. So a memory had persisted through thousands of bird-generations up to this. The memory born in the breast of a dove returning spent and desolate over a waste of water to a big wooden boat. . . . This bridging of an eternity sent a quiver through her body beneath the close feathers, a sweet fearful tremble.[31]

It is a mark of real writers that the flavour of the whole of their work can be communicated in a part; and this extract summarizes and transmits many of Stuart's most essential signals: exhaustion and suffering giving way to an intimation of an inner form, as distinct from the exterior forms and conventions of man-made value. Patrick Kavanagh once remarked that a poet's being was characterized by 'volatility', a lightness of being capable of realizing and integrating difference, and one can see this operating powerfully in this Stuart passage. The writing leaps across the gaps between the phenomena, to produce a fictional model of reality in which heterogeneous elements are conjoined. The darkness of separation starts to clear as the coastline grows more distinct, but also coming into view, through this most peculiar angle, is the fabulous sight of Noah's ark, still on the waters in the bird's senses. The writing involves us in this coming together of mind, emotion and memory.

Communion itself, as in all of Stuart's fiction, is a major theme in this novel. Ireland and her European allies are to be defeated in the war raging in Europe, and at home preparations are being made for the inevitable invasion. Ireland's identity will be swamped in the 'super-civilisation that was flooding towards [her] through Europe.' An ark, she will not survive. Catherine's, the young heroine's, hope is that they may persuade the invaders to allow small 'colonies' here and there throughout Ireland, in which 'picked communities' the Irish spirit will survive intact.[32]

In *Pigeon Irish* Stuart makes his hero, Allen, quite conscious of the dangers of the patriotic fanaticism possibly attendant on such concepts as the 'deep supremacy of the Irish spirit' which Catherine's envisaged 'colonies' are devoted to sustaining. But they are also imagined as places apart from the 'flood' of 'super-efficiency' which the new anonymous culture will bring with it. Catherine espouses martyrdom and suffering not simply for a nationalist cause, but because through this extremity a glimmer of the reborn self may be perceived. A memorable moment in the novel occurs when Allen, awake early one morning, goes for a walk in the Wicklow mountains, and sees her, outlined against the spreading sunlight, on a ridge. Without any allegorical machinery on Stuart's part, she becomes the *anima* or psyche, which the philosopher breathes out, according to alchemical lore, at the beginning of the *nigredo*.

The communities and communions of Stuart's novels always involve women. They are made up of fugitives, criminals, the tormented, the obsessed, who take shelter with each other in the prevailing indifference. They partake in a form of death; they die away from the illusory enticements of orthodox society which have been revealed to them as such by suffering, hunger and deprivation. Often their gathering places are 'tiny'; very frequently they gather in an upper room (as the disciples did after the crucifixion). In this atmosphere of quiet containment, they wait, they create a small world for themselves, a cleft over the abyss, or an ark upon the waste of waters. This life, then, beginning to be purged of all 'man-measured value' and certainly, outside the protective barriers society creates around itself, barriers of cliché, indifference and lethargy, acquires an inner glow, a special warmth, that makes each person, each thing, become alive in its own presence. Life becomes a shared communion, a sacramental awareness. Difference is merged; priest and murderer share a common sense of each other's claims to life. In *Redemption* Father Mellowes, the deeply spiritual priest; his sister Romilly; Ezra Arrigho, the Irishman returned from French-occupied Germany in disgrace; Margareta, a crippled girl whom he met in Berlin; and the murderer Kavanagh, all begin to live together in a community over Kavanagh's fish shop. It is a refuge:

> They felt the unexpected life of the little group encompass them. There was a dark and subtle field of power set up between those living in the house. Ezra was more conscious of it than the others. There opened before him vast and strange vistas. He saw that, after all, there were other modes of communion beside the old and played-out ones, other cults beside the marriage-cult and the family-cult. He said nothing, even to Father Mellowes.[33]

Romilly, the priest's sister, has turned her back on a safe marriage to a well-heeled colonel with a fine house. She has chosen the dark peace of this community and at the end marries the murderer, Kavanagh, knowing he is to be executed. The priest comments that 'in a marriage like this the sacrament is purified of all the misuse that has been made of it.' Kavanagh, astonished at this leap of charity in Romilly, reflects:

> Women were queer. He left it at that. There was nothing of which they were not capable. He felt a new breath of life in the very face of death.[34]

The new breath is that of the 'new man' of St Paul; of the spirit.

These themes of communion and sacrament are not, in Stuart, a quasi-theological apparatus through which he is processing his own religious preoccupations. They become active in the fiction, in the actual writing, and indeed in the style. This mood of intent and purified concentration gives the writing a quality of alert, luminous awareness, dispersed throughout the whole, in a kind of solemn joyful peace; and concentrated at particular points of intense understanding, often to do with the celebration of the female body. In *Redemption*, for example, Arrigho arrays his mistress, Margareta, for the marriage between Romilly and Kavanagh. Because she is crippled he washes her, having first stripped her of the clothes she has worn since she gained her freedom from the refugee camp.

> He spread the towel on the bed and put the basin on it and began to lave her as she lay there. He passed the sponge, that lay like a living thing between his hand and her flesh, over the breasts and her belly, her loins and flanks, slipped over the gleaming planes of her body and into the folded shadows, his hand moving heavy and brooding and yet light on the sponge on whose web the water had turned to balm.[35]

This writing integrates the different elements by means of a style which celebrates the movements described by linking them together into a unity: assonance provides a chain of links ('basin', 'lave', 'lay', 'planes'), which is set off against contrasting vowel and consonant colours ('sponge', 'thing', 'slipping', 'folded'); there are contrasts ('gleaming', 'shadows'); and there is an insistent weaving of the notion of interconnectedness ('spread', 'living', 'folded', 'web') in the passage. The writing studiously attends to and celebrates this simple activity, and makes it radiant with presence. We are invited to see it as a 'holy' act, because it seeks to depict an active, loving sympathy.

Over Kavanagh's shop they eat fish, the Christ-symbol, and the prehistoric one which the picnickers see etched on a rock in a cave at the beginning of the novel. The sharing of food is celebrated in this novel, which is appropriate, considering the attention devoted to the idea of communion; and throughout Stuart's fiction eating and drinking are characteristically treated in a sacramental manner.

In *A Hole in the Head* (1977), for example, the protagonist Barnaby Shane has lunch with the French girl Gilde and her lover:

> We had agreed, Gilde and I, to Combermale ordering a *Fondue* dish, which, when it appeared, consisted of a central tureen of simmering oil under which was a small blue flame, a side dish beside each of us of raw meat in

smallish dice-like pieces, an array of piquant condiments and, to be eaten apparently from the larger plate directly in front of us, a bowl of salad.

With all this went long, two-pronged, bone-handled forks with which the cubes of meat were held in the boiling oil until done to each of our taste.

At the Last Supper portions of bread had been dipped into what I imagined as a centrally-placed bowl of wine, between which sops, morsels of the Paschal lamb were eaten with the fingers.[36]

Or there is the haunting episode of the fried dumplings in *The Pillar of Cloud,* when the two girls, Lisette and Halka, eat the precious balls of flour fried in fat off a tiny table which Malone pulls up beside the bed.

The quiet intensity Stuart brings to these passages of what appear at first to be simple description, bestows on the events and objects described a luminous and sombre clarity. Eating, the preparation of food, even walking down a street, become detached from their everyday familiarity, and stand out in a radiant light, the 'pure ray' of Gascoyne's poem. The actual inclines towards the mythic and the legendary; and the opposite movement also takes place in the changing state of the fiction. In the passage quoted from *A Hole in the Head,* Stuart is associating the fondue with the central dish of the Last Supper, the one into which Judas put his hand, along with Jesus. Soon after, in explaining to Gilde and Combermale his role as go-between in the conflict in Belbury (thinly disguised Belfast) Barnaby Shane describes himself as a mediator which he is, he says, qualified to be because of 'a facility for entering into conflicting viewpoints. An aptitude for sharing extreme positions and attitudes, perfected during my recent illness.' (Shane, in his delirium, has had as companion Emily Brontë, to whom he explains modern things such as the motor car, and buys her a contemporary outfit.) In *The Abandoned Snail Shell* the effectiveness of 'a model of reality' is assessed by its ability to bridge the gaps between differentiated phenomena. The seamless garment is a better metaphor for existence than the watch. A writer of fictions may act as a mediator between opposed camps, each of which is intent on its own justice, if he can heal the separation, which is pain, by the communion which arises from prayer, suffering, waiting. Such a fiction may involve the unfolding of the Christ-self, which means losing man-measured value to gain life. In the cross, opposites intersect.

Towards the end of *Faillandia* the old monk, Frère Emmanuel, instructs Gideon Spokane and his 'dove' Pieta, on differing and opposed perceptions of time. In an aquarium he has some tiny ovaloid marine creatures descended from the tribolites of five or six million years ago; on the desk also he has an hour glass:

> Gideon thought he began to grasp the principle behind the old monk's discursive method. He did not concentrate exclusively on one subject, especially an urgent one, but surrounded it with other completely unrelated ones - such as the hour-glass and the fossils - steeped it, so to speak, in solvents which might cause it to vanish or could reveal something about it which was hidden from a direct approach.[37]

This passage, in a characteristically oblique way, explains Francis Stuart's narrative technique. He experiments with autobiographical fiction, surrounds the central self with the various solvents, the more apparently discrete the better (Emily Brontë/1970s Belfast; bestiality/holiness) and seeks an inner coherence. The old self is lost and a new self, a fictional one, capable of integrating past and present, pain and joy, comedy and tragedy, emerges; or, rather, begins to emerge. It is crucial not to write in a triumphalist manner about Stuart's interrogatory intuitions.

This narrative play across time, personality, casual sequence, is a *jouissance* of energetic unfolding. *The High Consistory* tells of the varied experiences of a painter Simeon Grimes in Berlin, Paris and Halifax, Nova Scotia. Returning to Ireland by air he is involved in a slight air crash, which disperses his memoirs. He collects them and has them typed up just as 'accident' has arranged them. Scenes in Berlin interact with events in Nova Scotia; his commission to paint St Thérèse interpenetrates with a love affair between him and Claire, from Halifax, who has sexual congress with an ocelot she has stolen from a zoo. Put down baldly like this the enterprise sounds like a zany one, but the different perspectives intermesh to reveal a consciousness flickering across different events; the style is one in which the reader is invited to participate in the criss-crossing of intuition, excitement, pain and longing. Oddly, too, a comic spirit is much in evidence. An extract from an interview with a woman journalist is included; she asks him what he would like to fulfil his 'fancies':

S.G. To be the dove in your cote, the pig in your sty.
W.J. That's not very nice, the last wish, I mean.
S.G. I'll try again: the third side of your triangle,
the barge in your canal lock.
Interruption as the wine bottle is brought.
W.J. Anything else?
S.G. The salmon up your weir.
W.J. That's better.
S.G. The cross-bar on your cross.
W.J. Don't go morbid on me.[38]

In the later fiction, especially, the writing becomes a space wherein different perspectives on the central self are revealed; heterogeneous events are brought together, in order that the writing itself become a kind of communion in which reality's different facets are lit, brilliantly, in a succession which proceeds according to a law of similarity or coinciding rather than causality. This writing invites the reader to experience the possibility of freeing his or her sense of reality as a fixed determined thing in order to allow for a less certain but more jubilant coherence.

According to the old way of thinking (St Paul's 'old man') reality is a hard and obdurate rock. Brief mention has been made of the fictional feasibility that in the rock face there may be a cleft; into which the imagination can creep for shelter, one of those 'tiny' places where a few people gather for communion. Always there is a woman, or women. In *Faillandia* 'Kathy was his dove in the cleft of the rock-face that fell away to nothingness.'[39]

In *The Pillar of Cloud* women are described as the 'living mystery . . . the inner sanctuary of the earth, the pale, fecund groves of the holy of holies.'[40] In *Memorial*, in a biological fantasy, Sugrue explains to Herra the opening of the wound in the smooth fabric of reality, the opening which is female:

'There came a moment on the warm sands when the longed-for penetrability of female flesh was no longer a

> joke or fantasy, and a sick one at that, very possibly, to certain conservative marine creatures, but fact, fact, fact.'[41]

At one point in *A Hole in the Head* Sammy, the paramilitary, asks the protagonist, Barnaby Shane, if he is 'cunt crazy'; and indeed Stuart's fictional heroes have an obsession with the cunt. H, in *Blacklist, Section H*, recalls how, as a child, he folded over a mattress in the attic of a house in Co. Antrim, and sought to penetrate the cleft, imagining it to be Tolstoy's Katusha in *Resurrection*. Sex is linked with suffering; sex is the rent in the fabric of reality. In Stuart the women embody pain, but, as we have seen, pain is the way out of 'man-measured value', and the confident sterilities of the righteous and the orthodox. Through pain the new man comes into being in the company of women, the women at the foot of the cross of Christ; or the 'holy sisterhood' described in *The High Consistory*:

> Thérèse Martin from nineteenth-century France in her white woollen choir habit, Katusha from nineteenth-century Russia in padded jacket and long, red-leather boots, a gift from Tolstoy, Libertus Schultze-Boysen in the blue ski-pants and high-necked jersey I'd last seen her in, the ocelot in his spotted ochre coat, the girl-patient from the asylum in Dublin, and Claire.[42]

These compose the picture Simeon Grimes has made for his 'sisterhood'; and in the foreground, he wonders, should there be 'some loaves, a couple of grilled fishes? No. A few bottles of wine and a dish of freshly opened oysters.' Nothing too obvious.

Stuart's fiction creates alternative models of reality, not to escape from actuality, but to find a way of holding it in a perspective that reveals a coherence and integrity not available to the standard, and he would argue, outmoded and exhausted, ways of looking. In a sense one of the 'last Romantics', he is also someone who promotes new and radical apprehension. He sought strangeness from the start; and he sought shame. He found both and interiorized them completely. His accounts of suffering and anguish persuade us because, to this reader at any rate, there is a strong refusal to enlist our sympathy for the suffering ego. Indeed, as readers, we are continuously invited to find it ludicrous. Instead there is a steady and sombre attention to waiting, suffering, pain, which opens into the redemptive power of love located in small, quiet and unsignalled private acts. Little comforts are exchanged in the privacies of tiny rooms on the upper floors of desolate houses; or in cellars or bomb shelters. These places, these interiors, then become sketches for the changed and illumined world that may come into being when man is reborn, often through a woman's unstinting kindness. The old self is lost and a new one arises, changed into a redeemed personality, in the fiction, which often, like the gospels, has 'the impact of reality'.

9

SAMUEL BECKETT

'Matrix of surds'

When Desmond Egan wrote to Samuel Beckett in 1985 to ask him which he thought more highly of, tragedy or comedy, Beckett replied as follows:

> Sorry I can't help with yr. problem. Democritus laughed at Heraclitus weeping + Heraclitus wept at Democritus laughing. Pick yr. fancy.[1]

In *More Pricks than Kicks* (1934) Belacqua seems to pick Heraclitus weeping, but that does not prevent him, lying on his back waiting for his operation in the story 'Yellow', from finding solace in the form of this paradox, 'its terms, the extremes of wisdom that it rendered'. However, anxious though he is, Belacqua presses the point a little further and hazards a paradox of his own, to set beside or against the one about Democritus/ Heraclitus, and it is that 'between contraries no alteration was possible'.[2] If there can be no 'stirrings'[3] between contraries, then there can be no movement; the thought is moving to stasis and fixity, just as, incidentally, Belacqua is proceeding, in the story, to his death. The surgeon, just back from a wedding where he has been best man, 'clean forgets' to check the heart-rate.

In an earlier story in this, his first, collection, Beckett goes to great lengths to explain the attractions of paradox, its relations to movement, and the lascivious and dangerous allurements of stasis. In the opening pages of 'Ding Dong', he reveals, in a prose energized by a tense and brittle wit, a great deal about his method and much too about his central artistic obsessions. Belacqua believes, at this stage, a stage before 'he toes the line and relishes the world' that:

> the best thing he had to do was to move constantly from place to place. . . . The mere act of rising and going, irrespective of whence and whither, did him good . . . asking nothing better than to stay put at the good pleasure of what he called the Furies, he was at times tempted to wonder whether the remedy were not more disagreeable than the complaint. . . . I know all this because he told me. . . . I have had glimpses of him enjoying his little trajectory. I have been there again when he returned, transfigured and transformed. . . . He lived a Beethoven pause he said. . . . One day, in a positive geyser of confidence, he gave me an account of one of these 'moving pauses'. He had a strong weakness for oxymoron. In the same way he over-indulged in gin and tonic water. Not the least charm of this pure blank movement, this 'gress' or 'gression', was its aptness to receive, with or without the approval of the subject, in all their integrity the faint inscriptions of the outer world.[4]

There is the strong temptation to stay put, not to become involved in this 'gression', a temptation to which Belacqua, and subsequently Murphy too, succumb. Let the Furies do what they will: the effort of going out is too great. But going out is the 'moving pause', a state of expectancy in which there is a certain freedom. The outgoing is a part of the trajectory of movement which only completes itself in the return: each part engenders the other, the contraries are active and interpenetrate, hence the 'aptness to receive', the alertness, arising from the movement from fixity. There are problems, in that the inscriptions visited on the subject happen with or without the subject's approval, so you do not know what you are letting yourself in for, but this procedure, the one that is 'blank' movement, that knows nothing, is the place to start. The paradox and the oxymoron are 'strong weaknesses' in that they initiate the freedom from fixity in which alertness may develop. The best thing to know is that you know nothing; rightly held, such a state of mind is one of readiness, as Beckett found when, after his mother's death, he sat down to write *Molloy*.

> I realized that I knew nothing. I sat down in my mother's little house in Ireland ['New Place', to which she moved when Cooldrinagh was sold] and began to write *Molloy*.[5]

But Belacqua, Murphy and Watt had themselves been travellers intent on the 'moving pause'; Beckett had prepared himself for the terrible trajectories of Molloy, Moran, Mahood, Worm and Pim, and their even more penitential stillnesses; as well as those of Vladimir, Estragon, Hamm, Clov and all the others.

Murphy (1938) expresses Beckett's impatience with the complacent assurance that underlies the avidity and greed of materiality and its representation. Who are you, he seems to say, to imagine that reality is such that it can be set down and represented as if it were out there, ready for the taking. Virtually everyone in the novel is trying to take Murphy over by making him part of a narrative that will obey the rules of realism and normality. Murphy, for the most part, wants to rock in his rocker; he wants to be, in his own mind, free of the rampaging wills of others. The transactions that go on in the world of 'intelligence and habit',[6] the 'normal' world, are by turns exploitative and sentimental (remember Joyce's incessantly repeated formula against the sentimentalist, who refuses the immense debtorship of the thing done[7]). This interchange is alluring, seductive and, in Beckett's almost Jansenist and certainly pitiless light, corrupt. It is what we see taking place between Miss Counihan and Wylie in Wynn's Hotel:

> oyster kisses passed between them. Wylie did not often kiss, but when he did it was a serious matter. He was not one of those lugubrious persons who insist on removing the clapper from the bell of passion. A kiss from Wylie was like a breve tied, in a long slow amorous phrase, over bars' times its equivalent in demi-semi quavers. Miss Counihan had never enjoyed anything quite so much as this slow-motion osmosis of love's spittle.
>
> The above passage is carefully calculated to deprave the cultivated reader.[8]

There is, here, a dig at Austin Clarke, who, as Austin Ticklepenny, is a ludicrous and lethal figure in *Murphy.* Clarke wrote a 'gaelic prosodoturfy'[9] that imitated in English some of the formal devices of bardic and accented Irish verse of the late medieval and early modern periods. In a footnote to his volume of 1928, *Pilgrimage and Other Poems,* Clarke had written that 'assonance takes the clapper from the bell of rhyme',[10] a phrase that, obviously, had afforded Beckett great amusement. Not because he disapproved of experimentation, but because Clarke seemed to view technique as a thing in itself, whereas Beckett's attitude was that technique is part of the whole exercise of the spirit, and to speak of taking clappers from the bells of rhyme, while prettily put, is to make the activity, which should be whole, partial and materialistic. Wylie is not as 'lugubrious' as Clarke, but his artistry, his technique, is drearily insistent on its own supremacy, its contrapuntal assurance. Compare Beckett's description of what the artist, the writer, does in his essay on *Proust* (1931):

> The only fertile research is excavatory, immersive, a contraction of the spirit, a descent. The artist is active, but negatively, shrinking from the nullity of extra-circumferential phenomena, drawn in to the core of the eddy. . . . We are alone. We cannot know and cannot be known.[11]

The 'nullity' of the sentimental assurance which the Counihan/Wylie passage mocks, Beckett harshly rejects. This kind of realism is conceited, as Beckett wittily indicates in the conceit of the contrapuntal oyster-kiss. Such transactions deprave, and they are particularly effective with cultivated readers, with refined 'tastes'. Such a comfortable interchange as that described has nothing to do with the penitential rigours of art which is, he wrote in the Proust essay, 'the apotheosis of solitude'.[12] Murphy prefers the cool solidity of his rocker, which reconciles activity and stasis, to the agitated suctions the lovers from Cork enjoy. (It may not be too fanciful to suggest that the Corkman Frank O'Connor's sentimental realism and its confident narrative stance are as much the object of Beckett's derision as Austin Clarke's 'prosodoturfy', in the Wylie/Counihan exchange.)

The Proust essay insists that the only worthwhile approach, for the artist, is excavatory; and with some degree of reluctance, as of one undertaking a particularly nasty task, Beckett gives an in-depth account of Murphy's mind. It is a place, not an instrument. The 'big world' of confident assertions and oyster-kisses insists that the mind is a functionary, so that Murphy in the asylum, where Ticklepenny gets him a job, finds his like amongst those freed from a 'colossal fiasco'.[13]

There are three zones in Murphy's mind, the third being the deepest, most immersed state. Here the ego has died ('the old ego dies hard' Beckett wrote in *Proust*[14]), the will to insist on this or that has disappeared. This place is the place not of conceit but of paradox – it is Heraclitean movement and interchange, an energy source where all is activity without the striving of will:

> a flux of forms, a perpetual coming together and falling asunder of forms. The light contained the docile elements of a new manifold . . . the half light, states of peace. But the dark neither elements nor states, nothing but forms becoming and crumbling into the fragments of a new becoming, without love or hate or any intelligible principle of change. . . . Here he was not free, but a mote in the dark of absolute freedom. He did not move, he was a point in the ceaseless unconditioned generation and passing of line.
>
> Matrix of surds.[15]

A movement which is a ceaseless stasis: these concepts are not clear in the normal sense, but then Beckett has said that he is no intellectual but on the contrary 'all feeling'.[16] The writing here reaches out to create a 'place' where movement is unconditional and generative, where the utilitarian will, 'a servant of intelligence and habit',[17] has no function: this place is the place of art, a matrix of surds. A surd is an irrational number: 2 is the cube root of 8 (2 x 2 x 2 = 8), the cube root of 8 is rational; but the cube of 9 is irrational or surd, occupying that infinity of the ever-receding decimal point. This place of movement is Murphy's third zone, and where Beckett's landscapes and visions come together and fall asunder.

In *Watt* (written 1942–4; published 1953) the central figure leaves the rational world of numbers, kisses, sentimentality and assurance to enter a place or state that is surd (Beckett's mathematics do sharpen our sense of the absurd): the house and gardens of Mr Knott. As with all of the travellers that traverse the Beckett world, Watt's locomotion is remarkable and difficult, a 'headlong tardigrade', an agitated oxymoron of ambulation:

> Watt's way of advancing due east, for example, was to turn his bust as far as possible towards the north and at the same time to fling out his right leg as far as possible towards the south, and then to turn his bust as far as possible towards the south and at the same time to fling out his left leg as far as possible towards the north, and then again . . . the feet fell, heel and sole together, flat upon the ground, and

> left it, for the air's uncharted ways, with manifest repugnancy.[18]

It is as if Beckett has tried to describe, through bringing to his prose a mathematical alertness and rigour, the three-dimensional geometry of the body's mechanics, so that he can take the reader *into* the hiddenness of motion. One could imagine now a computerized realization of this locomotor system which would be a commotion of vortices, vectors, the 'grey air aswirl with vain entelecheis'.[19] This is funny, too, but the humour is shot through with a painful attention to that which 'habit' and rational intelligence would regard as circumferential, a distraction: whereas Beckett is driven by the need to immerse himself in the continuously changing 'matrix of surds' that inheres in all activity, including bodily motion, in the 'nothing' than which, in a favourite tag of his from Democritus, nothing is more real.[20] At the risk of labouring the point it should be noted that the feet display 'manifest repugnancy' to participate in this swirling entelechy; they have that 'ataraxy'[21] (another favourite word, from Florio's Montaigne) or reluctant lethargy which balances hectic activity.

This kind of locomotion brings Mr Watt to Mr Knott's house, where he becomes part of one of Beckett's complex, meticulously arranged, but essentially baffling systems. As with Watt's system of bodily 'gression' what Beckett has done is take the doings of a family house, and by concentrated immersion, he reveals that the ordinary conceals what is surd. A life or consciousness that pays no heed to this concealment is therefore ab-surd; and not the other way around. In a perverse way Beckett might argue (not that he ever bothered overmuch) that his method, based on reality, the matrix, is *normal*, conducing to normality.

Mr Knott's establishment, like any other such, is based on comings and goings, dependencies on external agents, and maintains various rules governing proprieties extending from matters such as seniority amongst the servants, to the arrangement of furniture, cooking and the disposal of leftovers. But these rules, which the novel painfully rehearses (as if the iteration of these miseries might allay the sorrow that inheres in them) conceal under a front of rationality, a commotion of ceaseless shift and change.

When Watt arrives Arsene departs, and eventually too Watt

will leave. All normal enough, on the surface, but the writing slows everything down so that the inner space within all exterior arrangements can be explored. The story (if such it can be called) Arsene tells Watt before he departs touches on the kinds of shifts into the irrational to be found in the place to which Watt has travelled. One day, he tells the newcomer, sitting on the step in the yard, looking at the sun on the wall, something happened. Beckett's prose is needed to convey this illumination in which perception is transformed:

> The change. In what did it consist? It is hard to say. Something slipped. There I was, warm and bright, smoking my tobacco-pipe, watching the warm bright wall, when suddenly somewhere some little thing slipped, some tiny little thing. . . . There is a great alp of sand, one hundred metres high, between the pines and the ocean, and there in the warm moonless light, when no one is looking, no one listening, in tiny packets of two or three millions the grains slip, all together, a little slip of one or two lines maybe, and then stop, all together, not one missing, and that is all, that is all for the night, and perhaps for ever that is all, for in the morning with the sun a little wind from the sea may come, and blow them one from another far apart, or a pedestrian scatter them with his foot. . . . It was a slip like that I felt, that Tuesday afternoon, millions of things moving all together out of their old place, into a new one near by, and furtively, as though it were forbidden. . . . To conclude from this that the incident was internal would, I think, be rash. For my . . . personal system was so distended at the period of which I speak that distinction between what was inside it and what was outside it was not at all easy to draw. Everything that happened happened inside it, and at the same time everything that happened happened outside it. . . . This I am happy to inform you is the reversed metamorphosis. The Laurel into Daphne. The old thing where it always was, back again.[22]

But, like Belacqua after his trajectory, transformed. This is a realism attentive to the irrational basis of reality; a realism grounded in profound uncertainty; a writing based upon what is 'inside', because, at a certain point of concentration the distinctions between inner and outer dissolve to reveal Francis Stuart's 'seamless garment'.[23] In this very precise and exacting sense all of Beckett's writings are autobiographical because he begins with the penitential search for the matrix within, knowing, or rather hoping, that she will be the same without.

To tell a story, Beckett held, was a foolish business. 'Miseries', he called his writings, commenting 'it was not as though I wanted to write them.'[24] Nevertheless Beckett's stories got told, powerfully. But to tell a story was to embark upon sequence, to travel through time, because that is what narrative does. As well as that it was to court all the dangers inherent in narration, such as causality, arrogant representation and superficial realism. How to remain true to 'how it is', with all its commotion of uncertainty, and yet proceed with a story? As Sam, who writes down Watt's story, is all too keenly aware, it is very easy to distort a story from its truth, which must rest upon a scrupulously maintained *uncertainty*:

> it is difficult for a man like Watt to tell a long story like Watt's without leaving out some things, and foisting in others. And this does not mean either that I may not have left out some of the things that Watt told me, or foisted in others that Watt never told me, though I was most careful to note down all the time, in my little notebook.[25]

The transitions between the so-called events in a story, their relations with each other, the temper of the voice which rehearses them: all of these are not only liable to shift and movement, it is their very nature that they will so move, so shift. In the empty space between the voice telling the story and the ear attentive (or not) much can go wrong; and in the mind or intelligence that receives, the opportunities for malfunction, misprision and deceit are limitless. The telling of a story, in Beckett's space, in the place where these narratives grow, change, shift and develop, is a continuous coming together of the elements, of words, figures, locations and a continuous sundering. His narratives subject storytelling itself to the same Heraclitean enquiry as he subjects Watt's walk.

Not that Beckett is drearily obsessed with drawing the reader's attention to the fictiveness of narrative as an end in itself. The writing is too engaged, too desperate for ludic consolations or postmodern delectation. This is how it is between us, he says; listen, study and pity. The effort will be a cleansing of perception, so that it may become clear what is required in really paying attention. A powerful extended figure or trope over half-way through *Watt* conveys the expense of storytelling and listening.

Watt and Sam are living in different pavilions, each with its own grounds, which are enclosed by high barbed wire fences. This in-between space is narrow, no wider than the human body, but it is where Watt and Sam communicate. With their hands on each other's shoulders, facing each other, they walk, one going forwards, the other backwards up to the point where the fences diverge; as soon as that point is reached the movement is reversed until the other point of divergence is reached. Watt speaks and Sam makes notes, stopping to do so, but Watt never takes his hands from the auditor's shoulders. In this figure movement and narrative are linked. Only in this lonely space, between the rusting barbed wire fences, does contact take place; nor are there any unwary assertions about this contact. It takes place, but it is, of course, imperfect. Sam can understand some of Watt's pronouncements, but some are 'so much Irish' to him.[26]

Mostly what the Beckett voices speak of are journeys, during which there are encounters. The voices attend to the business of trying, as best they can, to present these encounters faithfully, without too much 'literature': 'it is not at this late stage of my relation that I intend to give way to literature', Moran comments in *Molloy* (published in French 1950; in English 1955), after explaining that he cannot account for the fact that he finds a man he has previously met in the wood with his head beaten to a pulp.[27] Literature would be explication, it might be 'worth reading'; but that is not what these stories are about.

Moran, in part two of the novel, is in receipt of instructions to find his mother. Molloy tells us, however, that he has always done very little else other than that: 'all my life, I think I had been going to my mother, with the purpose of establishing our relations on a less precarious footing.' However, he leaves her without accomplishing anything; and once he is away from her he starts on his way back. But even that uncertainty, that failure, is too confidently asserted. Molloy, in speaking of Molloy, or in saying he did this or said that only finds himself 'complying with the convention that demands you either lie or hold your peace. For what really happened was quite different.'[28]

Here Beckett is intent on taking the supremely daring swerve of trying to say what 'really' happens when someone says they did this or said that; he is attempting to unfold the basis of narrative itself, how the I ventures in the systems of language. Molloy tells us that when he says 'he has the impression that'

> I had no impression of any kind, but simply somewhere something had changed, so that I too had to change, or the world too had to change, in order for nothing to be changed.[29]

Whatever the I is it is not fixed; and inside and outside are not differentiated clearly, as convention demands they should be.

These linguistic 'canters' (as such diversions are called[30] in *Waiting for Godot* (published in French 1953; in English 1954)) are a prelude to the final figure of Molloy's narrative. Schooled in Beckett's rigour, distrustful of narrative, conscious that he who dares to speak of this or that, his mother or himself, does so in an arrogance that neglects life itself, for which Beckett has nothing less than a profound reverence and awe, we now are given one of the most terrifying visions in modern writing: Molloy flailing through the undergrowth on his belly, using his crutches like grapnels to haul himself forward towards (he says to encourage himself) his mother. Speech, language, writing, take too little note of this:

> Flat on my belly, using my crutches like grapnels, I plunged them ahead of me into the undergrowth, and when I felt they had a hold, I pulled myself forward, with an effort of the wrists.[31]

Molloy, early on in his narrative, says that his 'sense of identity was wrapped in namelessness'.[32] *Malone Dies* (published in French 1951; in English 1956) and *The Unnamable* (published in French 1953; in English 1958) subject the 'I' of the storyteller to increasingly relentless scrutiny.

Malone, the old ego, dies hard. While waiting he tells himself stories, as best he can. He makes a few scattered attempts to write narratives that would be conventionally recognized as such but fails; he hasn't the heart for them: 'In this country the problem – no, I can't do it. The peasants. His visits to, I can't!'[33] Nor is Malone himself the subject in that the story spends no time rehearsing the details of his life; rather is it something or someone else, inside Malone's ego, or beneath it:

> My concern is not with me, but with another, far beneath me and whom I try to envy, of whose crass adventures I can now tell at last, I don't know how. Of myself I could never tell, any more than live or tell of others.[34]

There is an I or perhaps a series of Is within Malone, so monolithic and intact at first to all appearances. There are many worlds within Malone, just as within Molloy there were many persons: 'a rubble in [the] head, what a gallery of moribunds. Murphy, Watt, Yerk, Mercier and all the others.'[35] These 'others' are all the creatures of Beckett's stories who inhabit the place which he incessantly describes through all his fiction, and which he puts before the eyes in the stark theatrical worlds of *Waiting for Godot, Endgame* (published in French 1957; in English 1958) or the late television plays, *Ghost Trio* (1975) or *. . . but the clouds . . .* (1976). They come from 'beneath' the upper layers of consciousness: Murphy, Watt and the 'others', including, for example, the terrifying figure that beats along the road towards the station in *Watt* at a fierce pace. The hero watches this frenetic ball of activity only to realize that it is not getting any closer. They are baffling and inscrutable, from the depths. At the beginning of *Molloy* the narrator recalls an evening when he stared at the road, watching two figures, one walking away from the town the other towards it. This scene has the typical Beckett air: tension, uncertainty, evening or twilight, confusion. Molloy then goes on to reflect that he may be confusing several different occasions, times, figures. They originate, he says, 'deep down, and deep down is my dwelling, oh not deepest down, somewhere between the mud and the scum. . . . No matter, no matter, let us go on, as if all arose from one and the same weariness.'[36] This place is another version of Murphy's 'matrix of surds'; and it is the deep of consciousness into which the stories try to reach. Malone himself speaks of a hand plunging into him, up to the elbow, 'delving feebly in my particles';[37] but this hand also 'ravages', 'clutches'. The world of Beckett's fiction and drama brings into consciousness voices, figures, locations that lie deep in the interior world of the twentieth century. They act strangely; speaking, they break off; they go on journeys; they start and abandon narratives; they are full of energy and rage, then they shift to tiredness and ennui; they laugh; they despair. They are how we are in the deep, unvisited mostly and neglected, these little ones, these lost ones, who stare back at us bleakly out of Beckett's narratives, or from his stage, reminding us how far astray we are from language, real speech, real understanding. Their ineffectuality rebukes our driving greed and appetite; their silence comments on our endless blaring of words and emitting of images. Their multivalence, their unfixedness and plurality calls into question our confident assurance that we are who we say we are and that we are what others, involved with us in our direful need for mutual deceit, say we are.

Malone is restricted to his bed; he cannot move, but he can write. And his writing is his trajectory, his venture. Not that he contemplates the thought of writing and developing stories with any pleasure - it will pass the time - but it gives him the opportunity to engage in the painful kind of research Beckett described in *Proust*: 'excavatory', 'immersive', 'a contraction of the spirit'. He knows about this method:

> To speak for example of the times when I go liquid and brown like mud, what good would that do? Or of the others when I would be lost in the eye of a needle, I am too hard and contracted? No these are well-meaning squirms that get me nowhere.[38]

His compulsion (not desire) is to go deeper still, into the mud-matrix of the pool of darkness at the centre, the arena which is unvisited and which has grown stale if not corrupt.

In there identity is an unfixed pronoun, a changing consciousness, a 'namelessness'. James Clarence Mangan tried to describe this vacancy and fluidity of self: he presented it in poems and translations which he 'foisted' (a favourite Beckett word to describe these tricks) on others; he invented passions which he utilized; and, in his prose, in 'An Extraordinary Adventure in the Shades', for example, he communicated the unsettling implications for narrative of an ego that has entered into dissolution.[39] Mangan, more so than any other Anglo-Irish writer, is Beckett's forerunner, more so even than Joyce. How close Beckett is to him can be seen in 'The Nameless One', a poem which questions the assurance of identity, and looks into the depths opened when it is called into doubt:

> And tell how now, amid wreck and sorrow,
> And want, and sickness, and houseless nights,

He bides in calmness the silent morrow,
That no ray lights.[40]

Beckett: 'no things but nameless things, no names but thingless names.'[41] All the stories that Malone invents, or Beckett, are attempts to open up this depth of namelessness. No 'legend', no song of the self is to be found, but intimations of the unvisited worlds within, the inner space which is 'surd': 'All the stories I've told myself, clinging to the putrid mucus, and swelling, swelling, saying got it at last, my legend . . . has anything happened, anything changed? No.'[42] This arena is not an armoury for the ego; it is the place of patience and of waiting. What we see in Estragon and Vladimir, Hamm and Clov are figures of this depth, figures which tend to be binary.

If we return to the idea of the surd it may help us to understand why these figures at these depths tend to be binary. The cube root of 9 is somewhere in the vast hinterlands of decimal between 2 and 2.1: 2 x 2 x 2 = 8; 2.1 x 2.1 x 2.1 = 9.261. It is in this hinterland that the Beckett characters speak and move, and they are there by virtue of a space, an infinite space, between one thing and another; between each of the figures in the binary. Estragon and Vladimir have dialogue only because of the gap between the two of them, an unbridgeable gap of limitless extent which is indicated, hinted at, by their speech and presence, their various ruses for passing the time. The Beckett storytellers in the fiction are dependent on the same binary presence. Malone is 'there', in the writing, but he has no illusion about identity or fixed value. He can only get going once he starts involving some other, some little one of his very own, 'a little creature';[43] because then there is the beginning of the binary relation between storyteller and figure, and that 'between' is the object of Beckett's 'excavatory', 'immersive' research.

The figure Malone finds is Macmann or Sapo, but he settles for the name Macmann. Once he enters, the narrative, such as it is, can go deep. The other objects for Malone's narration, the list of his possessions, for example, do not give him anything like the same freedom to invent. An inventory, listing, description, are tedium; the interchange Macmann makes possible between Malone and his 'little creature' is much more penetrative, the space the binary sets up being more extensive. Of course there is an element in this comparison which is unsatisfactory: Malone is not an analogy of a real number, because he himself is in the arena of the matrix, as indeed is Macmann; but within the matrix they are oppositional coordinates for intensified exploration, just as Estragon and Vladimir are in *Waiting for Godot*. So they are less rational than the rational figures 'convention demands', but they allow other stories, other probings, to proceed. These stories are often about ostensibly very little. Deeply moving, for example, is the account of Macmann's coat which, in various forms, surfaces throughout Beckett's writing from *Watt* through to *Company* (1979). It is difficult to explain why this coat should engage our attention and our feelings so much, but it does.

It is a greatcoat, in *Watt*, 'still green here and there'; it is long, right down to the ground; there are nine buttons, which fasten the coat from ground to throat; the skirts do not divide; and, the *coup de grace*, 'aloft in the flower-hole brooded the remains of a factitious murrey chrysanthemum.'[44] Thus Watt stands in his greatcoat, in the kitchen of Mr Knott's house, a figure of totally forlorn isolation. Willing to go, thankful even that his time is at an end, he embodies the sadness of all severances. The coat (although Beckett warns 'no symbols where none intended') is the coat we will wear for the road; whether with anything like Watt's fortitude remains to be seen.

Before he describes Macmann wearing this coat, Malone tells us:

> I have taken a long time to find him again, but I have found him. . . . I slip into him, I suppose in the hope of learning something. But it is his stratum, strata, without debris or vestiges. But before I am done I shall find traces of what was.[45]

Malone will not give up the search for self so easily: the old ego dies hard. More significant than any 'traces of what was', any recollection, is the powerful evocation of this figure of the depth, this other from Malone, which releases the writing to the spaces between:

> most remarkable of all is his greatcoat, in the sense that it covers him completely and screens him from view. For it is so well-buttoned, from top to bottom, by means of fifteen buttons at the very least, set at intervals of three or four inches at the very most that nothing is to be seen of what

> goes on inside . . . the hands too are hidden . . . [but] the head emerges, lofty and impassive.[46]

In *Company* the figure appears twice: first when it sets out, in the evening, after pulling the front door gently to behind it. In *Company* the voice speaks, in the text, to a 'you', lying on its back in the dark:

> You lean back against the door with bowed head making ready to set out. By the time you open your eyes your feet have disappeared and the skirts of your greatcoat come to rest on the surface of the snow. The dark scene seems lit *from below*.[47] (my italics)

The second sighting of this figure in *Company* is even more haunting:

> A strand. Evening. Light dying. Soon none left to die. No. No such thing then as no light. . . . You stand with your back to the wash. No sound but it. Even fainter as it slowly ebbs. Till it slowly starts again. You lean on a long staff. Your hands rest on the knob and on them your head. Were your eyes to open they would first see far below in the last rays the skirt of your greatcoat and the uppers of your boots emerging from the sand. Then and it alone till it vanishes the shadow of the staff on the sand.[48]

In *Company* the binary opposition is between this figure (and others such in the text) and the voice which speaks incessantly. It is difficult and probably impossible to say what this figure means: as Beckett said in an interview with Gabriel d'Aubarede if he could have expressed his meaning philosophically there would have been no reason to write fictions.[49] Very possibly it has, as one of its antecedents, Yeats's coat:

> I made my song a coat
> Covered with embroideries
> Out of old mythologies
> From heel to throat;
> But the fools caught it,
> Wore it in the world's eyes
> As though they'd wrought it.
> Song, let them take it,

For there's more enterprise
In walking naked.[50]

We can see the sardonic Beckett eyebrow lifted at the declaratory tone, the sheer ego, of the last lines. We can imagine him scoffing, ever so slightly, at words like 'enterprise'; 'going naked'. Yeats never went naked, nor does anyone. Words cover everything. The Beckett coat is far from being covered with mythologies; it's covered with grime and filth, and the ordure of many bitter rains. It is a cross between a cloak and a monkish habit; and may have another literary antecedent, Mangan's cloak. Mangan was known as 'the man in the cloak' from the pseudonym he used for some arcane and eccentric writing published in Dublin journals.

One of the last sightings of this figure in Beckett is in *. . . but the clouds . . .* (1976), a play for television. The set is a circle, a pool of dim light, surrounded by deep shadow. This circle, the space for action, is the broad end of a cone of vision of which the camera is the apex: a televisionized Yeatsian gyre. (The diagram in the Faber edition makes the allusion quite clear.) A man in the Beckett greatcoat and hat comes and goes throughout. He comes in, it is nightfall; he sheds his hat and greatcoat, assumes a 'robe and skull'; then, crouching in his sanctum, implores 'her' to appear. This imploring is a 'begging of the mind'. Or that at least is one version of what he does, before leaving again, at break of day, to walk the roads, the 'back roads'. According to another version he implores, she doesn't appear, and he busies himself 'with something else, more . . . rewarding, such as . . . such as . . . cube roots . . . or with nothing, busied myself with nothing, that MINE' until it was time to put the greatcoat on again and set forth once more. In another version of what happened (this tiny play contains four separate options: you 'pick yr. fancy') she does appear, a 'close-up of a woman's face reduced as far as possible to eyes and mouth': the matrix. This face is held in a single shot and she speaks:

. . . clouds . . . but the clouds . . . of the sky . . .

The lips first mutter inaudibly, then, synchronous with them the *man*'s voice utters the words, as we see her lips move. At the end of the play these words are expanded, revealing themselves to be Yeats's from the last section of 'The Tower', in which Yeats contemplates the dissolution of his ego, peacefully, free of longing. Again it is the man's voice which speaks:

> . . . but the clouds of the sky . . . when the horizon fades . . .
> or a bird's sleepy cry . . . among the deepening shades . . .[51]

The man has begun his travels again, his greatcoat on, while these words are spoken.

In . . . *but the clouds* . . . the same gestures of divesting, moving to the 'sanctum', moving back to the centre, are repeated over and over, so that the effort is to draw the viewer into a focused though uneasy attentiveness to movement itself, its variance and repetition; on words, their ability to occlude, entrance, express; and on the human figure, male and female. Having created the required atmosphere of tension and entrancement (Beckett said he wrote in a kind of trance), the viewer can *behold,* can contract the spirit, reduce the thought pulse to a receptivity: the kind of receptivity Belacqua has in his 'gression' because it is 'exempt from destination'[52] and the clamour of habit.

These wearers of the Beckett greatcoat are capable of stillness. Once invoked successfully they allow the writing to deepen and to expand inwardly: Malone, for example, envisages Macmann's calm to be so steady that it can dilate within the instant itself:

> perhaps he has come to that stage of his instant when to live is to wander the last of the living in the depths of an instant without sounds, where the light never changes and the wrecks look all alike. Bluer scarcely than white of egg their eyes stare into the space before them, namely the fullness of the great deep and its unchanging calm.[53]

In *Company,* after the man in the greatcoat leaves the house, he walks through a landscape recognizably that in 'Walking Out' in *More Pricks than Kicks.* The whole scene is now more powerfully charged, more alive to the feeling tonalities of the place. Immediately following this excursion, involving the interplay of the binary between the voice narrating and the figure evolved, the writing is ready to venture inside another instant, one of the strongest pieces of writing in all of Beckett. The attention has been roused; the thrusting of the will stilled, to an extent; query has been silenced, for the time being at least; all of this preparatory to an evocation of the summerhouse at Cooldrinagh, a father, a little boy, a mother:

> She joins you in the little summerhouse. A rustic hexahedron. Entirely of logs. Both larch and fir. Six feet across. Eight from floor to vertex. Area twenty-four square feet to furthest decimal. Two small multicoloured lights vis-a-vis. Small stained diamond panes. Under each a ledge. There on summer Sundays after his midday meal your father loved to retreat with Punch and a cushion. The waist of his trousers unbuttoned he sat on the one ledge turning the pages. You on the other with your feet dangling. When he chuckled you tried to chuckle too. . . . The years have flown and there at the same place as then you sit in the bloom of adulthood bathed in rainbow light gazing before you. She is late. . . . You open with quickening pulse your eyes and a moment later that seems an eternity her face appears at the window.[54]

The writing is inside time, inhabiting a place of change and transformation; where things come together, fall asunder.

In *The Unnamable* voice succeeds voice in a torrential flow of rage, despair, abuse. There is the narrative voice, and the figures it evokes: Mahood, Worm and so forth. But the distinctions between these different voices and the narratorial one continuously dissolve, reseparate, then dissolve again. There is no fixed stance whatever; and *The Unnamable* involves us in even greater uncertainty by asserting that the voice which drives *The Unnamable* had, earlier, made use of the guises of Belacqua, Watt, Molloy, Moran, Malone, Mercier and Camier, and so on. The narrative has a released intensity that is moving in the direction of the third zone of Murphy's mind: 'nothing but commotion and the pure form of commotion. Here he was not free, but a mote in the dark of absolute freedom. . . . Matrix of surds.'[55] This voice, which moves in and out of other voices, is astonishing in its range and incessant energy. At one point, an 'instant', in which it has been Mahood, it says that it/Mahood was coming to an end of a world tour, two or three centuries ago. It has been on an exploratory trajectory, to Java, the Pacific, the Indian Ocean; it/he has lost a leg. It has also been involved in a gyration of contraction and expansion, another parody of the Yeatsian historic process:

> I must have got embroiled in a kind of inverted spiral, I mean one of the coils of which, instead of widening more and more, grew narrower and narrower and finally, given the kind of space in which I was supposed to evolve, would come to an end for lack of room. . . . But a difficulty arises here. For if by winding myself up, if I may venture that ellipse, it doesn't often happen to me now, if by dint of winding myself up, I don't seem to have gained much time, if by dint of winding myself up I must inevitably find myself stuck in the end, once launched in the opposite direction should I not normally unfold ad infinitum, with no possibility of ever stopping, the space in which I was marooned being globular, or is it the earth, no matter, I know what I mean. But where is the difficulty? There was one a moment ago, I could swear to it.[56]

This contraction/expansion unites the Belacqua trajectory with Yeats's expanding and contracting cones, his gyre-force. But why? The voice does not tell us. What is brought home to us is the terrible liberty of the mind, as Beckett sees it. The view of Arnold Geulincx, the Antwerp philosopher, that we cannot claim to control what our minds do, was one that troubled Beckett greatly. In *The Unnamable* we see it moving through a series of voices, rehearsing stories, abandoning them, contradicting itself, turning upon itself with rage, then giving in to self-pity or self-congratulation. It sounds chaotic and uncontrolled, but *The Unnamable* is not that, although its method is one which deliberately undercuts the conventional notion of control and order in a more extreme fashion than any other previous work of Beckett's.

In *Proust* he wrote of the breakdown of the object,[57] maintaining that in the modern world we cannot be assured of the traditional relations between subject and object, inside and outside, upon which normal activity depends for its security. Beckett attacked the sentimentality of conventional notions of realism in his earliest writings, and the objective world increases in uncertainty from Belacqua's to Malone's to that experienced by Vladimir and Estragon. By *Endgame* its supremacy is well and truly over. But the subject is broken down too; the old ego may die hard, but its dissolution, in the Beckett universe, is inevitable.

But what strikes us about *The Unnamable* is the wilfulness of its vociferations (a favourite word of Beckett). It cannot be stopped. This voice (and we may use a singular, because despite its multifariousness, it subjugates everything to its narrative) is insistent and seems like it could go on forever. This drive, of vociferation, is continuously undercut by the way in which it shifts its own ground. It moves, continuously; the basis of its movement is that it drifts from identity to identity. There is no subject, and it is that very absence that drives it on to take on yet more personae, voices. Mahood, for example, tells it, the voice, stories about itself; Mahood

> lived in my head, issued forth from me, came back to me, entered back into me, heaped stories on my head. . . . It is his voice which has often, always, mingled with mine. . . . until he left me for good, or refused to leave me any more, I don't know. Yes, I don't know if he's here now or far away. . . . it will disappear one day, I hope, from him, completely. But in order for that to happen I must speak, speak. And at the same time I do not deceive myself, he may come back again, or go away again and then come back again. . . . But now, is it I now, I on me?[58]

Here a linguistic space is being created in which there is no differentiation between one voice and another. The binary interplay, between narratorial voice and figure (Mahood, later Worm, earlier Basil) is so intense that the coming together and falling asunder happens incessantly. All of this speaking takes place, too, in a manner which asks the reader to make a huge effort of concentration, and forgo all the normal expectancies of sequence and identity. Time is also away. Hundreds of years are mentioned; or it all takes place in an instant – 'Pick yr. fancy':

> This transmission is really excellent. I wonder if it's going to get us somewhere. If only they would stop talking for nothing, pending their stopping everything. Nothing? That's soon said. It is not for me to judge. What would I judge with? . . . Sometimes I say to myself, they say to me, Worm says to me, *the subject matters little,* that my purveyors are more than one, four or five. But it's more likely the same foul brute all the time, amusing himself, pretending to be a many, varying his register, his tone, his

> accent and his drivel. . . . Mahood I couldn't die. Worm will I ever get born? It's the same problem.[59] (my italics)

Beckett's writing here, and throughout *The Unnamable*, occupies an imaginative dimension of language which contemplates the dissolution of the individual, not with equanimity, but with a kind of satisfaction. All the insistencies of the ego, the huge efforts of property, system, government, ownership, control, are set at nought. There are separate concentrations of energy, which move apart and come together again. But individuals? What importance can we attribute to them? Beckett, as well as being in touch with the rigours of Zen Buddhism, with its emphasis on the extinction of self, has also got in him an Irish Jansenist streak, which he shares with Denis Devlin, a poet-friend of his in the 1930s, whom he greatly admired. This intolerance of the vanity of ego, its pushy assertiveness, its presumption to significance and even to grace, is something very old in Irish culture, which Devlin recognized, in poems like 'Lough Derg' (1942); and which Beckett, too, distrustful though he was of all soft continuities, would be aware of as being a major element in Irish religious feeling from the Culdees down. What else drove men to live on Sceilg Mhichíl, other than a revulsion with sordid confidence and the bounding vitality of arrogance?

For confidence Beckett offers interrogation, and for vitality he offers desperation or the frenzy of exhaustion; subject and object recede to leave only words:

> I'm in words, made of words, other's words, what others, the place too, the air, the walls, the floor, the ceiling, all words, the whole is here with me, I'm the air, the walls, the walled-in one, everything yields, opens, ebbs, flows, like flakes, I'm all these flakes, meeting, mingling, falling asunder, wherever I go I find men, leave me, go towards me, come from me, nothing ever but me, a particle of me.

But then, also:

> a quite different thing, a wordless thing in an empty place, a hard shut dry cold blank place, where nothing stirs.[60]

In turning the first statement around Beckett describes, in miniature, the method of *The Unnamable*, which is to accomplish a trajectory between two opposite viewpoints, and to make this trajectory the material, the writing. So that the writing leaves a space for the mind to embark upon the 'contraction' and 'immersion' which accompanies proper research, which is thought appertaining to 'how it is' in being.

In *How it is* (published in French 1961; in English 1964) the figures are in the mud, not between the mud and scum, as in *Molloy*:

> here then at last . . . where I have still to say how it was as I hear it in me that was without quaqua on all sides bits and scraps how it was with Pim vast stretch of time murmur it in the mud to the mud when the panting stops how it was my life we're talking of my life in the dark in the mud.[61]

The form which Beckett uses in *How it is* allows him to give each instant of the narrative, each flash of pain, each surge of telling, in a bare stripped down presence. Punctuation has disappeared, but instead of the torrent of *The Unnamable* there are the isolated paragraphs, each one a 'point' in the 'unconditioned generation and passing away of line'.[62] The narrator is in the matrix, and yet this geography is far from being disordered and chaotic; or at least it goes to great lengths to establish an order and sequence in this place, only to abandon it, though not quite: such qualifications are always necessary in Beckett.

The narrator, a 'he', is in the matrix herself, but that is not to say he is directionless:

> here confused reckonings to the effect I can't have deviated more than a second or so from the direction imparted to me one day one might at the inconceivable outset by chance by necessity by a little of each it's one of the three from west strong feeling from west to east.[63]

From Ireland towards Europe initially; but also now away from the monuments to European ego and individualism, its self-satisfied freedoms and self-advancements, to the east.

The novel is in three parts, each to some extent observing a place in a temporal sequence. Weaving and unweaving a continuous rehearsal of itself the narrative moves from a time before the narrator came to Pim, a time when both he and Pim are together, when he is Pim's torturer, then to a time after Pim. But there are other figures and the sequence is fugally reiterated with an exchange of roles; others come in who participate or who do not. The idea that there is such a thing as a 'time' when any event or person arrives or is present is one which the penitential interrogation of this fragmented narrative displaces. In a sense all that is described is described in a continuous present. But even that comes under question, because if there is a present, then there must be a presencing, either a self or an essential, and that is what appears to be lacking: 'the essential would seem to be lacking.'[64] Or if not that then some other to perceive its absence. But how can absence be perceived? If anything is there it will be perceived ('to be is to be perceived' Beckett took from Berkeley); but if there is no sure presence, no perception, how can anything be at all? Is everything just a continual and lawless surging of chance and accident? Beckett, of course, provides no answers to these trite questions, but the narrative brings the cold interstellar space of fundamental thought, where basic intimations between form and chaos, line and point, being and becoming are apprehended. No formulaic consolations are vouchsafed: just hard, pure questioning, that induces in the reader something of Beckett's awe and reverence for life; and communicates his intense loathing of flaccid moralizing, easy answers:

> never anyone never knew anyone always ran fled elsewhere some other place my life above places paths nothing else brief places long paths . . .
>
> here all self to be abandoned say nothing when nothing.[65]

Lest we be in any doubt of the intensity of this scepticism he repeatedly reiterates: 'never was only one voice my voice never any other'.[66] Which is not to say that Beckett's writings are autobiographical, although in a certain sense they are, but that this writing winnows life so finely that differentiations between individual consciousnesses dissolve in a rapport of shared effort and cold light.

'All that not Pim I,' he writes, which draws on a kind of structural linguistics to say that Pim, the word, is Pim by virtue of all that is not Pim, which is the 'I'. But Pim, Bom, Bim, Krim, Kram all merge: 'no Pim no Bom and this voice quaqua of us all never only one voice my voice never any other.'

Only one voice, maybe, and yet in part three he says that there are millions of them like the grains of sand in Arsene's story in *Watt*. There are millions there in the matrix, moving one from the other 'wending from left to right straight line eastward strange in dark the mud',[67] the one who was tormentor in the previous relation, now becoming victim, and vice versa. It is how it is, how it is in the absolute justice of what is, without asservations, pieties, imprecations: 'the terrain the terrain try and understand no accidents no asperities our justice.'[68] 'The terrain the terrain' is the place this kind of writing has made for itself. It is an uncomfortable place, a place of penance. From it these sounds and cries go up to where

> there is an ear a mind to understand a means of noting a care for us the wish to note the curiosity to understand an ear to hear even ill these scraps of other scraps of an antique rigmarole.[69]

It is a place of waiting, of dry unconsoled terror, of tiredness: it is the interior of Western *man* in the twentieth century. This writing does not give pleasure, in the way that novelists as different as Francis Stuart or Saul Bellow can communicate a sense of vital spirits. These plays and fictions are the opposite of that: they require nothing less than a 'begging of the mind', an imploring conducted by the feelings. Their figures move slowly, or do not move at all; but all the time a trajectory is being inscribed, departing from the known to what is not known; returning to silence, broken by voices, which go silent again.

Occasionally, just occasionally, the vision breaks through: some special ordinance in being itself rewards the patient scruple of the watcher; as must have happened in the bleak dawns of Sceilg Mhichíl in the sixth century. It may be a globe, surfacing in water in *Molloy*; in *How it is* it appears as follows:

> We are on a veranda smothered in verbena the scented sun dapples the red tiles yes I assure you the huge head bathed with birds and flowers is bowed down over my curls the eyes burn with severe love I offer her mine pale upcast to the sky whence cometh our help and which I know perhaps even then with time shall pass away.[70]

Beckett shows us the way things are (how it is) *without* this transforming vision.[71] Relentlessly he keeps his attention focused, so as to check the vanity of the mind and the assurance of judging.

From 1950 to his death in 1990 he was a mixture of Culdee and

Irish Zen master, resident in Paris, translating the lost world, the world of loss, of James Clarence Mangan and William Carleton from vacancy into French, then from French into an English chastened by an Irish sense of absence.

10

MÁIRTÍN Ó CADHAIN

'Repossessing Ireland'

In August 1969 Máirtín Ó Cadhain delivered a lecture in Donegal under the title 'Gluaiseacht na Gaeilge: Gluaiseacht ar Strae' ('The Irish Movement: A Movement Astray'). It is an uncompromising statement of his convictions about the Irish language and its importance in the struggle for independence. His views, expressed in this lecture given in the year before his death, are substantially the same as those he held as a young man when, in about 1932, he took the oath of loyalty to the IRA at the gate of his house in Camus in Connemara.[1] In the 1930s he held the rank of captain, and the local guards, under the command of Chief Superintendent Bracken, Brendan Bracken's brother, kept him under constant surveillance. In 1969, in the Donegal lecture, his analysis of the Irish problem is fierce and single-minded, as it had been thirty odd years before as a young teacher in Connacht. The passion and commitment are unambiguous:

> Not only should those involved in the Irish language movement take part in the war for the repossession of Ireland - which is the only thing worth participating in in Ireland - but it is our duty to lead this war and direct it. Let the Irish language command the revolution, and in this way Irish will be amongst the most progressive ideas in the country: in this way the language will be saved. Irish is the Repossession of Ireland and the Repossession of Ireland is the salvation of the language. The people's language is what will save them. Therefore, wherever the conflict is at its most intense there should Irish posters be seen, there should be heard the Irish-speaking voice.[2]

In 1969 he spoke as someone who had become Professor of Irish at Trinity College, Dublin; but in 1936 he was sacked from his post as a schoolteacher in An Ceard Mór for being a member of the IRA. He moved to Dublin where he worked as an organizer and recruiting officer for the IRA and as a teacher of Irish on a casual basis. His awakening as a writer he attributed to his discovery of a French translation of a story by Maxim Gorky, which he found in a journal picked up in a second-hand bookshop in Augier Street for a penny. He describes the shock he experienced reading Gorky, in French, lying on his bed:

> I jumped up in the bed. . . . Why didn't anyone tell me there were stories like this? 'I could write that', I said to myself. 'That's what my own people do except they have different names.' A kind of hunger came over me, a hunger more intolerable than that which I'd get in my belly from time to time. Cois Fharraige [his native place], its stony fields, its bare rocks, its fjords, streams, lakes, mountains, the faces of its men, women and children, started to form themselves behind my closed eyes. That magazine was in my pocket, and not much else, the day I was interned.[3]

He was seized in 1939 and held in Tintown, the internment jail in the Curragh, Co. Kildare, until 1945, by which time he had become a writer.

No other writer in modern Irish literature has Máirtín Ó Cadhain's mixture of rage and compassion. No one else conveys the texture of life in the Gaeltachts of the western seaboard with the agonized intimacy he does. His accounts of this life carry the salt sting of harsh reality. His work, though intensely alive to particulars of all kinds, is not reportage: it is an anatomy of a culture, done from the inside, but of a culture which is in its death throes. His analysis mixes despair and love; but there is comedy too, the wild, shocking comedy of the Gaelic world, which is identical to that in all of Irish life when the layers of respectability are peeled off. So that reading him in Irish one is amazed at the familiarity of the thought and speech patterns he has set down, because they are the thought and speech patterns of the great majority of Irish people in all of Ireland, even when they are speaking English. Reading him one is made aware of how much Irish writing in English, for all its linguistic and intellectual energy, *excludes*: the intimate flow of Irish speech, its twists and turns; its capacity for holding back information until the drama of the sentence has been allowed to accumulate; its readiness to make use of rapid emphasis; its swift rhetorical assertions; its open and shocking mockeries; its ability to shift its point of view. And so on. This speech craft is the method and substance of Ó Cadhain's novel *Cré na Cille* (1949) (*Churchyard's Earth*); but his short stories, from *Idir Shúgradh agus Dáiríre* (1939) (*Half-Joking, Half-Serious*) onwards, delineate the mentality and outlook of which this speech is both the expression and source.

An early story 'An Geis' ('Tabu') from the second collection of stories *An Braon Broghach* (1948) (*The Dirty Drop*) illustrates certain aspects of this mind: superstition, fear of the otherworld, annoyance at the presence of others, yet the dependence on them in a close community. All of these have been described before, in Yeats, Lady Gregory, Patrick McGill in *Glenmornan*, Tomás Ó Criomhthain in *An t-Oileánach* (*The Islandman*); but where Ó Cadhain differs is in the degree of intense detail he gives. He takes the reader into the interiority of the situation; so that, while the situation is traditional the method is modern. His fiction is an anthropological searching in words, a reach of the creative imagination into the landscape of feeling, thought and sensation as it unfolds in the minds of his characters. The reader is always being surprised but what is shocking is the familiarity of this interior world which Ó Cadhain's writing, densely packed, but with an awesome linguistic scope, reveals.

In 'An Geis' (superbly translated by Eoghan Ó Tuairisc in his collection of versions of Ó Cadhain's early stories, *The Road to Brightcity*), a woman, Neile, has built a new house. Her only son, Sonaí, has gone off on a sea-trip with two friends of his from the Training College in Dublin. He has been sent there on the proceeds of a huckster's shop she has kept going since the drowning of her husband twenty-one years ago. She is all flurry and anxiety at the move, and about the tide which can be dangerous. When her husband drowned we are told, a fairy wind shook the whitethorn growing out of a bank at the rear of the house. It is still growing there, terrifying her, just as it did on that day when 'black fate came laughing at her,' a fine summer's day, like the present one. Irritatingly a young man, Maidhcín Pheadair Anna, comes to the shop to buy a Player's Weight. Flustered by his chat, she sweats and becomes clumsy, and has to put her two elbows on the counter, so she can rest and calm herself: 'Her ear is now level with the tiny window.'[4]

Ó Cadhain gives us these details so that her next reactions are fully encircumstanced. Maidhcín, looking out himself, remarks: 'You'd think there were little whirlwinds out there . . . fairies shifting about.' He laughs foolishly at the dust, leaves, bits of straw swirling with a slight noise outside in the sunlight. When he leaves, to her relief, Neile, on an impulse, throws out the mashed potato she has been preparing, and, with a glance at the empty new house, she goes into the haggard for the axe to cut down the whitethorn. She has broken the taboo.

Neile's thoughts about her dead husband, the dangers of the tide, the fairy wind and the whitethorn, the annoyance at Maidhcín, are all swiftly presented in a style packed with awareness. The way the sea looks to her, or the whitethorn, as things animated by a life which she must face up to or be conquered by, is presented in a writing which is accurate by virtue of its intimacy.

No other modern Irish writer can convey the sheer physical hardship of Gaeltacht life. Ó Cadhain's descriptions of work are stripped of any romantic or nostalgic aura and the crushing pressure of unremitting effort is presented. Endurance, toughness and animal energy are what the bare stony fields and the shores with their narrow inlets require of the man or woman who wants to survive. Often Ó Cadhain writes of the exhaustion caused by endless toil without rest. In 'An Taoille Tuile' ('Floodtide') Mairéad and Pádraig, a newly married couple, go seaweed-gathering with their neighbours, the Lydons. The seaweed is needed to fertilize the tiny potato fields. They take advantage of the low spring tide to get out amongst the long deep inlets where the best and thickest weed can be reaped. Mairéad, having spent years in America keeping true to her promise to return to Pádraig, is unused to the heavy work. The story depicts her growing exhaustion and clumsiness.

There is no pathway from the shore down to the long inlets where the weed is gathered, so they cannot use an animal to carry the creels. They must be carried, full of the wet and heavy weed, by the women on their backs, holding them steady as best they can by means of straps slung over their shoulders. Mairéad carries the first load up to above the shoreline, to 'ionlach na feamainne' (the spreading ground), about nine or ten yards from the high water mark, easily enough; but with each load the distance becomes greater:

> She felt the teeming sweat lessening the cold of the sea which had penetrated every limb. The strap started to raise blisters on her palms and the sea was burning into the joints of her fingers. Her back was stiff and her legs – she could leave them out of the story altogether. . . . Every time she came on a sharp pebble she'd clench back her foot in the shoe, so that her instep formed a hump under the laces.[5]

As the tide begins to turn the two men, her husband and Lydon, start hauling the creels up with the women, so what they have stripped from the rocks will not be swept away. The trip up and down with the creels seems not to bother the men, or Cáitín Lydon, who can keep pace with them. Mairéad is so tired that she closes her eyes sometimes

> when she'd come to the edge of the sandy beach so that the last stretch of her journey would not torment her.[6]

At the end of the story she goes out into the increasing tide with Pádraig to gather up the last clumps of weed, now starting to float away. Pádraig snarls at her:

> 'Out of my way', said Pádraig, and went up to his thighs to sweep the last of the harvest from the devouring sea. Mairéad straightened; on the instant her mind leaped at that tone. A harsh strange voice. A voice from a world other than the world of his lamenting letters, the world of lovemaking and softness, the world of the pillow. With the shock that struck her a little bubble of seaweed burst between her fingers and a jet of dark slime shot up to her cheek.

Mairéad's failure to cope physically with the demands of this life, so harshly different from her life in America, itself having been demanding enough, means that the system of shared labour is impaired. Pádraig will need to work harder, unless she toughens herself. The close-knit community is an economic necessity and a means whereby the task of survival is eased. But that depends on each member being up to the demands the community makes on him or her. As well, therefore, as being a network of mutual assistance the community is a system in which people are on the lookout for weaknesses in others. A flaw in someone else can undermine you, if you are reliant on that person; or it can be to your advantage if you can exploit it. In addition, within the broader community, of an area or a village or an extended family, there are smaller, family communities, always watching each other, ready at the earliest opportunity to seize the least advantage that arises. Where people are so deprived, where there is so little to be had, the competition amongst the conflicting interests for what there is is fiercely and remorselessly engaged. Ó Cadhain's writing brings forward this aspect of Gaeltacht life with a sorrowing intensity never before so unflinchingly ventured; thereby issuing a profound corrective to modern romanticized notions of the 'Western World'.

Ó Cadhain's Gaeltacht people mostly hate each other. Almost everyone is an enemy apart from the immediate family, and it is dangerous even to count on all of them. *Cré na Cille* is based on the hostility of one sister for another: everything the other one does is hated, envied and mocked. At the core of the novel is a kinship system in which the individuals, living and dead, are locked in a set of antagonisms radiating out from the central opposition between the sisters, Caitríona and Neil. This family of hate, and the community around it, is revealed to us by the voices of *Cré na Cille,* all of which are the voices of the dead. Caitríona, her crony Muraed, Nóra Sheáinín, the despised mother of her detested daughter-in-law, are all dead. They talk incessantly, and crave news of the other world, in this instance the world of time and work. All information comes from the newly dead, who arrive throughout the book, bringing information about the doings above ground: such as whether Caitríona's headstone of island greenstone is yet arranged; or whether Caitríona's sister in America, Baba, has died; or whether Tómas Taobh Istigh, a relative, has left his house and land to Pádraig, Caitríona's son, or to Peadar, Neil's boy.

This dynamic set of antagonisms may be set out in diagram form (see opposite).

The hate between Caitríona and Neil had its origin in the fact that both of them loved Jeaic, a wonderful singer, capable of thrilling women with his voice. Neil gets him, because her father insists that the eldest girl must marry first. Muraed explains to her dead listeners:

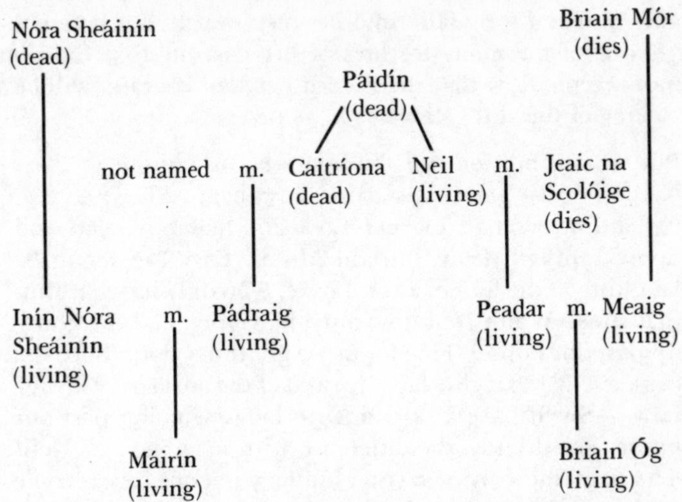

– The night of the wedding at Páidín's Caitríona was stuck in the corner in the far room with a face on her as long as a shadow at midnight. There was a gang of us there. Neil too. She started making fun of Caitríona:

'I don't know but you should marry Briain Mór Caitríona', says she. Caitríona had turned him down before that.

At this point Nóra Sheáinín comes in:

– I was there Muraed. 'I have Jeaic', says Neil. 'We'll leave Briain Mór to yourself Caitríona'.

– Caitríona went mad. She tore out and she'd not come back into the room again till morning. And she didn't go to the chapel the next day.[7]

The phrase 'I have Jeaic . . . We'll leave Briain Mór to yourself Caitríona' torments Caitríona throughout the book, in death as much as it had done in life. Neil's good luck continues, and her son Peadar marries the girl Caitríona had hoped Pádraig would marry, Meaig, the daughter of the man she refused, Briain Mór. Meaig is a superb housekeeper, energetic, economical and clean; whereas the girl Pádraig marries, Inín Nóra Sheáinín, is, Caitríona thinks, a slattern and useless; that is until later in the novel, she hears that her daughter-in-law has the gumption to assault Neil and throw her into her own hearth. But before that she is one of the many features of her past life that Caitríona cannot accept. Now that she is dead her son, Pádraig, will be at the mercy of the slut ('slamóg') he is tied to:

> But what condition can the house be in without me. . . . Neil will take great satisfaction anyway. . . . Let her. She has a fine woman on her floor for making bread and housekeeping: Meaig Bhriain Mhóir. Easy for her to be laughing at the fool of a son I have, who only has that slut, that streel. Won't Neil now often be saying, and she going up past our house? 'Fine for us we got thirty pounds for the pigs. . . . It was a fine fair, if you had the animals ready for it. . . .' She'll have a skirl now in her arse going past our house. She'll know the difference with me gone. . . . Neil! The slag! She's my own sister but may not one corpse come to the cemetery before she does.'[8]

She accuses Neil of all kinds of wrongdoing and mischief, including the curing of her son Peadar of his broken hip by getting the priest to give her the gospel of St John, thus allowing her to strike the bargain that this drastic form of healing involves. The sick person, in this case Peadar, who has been knocked down by a lorry, is healed through the efficacy of the gospel; but someone else's life must be taken in exchange. The life she claims Neil will offer is that of the man they once competed for, Jeaic na Scolóige, her own husband. Whether this is accurate or not is never revealed, although Jeaic does join the dead in the churchyard later in the novel. What Ó Cadhain is presenting to his readership is the mind of the people he came from, that he knew as intimately as he knew his own turns of thought. And this cast of mind is, or can be, extraordinarily cruel. Amongst a deprived and demoralized people, where survival is what counts, an old man, Jeaic, is of much less use than a younger man in his health. For all the respect given to the wisdom of age in traditional communities, where economic necessity is involved the young will have pre-eminence, and particularly the young men. Women are marginalized in this world; they are beasts of burden, breeders, talkers, arguers. And older women, or women who are sick or weak or ineffectual, are pushed aside even more. So that Caitríona's amazing linguistic energy, her powers of excoriation, her floods of vehemence, are an assertion of her presence, her refusal to shut up or be shut up, even in the cold earth of the churchyard. At least she has her hate, like the dancers in W.B. Yeats's 'Crazy Jane Grown Old Looks at the Dancers':

> For no matter what is said
> They had all that had their hate.[9]

It is not only Caitríona who is locked in this harsh geometry of hatred. It pullulates everywhere. The local shopkeeper has died and she is accused of cheating during the period of rationing that the Second World War necessitated, in Ireland as in England. One of her customers accuses her of killing him by depriving him of 'fags'. He died 'ceal fags' - for the lack of fags:

> You had them under the counter. . . .
> 'Where would I get fags', says you. 'Don't you know I don't make them.'
> 'If I could give you four or five shillings a box for them', says I . . . 'You can keep them.'
> I went home.
> 'You'd better put that spread of seaweed you left after yourself below out onto the field east', says my mother.
> 'Seaweed', says I. 'The last of my seaweed's out, mother.'
> I spat out a lump of phlegm. It was as hard as a male bollock.
> May I never leave here if it wasn't. There was a little kitten on the hearth - and he started licking the spit. He started a fit of coughing.[10]

Thus do the voices in *Cré na Cille* rehearse their grievances endlessly, fading in and out of the narrative, going over their obsessions, disappointments, never letting the dead bury the dead. At first the method seems very like that of Beckett but Beckett's figures know the hell that the perceptions of others can create for the self, and strive to break free; whereas Ó Cadhain's characters or voices speak out of that hell itself. *Esse est percipi*, as Beckett had it out of Berkeley; and in Ó Cadhain that is that. Stasis. The complete lock of immutable unchanging hate. If, in George Moore's words, 'the law of change is the law of life,'[11] then *Cré na Cille* is the obverse of *Hail and Farewell* within modern Irish literature. Seán Ó Tuama put a crucial question about *Cré na Cille* when he asked if a work of literature could be called an achieved work of art if it accomplished no development and the characters experienced no major change in perception or outlook.[12] Certainly *Cré na Cille* encompasses no change of this kind. There is not the slightest hint of moral transformation. The situation is now, in the narrative of the dead, as it always was, and such it will always be. But this rigid system of hate, this unchanging set of coordinates as depicted in the diagram, is challenged by and releases the flood of speech that washes over it. Caitríona's speech, that of Nóra Sheáinín, with her 'Honest a Dotie', or the lubricities of the schoolmaster with his recollections of his library of soft porn - all these are a ceaseless fructifying energy of speech that breaks over and through the static solid geometry of a petrified moral universe. It is as if one begets the other: the Byzantium of stasis begets the sea of speech. And it is a speech that voices and inscribes the speech and thought patterns of all Irish people; in it is revealed the impetus inhering in Hiberno-English, English as it is spoken in Ireland by the great majority of its people, that is all those who live outside the confines of Dublin 4, Montenotte or Malone, either in body or in spirit. The present writer can hear his grandmother's and his mother's voices, in English, moving inside Caitríona's speech, inscribed in Ó Cadhain's prose.

While there is no development in Ó Cadhain's novel this does not mean it has no structure, simply that the structure is built upon an opposition between linguistic energy and moral paralysis, each one 'dying [the] other's life'.[13] Furthermore, it is not without interest that the prevailing voice-energies, here and throughout Ó Cadhain's fiction, are female. In the harsh world of economic necessity and survival, which is the backdrop to the stories, women, the marginalized, the dependants, are in fact the energy-source, the speech-lode. It is as if the women are themselves the emblems of the marginalized and all but defeated civilization that Ó Cadhain sorrowfully, magisterially, depicts. It is on its last legs, but it is not over, yet.

'An Bóthar go dtí an Ghealchathair' ('The Road to Brightcity') perhaps one of his finest stories, gathers together these themes. With graphic attention to the details of utter physical exhaustion, it describes a nine-mile walk from the Gaeltacht into Galway for the market, where Bríd, mother of two children, with two others having died on her, will sell the eggs she has coaxed out of her hens with loving care and attention, and the butter in its creel, with the delicate imprint she has stamped upon it. Ó Cadhain's writing is a kind of walking with her; it is not a description of a long and arduous journey on foot, it is a 'comhbháidh' with it – a sympathetic re-enactment to take the reader into the vivid suffering of each phase of the walk, from the dark mysterious start in the night with the moon-shadows making the familiar strange, through the heartbreaking longing for a lift from someone with room on his cart, to the eventual delight of the last stretch into the city itself. The writing is all awareness, an enlivened sensory and moral attention that is totally exposed nerve. This is Bríd passing through her own little village, in darkness, having left behind her man and the children:

> there were bright moonlit spaces between the houses and byres, and terrible lines of shadow from the gables out. The rays of the moonlight concentrated in the grains of the granite boulders. And from them shone a cold threatening radiance.[14]

All along the way she hopes for a lift, knowing it is likely she will not get one until she is quite near to the city, when someone may offer her space seeing as, by that stage, it will not be fair to charge the passenger for the ride. There is no question of her being able to afford to pay.

She is climbing an incline when a number of cars come up behind her, but she does not look back, not wishing to give the impression she is desperate. Then, near the top of the hill she hears another cart: this time she looks around, despite herself, and her heart jumps. She recognizes Peaid Neachtain, who has, many times, warmed himself at her fire. But he passes her by, flicking the reins at the horse, setting it to a gallop. Bríd curses the look she gave back, a weakness. Will she ever be like the older women, tough and leathery, striding on remorselessly, seemingly incapable of tiredness? This is how she imagines them:

> Would the creel's hump come on her . . . ? Or the fierce drive of the walk? Or the bleak sharp jawbones like the beak of a currach? Or the cheeks like parchment, and printed on them goosefoot marks like those on the milestones? . . . That was what the middle aged women she knew were like, the soft looks beaten into an ironhard edge by the weekly managing and the slaughtering Saturday walk.[15]

Endurance, joyless survival, cruel and heartless behaviour: this is her lot, and she is not sure she can take it. But this Saturday she manages the journey. At the summit of the hill before the descent into Galway she stops to check the butter and eggs:

> A waterdrop in the printmark, and the butter firm and solid unlike the oily mess summer butter makes. She took the straw and paper from the eggs and counted them again. There they were, three score of them, scoured clean and lovely: some white, some yellow, some pale blue. Even though they were in no particular order, she easily knew every hen's egg. The little grey pullet's egg; the speckled hen's egg, with its delicate thin shell; those of the crested hen, brown and big as duck-eggs, which she liked so much, she'd have loved to boil one for herself since the Dry of the Hens came on, only she didn't like to do it on the quiet.[16]

Their beauty and their value, and the fact that the nine-mile walk is over, for a while, lift her heart. Ó Cadhain does not allegorize Bríd, but because of the way in which the writing registers her epic and yet totally mundane suffering, she embodies a quality of patient irreducible energy, a readiness to absorb difficulty, which is very powerful. She has life in her care and she goes on looking after it. However reduced her circumstances, however beaten the people she represents, she does not shirk the effort needed to survive. Her culture, the culture of Gaelic Ireland, survives, despite the economic realities that have driven it up against the wall, the onslaughts on it by British and Irish administrations, and the indifference of post-Treaty Ireland which is perhaps crueller than colonial hostility. This culture survives marginally perhaps, but not vestigially, as the density and sweep of Ó Cadhain's own style asserts. There is a sense in which Ó Cadhain writes his 'crua-Ghaeilge' (his hard Irish) in order to emphasize that Gaelic life, though pushed out to the edge of a driving and a driven Europe, is still there, still capable of the act of self-expression which is essential to survival. There is a sense therefore that his profound awareness of female endurance integrates with and informs his own experience of writing against the odds, enduring shame, indifference, the hostility of those who cannot or will not take into account the fact that Irish civilization, the fabric of Irish life itself, is crucially informed by

Gaelic culture and by the Irish language. In *Páipéir Bhána agus Páipéir Bhreaca* (1969) (*White Pages, Written Pages*) he wrote:

> [Irish] is mine, something I cannot say about any other medium. In the loneliness of my heart I heard – I always hear 'the sharp whistling of the blackbird of Leitir Laoigh' [a quotation from the Ossianic lays]. I am then in possession of the antiquity of the Hag of Beare, of Newgrange, the Irish elk. Two thousand years of that foul sow that is Ireland is going round in my ears, my mouth, my eyes, my head, my dreams.[17]

A nightmarish late story 'Aisling agus Aisling Eile' ('A Vision and Another Vision') in *An tSraith dhá Thógáil* (1970) (*The Sheaves being Stacked*) explores the parlous state of Irish culture, both English- and Gaelic-speaking. A scholar/poet is visiting the Gaeltacht with a map of the Irish-speaking areas according to the latest government surveys and statistics. He is testing the map against actuality, or at least that is what he pretends to himself. He also fancies that he is looking for a real Gaeltacht, which would correspond to his own ideals of purity and authenticity, but in fact he is preoccupied with his obsessions, which revolve around his writing, and a neurotic fixation with *dán dírech* – syllabic poetry. He comes, eventually, after a number of miserable encounters in hapless bars, where the scant clientele stare at the sexy gesturings and provocative clothes of a TV actress (one of the *aislingí* or visions), to Lappin's hotel, where, he is told, he'll find proper Irish. Lappin is a cripple. The hotel is a sordid and filthy place, poorly run by Lappin's overworked and exhausted wife, who, as well as cooking and cleaning, also looks after a filthy chain ('slabhra') of snotty children, who hang out of her constantly. The scholar/poet's sensitivities are outraged by the filth and squalor. His bacon is fat and greasy, he finds excrement on the towels, the smell of urine and faeces permeates everything. Watching the cripple climb the stairs ahead of him his hysteric disengagement from normal humanity, and his preoccupation with his own reactions manifest themselves in frantic laughter at the disabled man's slow progress up the steps, and in a baroque fancy that this uneven ascent can be linked with the metric schemes of syllabic or bardic poetry:

> He put the good leg first on the steps of the stairs. The

> stranger could see why: it was an attempt to get an advantage. The short leg would not be able to pull up from the lower step. But the pull up was embarrassing and the letting down of the gammy leg was heavy and resounded as it came up to the same level as its companion, before he'd embark on the next step up. The pull up and the letting down of the disabled leg were hesitant and uneasy. The stranger had his middle finger pressed against his Adam's apple but laughter erupted out of him nevertheless. . . . A demented notion came on him once or twice to give a hard kick to the good leg to destroy the airy, accentual lyricism it conveyed . . . that would make a *rannaigheacht bheag* [a regularly paced bardic metre] out of Lappin's clumsy *deibhí* [a bardic metre with an uneven lyric pulse].[18]

This heartlessness, this contempt for the actually human, illustrates what Beckett has called, in that searing phrase ablaze with shame, the 'loutishness of learning'.[19] The scholar/poet has no imaginative relation with the world outside him, although his ostensible and conscious aim is to relate the map he carries, which is an intellectual formulation about reality, to the actual condition of people and the words they use. His words, his language, are literary, in that they are a discourse taken from the learned journal, the grammatical note, the metric analysis. All this time, dominating his awareness while he is in the Gaeltacht, is what he will say to An Fear Mór (The Big Man), his mentor, editor and authority, when he gets back to Dublin. Ó Cadhain's writing reveals, through monstrous parody, the scholar/poet's dereliction: he takes his language from others, he is stuck in a discourse, a set of attitudes, that prevents any normal engagement with the people he meets. The experiences he has are, to him, either contemptible or ridiculous. In a sense he has no experiences at all; what unrolls in his mind is his own kaleidoscope of obsessions about his avid scholarly and poetic interests. There is no mind or thought of his own; for all his Gaelicism he is well and truly colonized, if by that one can infer the lack of any means of self-expression or authentic experience. His language, an Irish intent on purity, is a sterile hell of static self-involvement. He is as much concerned with his clothes, his elegant car, as he is with syllabic poetry and Irish.

If the scholar/poet is dominated by An Fear Mór, Lappin's

wife is oppressed by the cripple, her husband. Exhausted by day looking after the children and the hotel, she gets no peace at night either, having to acquiesce to the cripple's insatiable sexual demands:

> [Lappin's snoring] was part of an interminable ritual, a ritual that would begin with him turning to her and would end with his turning away and falling asleep . . . it was always the same outcome, another child . . . She had no rest. There was only work, in bed or out of it. The children always in her way during the day. Himself before her sitting on the edge of the bed at night, his gammy leg like some form of tentacular growth, ever active, barring the way on her out of this lair of Polyphemus, except for the brief respite afforded at the birth of another child.[20]

She dreams of an alternative life of luxury, energy, delight and pleasure, which the scholar/poet embodies for her. Her thoughts run wild, and she imagines, as she serves him breakfast, what it would be like if she were to go off with her guest. She thinks of the glances between them, the erotic signals, she putting on lipstick seductively with him looking at her, desiring, as she concentrates on her image in the mirror. She does not charge him for his board and breakfast, but her urgency is completely lost on him, who has always said to An Fear Mór that a syllabic poem in the *deibhí* metre is a greater passion in itself than the love of any woman.[21] On the way back to Dublin, in the car, as he reaches into his overcoat pocket for a watch, he finds a grubby folded piece of paper, and written on it the following: 'Missus Molly Lappin, The Narrow, Mawmore'. His reaction is utter disgust: the paper brings back 'the sidelong glance, baking, screeching, snot . . . fatty bacon, the smell of excrement.' That this communication is in English confirms his view of the falsity of the Gaeltacht, its failure to live up to his idealized version of it. He tears up the note and throws it away, 'then he started scratching above his coccyx as he went back in his mind to the last part of his book'.[22] Thus the story concludes with a picture of utter futility and static obsession; the complete breakdown of communication.

Ó Cadhain's study of cultural petrifaction and stasis in this story reveals a crucial psychological knot in Irish thinking about the Irish language and Gaelic culture. The more disappointing one's encounter with the living language, such as it is, and the people who speak it, however patchily, the more one's own sense of cultural purity is enhanced. The 'real' culture then, the 'essence', becomes the preserve, in all senses of that word, of a chosen few, and a very few at that. The more vestigial the language, the more remote its culture, the greater the intensity of the devotion given it by the dedicated initiates. This is a cultural attitude that is animated only by the thing which is dying; the fact that it is dying makes it all the more valuable. Taking this thinking to its logical conclusion, one arrives at the proposition that Gaelic culture will be perfect when it is dead and gone forever. Then it can be worshipped as such, its grammar totally explicated, its mysterious syntax probed, in the reassuring knowledge that no living person speaking the living tongue can usurp these funerary meditations.

This cultural attitude has been stated in its extremest form but only to emphasize the danger of cultural puritanism of this sort. Ó Cadhain's story 'Aisling agus Aisling Eile' is a blast of white-hot rage at these loutish and funereal obsessions. The attitudes he excoriates are those of cultural and psychological paralysis; and he also attacks the inhumanity that accompanies this hemiplegia. The writing is vital, dynamic and moved by an outraged humanism. Life has more than these emotional and cultural locks, whether of obsession or fantasy.

Ó Cadhain, as is the case with most good writers, avoids explicit statements about what that 'more' is or could be. It is implicit in the vitality and energy of his writing; in his attentiveness to the human voice in all its phases of speaking; in the living depictions of the endurance and patience of women; in his alertness to the intricate, even microscopic details of west of Ireland life. But in a number of late stories, and particularly in his breathtaking devotional prose poem 'Rinneadh', the sacredness of being itself is evoked, in a language that unites the fervour of Aodh Mac Aigil with the intellectual urgency of Pádraigán Haicéad, two seventeenth century divines and poets. But also animating this extraordinary account of Joseph's vision of the Virgin Mary at the Annunciation is a Mallarmean delight in the evocative and suggestive powers of words, their ability to evoke a sensuousness invigorated with lucent, intensely textured variety.

An ageing man is returning home at noon, from a hard morning's work: it is Joseph, the place is Nazareth, but that is kept from the reader until the end of the story. He is, like so many of Ó Cadhain's figures, exhausted. Life is endless toil. Sweat and effort, all week long, are required to keep something on the table. Then the situation is transformed. Coming close to the house he sees, to his astonishment and bafflement, that great streams of sunlight, like huge tresses, are vibrating round the house, as if caressing it. The garden is a living harp of birdsong, odd and strange at this time of day:

> The apparition was becoming clearer. He could see, through the thick wall, through the curtain which had not been drawn, into the sunny terrace inside: a table of mountain whitewood - which he had made - and on it a bowl of local fruit. Other things were revealing themselves out of the pool of intensely bright light, by the table, in which starlike flashes burned in jewelled fire. There was an uncertain shape, which moved according to a solemn music. And there was yet another form which was only evident in the pulsing in which the sonorous music could be heard. The wash of light was so intense that no eye could bear to look at it. The shape within the light softened and moved. . . . Joseph of Nazareth had forgotten the timber and wood, which was his portion of life, looking on the woman shining as the sun, Mary: the Mother of God.[23]

This is the centre of Ó Cadhain's vision, that sacred mystery which the rage and casualness and inertia of life flout at their peril. It is intimately involved with what language is and what it does: in the Virgin the Word was made flesh. Language involves us in being. A people's language is involved with how they are, at the deepest level of awareness. To begin to realize that, for Irish people, is the beginning of the repossession of Ireland. Seen in this radical, indeed revolutionary way, life has the potential of transformation, in time, in the harshness of the actual.

11

SEÁN Ó RÍORDÁIN

'Renewing the basic pattern'

Seán Ó Ríordáin (1916–77) was born in Baile Bhúirne (Ballyvourney) in Co. Cork and moved to Cork city with his family when he was 15 years of age. He went to school in the North Monastery, a Christian Brothers school on the north side of the city and subsequently joined the staff in the City Hall, Cork, where he worked as a clerk in the Motor Taxation Department until 1967, when he retired on health grounds. He suffered from pulmonary tuberculosis for a great part of his life and was often in terrible pain. He was unmarried and lived on the outskirts of Cork city, at Iniscarra, in a small house. From 1969 he had a part-time, advisory post, attached to University College, Cork, which he obtained through the good graces of an old schoolfriend, Tadhg Ó Ciardha, then Registrar of UCC, Professor Risteárd Breatnach, Head of the Department of Irish, and Professor Seán Ó Tuama, Professor of Modern Irish Literature in the same Department. He is amongst the great Irish poets of this century, and perhaps the finest in Irish since Aogán Ó Rathaille.

And yet outside Ireland he is virtually unknown, the reason being that he wrote exclusively in the Irish language. Even among his devoted band of readers, not all of his work has received full appreciation, because he is sometimes accused of abstraction and of outmoded religious feeling.

He grew up in the Ireland of Eamonn de Valera. He was 21 when the Irish constitution was published in 1937 and he was deeply affected by the idealistic republicanism of post-Treaty, Fianna Fail Ireland; by its adoption of a policy of detachment from many aspects of contemporary life, and by its emphasis on moral rectitude and purity. Detachment and republicanism combined in the Irish attitude towards the Second World War. Some Irish people were sympathetic to Hitler, as England's enemy; Ó Ríordáin, in some moods, shared this attitude, but for his own personal, discontented, reasons. Ó Ríordáin came to maturity during a time when Ireland was trying to make a human reality out of theoretical independence.

Ó Ríordáin's nature was primarily a religious one, if we understand that word in the simplest sense of 'binding together'. And his poetry explores the nature of binding and relationship between man and man, man and God, outer and inner, past and present. The set of his mind, the nature of his personality, was such that he set out to experience things as fully as possible, and in this way come to know them. This outward pulse of his mind and intelligence was complemented by a sometimes equal, sometimes unequal impulse inwards, to re-search the self, its moods, passions, hates and loves. This inward pulse is reflected in his Diary, which he kept continuously up to his death. The Diary remains unpublished, and may have to for some considerable time yet because many living people are fiercely treated in it, but judging from the extracts he published in his own lifetime, and from the pieces Seán Ó Coileáin prints in his indispensable biography of the poet, the Diary, which is in many volumes, has a power and literary excellence of the sort we find in the *Essays* of Montaigne. There is the same merciless instinct for probing the recesses of the self, to scour out the filth of the personality, to anatomize pride and meanness; but Ó Ríordáin is without the composure of the Renaissance Frenchman; his is the anguish and self-doubt, the fear and trembling, the deep not-knowing, of Baudelaire or Kafka:

> 14 August 1968, 5.35 p.m. – a fine day again, but a day of despair. As bad as yesterday was, today is worse. I am in the bottom of hell.
>
> Rover was a stray dog. I say 'was' because maybe he is no longer with us. He was here with me first. He came to me in the winter of 1966/67 and stayed with me. And then I brought him up to Mayfield to my brother's house. He's been there since. He'd always welcome me when I'd go there. The woman of the house was getting sick of him because he'd snap at strangers. I brought the creature to the dog's home today. Three of the children went with me. But

> the dog watcher put a halter on him and he had to go in. I've used up so much of the welcome of the world, and the welcome it offers you does not increase with the passing of the years. No wonder I'm heartsore. I'm a kind of Judas.
>
> If despair entangles itself more deeply in me I'll go mad. I lack charity and that is why I have an emptiness in my heart.
>
> Poor Rover was friendly and affectionate. His affection, maybe, was what left him in the dog yard playing with his destroyers. If he's alive yet he's waiting for death in captivity. It was a fine summer day. I saw him playing with two children about 2 p.m. He welcomed me. I sat in the small grassy patch behind the house. He lay down near me, his head on my knee, full of trust. He must have been thrown out when he was a stray, because he was trained like a housedog.[1]

This experience lies behind one of the poems in the volume *Línte Liombó* (*Lines from Limbo*) (1971), 'Tar Eis dom é Chur go Tigh na nGadhar' ('After I Took Him to the Dogs' Home'):

> You had a housedog's ways
> And the shyness of a stray;
> Tonight, all that remains of your
> Impulsive love's destroying my heart.[2]

Ó Ríordáin made absolute demands on himself and sometimes upon others. In many respects he's the opposite of Yeats in his triumphal mood of self-forgiving, self-rejoicing:

> I am content to follow to its source
> Every event in action or in thought;
> Measure the lot; forgive myself the lot!
> When such as I cast out remorse
> So great a sweetness flows into the breast.[3]

Yeats is in his dominant, rhetorical mood here; Ó Ríordáin rarely, if ever, allows himself such triumphal claims. For him the event, or hurt, or mood ramifies, expands and may take over. It may render the personal will powerless to act: 'Bíonn clann ag gach gníomh' ('Every action has a progeny'), and there's no knowing what the progeny will be like. Of one particular action he says, in the Diary for 28 June 1943:

> The accursed offspring of this action gathered round me and abused and reviled me to such an extent that I will not forget it for a long time.[4]

That actions, events, things and animals should be instinct with a life, mood and personality of their own was basic to Ó Ríordáin's thought, and takes us back to the beginning of his career as a published writer.

In the long, considered preface to his first volume of poems, *Eireabaill Spideoige* (*A Robin's Tail*) (1952) he outlined an aesthetic, the implications and depths of which he explored for the rest of his life. This preface is an extraordinarily coherent and shapely thing, entirely rational, perfectly clear and very disturbing. Drawing upon the aesthetics of Plato, Aristotle and Hopkins, the theology of St Augustine, St Thomas, the linguistic theory of Raissa Maritain, and the philosophical insights of Stephen McKenna (the translator of Plotinus who wrote in Irish), he forges a personal credo about artistic expression and its relation to being.

At the heart of this theory is the simple yet profound notion that an essential quality of poetry is the open mind of a child. Imagine, he writes, two people in a room, a child and his father, and a horse going by on the road outside:

> The father looks out and says, 'That's Mr. X's horse going to the fair'. That's telling. It appears that the father loses the horse because he remains outside it. Say that the horse is a disease. The father doesn't get that disease. The horse does not enrich the father's life. But the child – he hears the sound of the horse. He tastes the sound of the horse, for the sound's sake. And he listens to the sound diminishing and falling back into the silence. And he is awed by the sound and the silence. And he looks at the horse's hindquarters and is awed by their authority and their antiquity. And the world fills with horse-awe and trotting-magic. That is being, to be under another aspect. And that, I think, is poetry. . . . Poetry is being, not telling.[5]

Poetry is the apprehension of being something else. The word Ó Ríordáin uses is 'ionadh' – wonder, awe – for this apprehension.

To apprehend something else is to sense its basic pattern, its form, its essential being, its other-ness. And each thing, each person, each place has such a pattern, a mould, and this pattern or mould or form, Ó Ríordáin says, is the prayer that that thing, person or place, transmits. The child looks at the horse, is involved with its basic pattern, strives to close the distance between his own being and that other being, and seeks to unite his prayer to that of the horse. Again the word 'prayer' is Ó Ríordáin's: 'Ba mhaith liom paidir a thabhairt ar an rud dúchasach, an sainrud, a thagann as an múnla.' ('I'd like to call the traditional thing, the essential thing, that arises from the basic pattern, a prayer.')

> Each mortal thing does one thing and the same
> Deals out that being indoors each one dwells:
> Selves - going itself; *myself* it speaks and spells:
> Crying, *What I do is me*: *for that I came.*[6]

Ó Ríordáin cites this poem of Gerard Manley Hopkins as part of his argument. Each thing selves itself, it 'goes' itself, and in doing so Ó Ríordáin's idea (and ideal) is that poetry is a reaching of the basic pattern of the poet himself towards that form or basic pattern of the other. To accomplish this reaching, in language, is to find the creative shape of poetic form in language. And then the language itself, poetically alive, starts to achieve its own doing, its own selving. Put down in this way, it sounds very abstract, but Ó Ríordáin has the capacity to ignite his philosophizing through concrete images:

> Often I felt that I was engaged upon an extraordinary activity when I was composing; an activity other than writing or inventing; an activity that was closer to cleansing. I think I was like someone cleansing rust or dust off an image, looking for and renewing the basic pattern - looking for the patterns on the sea floor. If this cleansing, this scouring, is compared to a cough during a cold, then the basic pattern can be imagined as a lung. Or the activity can be thought of as a blind man reading Braille. We all know the pattern, this form which has been separated out from all other forms; we do not know how we know it; but we know it as being old, basic, authoritative, persistent, beautiful,

> and it is not possible to contact it without experiencing a thrust of joy.[7]

The last phrase in Irish is superbly vivid: 'ni féidir teangmháil leis gan geit áthais'. This searching of the sea floor for a thing or an experience (a horse, a love affair, despair) is the poetic activity. It is an objectless activity, in that it does not seek a particular transitive object; but it is a waiting for the 'geit', the thrust, of creation. No true poem, Ó Ríordáin says, is born without a 'beo-gheit' - a life-thrust.

Each being deals out of its own being, that which dwells indoors in 'each one'. But this 'being' is normally hidden, in the way that, according to the old philosophical maxim, truth takes care to keep itself hidden. The poetic activity, which is childish, ancient and basic, looks to being in this sense. Ó Ríordáin, in a daring move of the argument, not entirely worked out logically, then says that that being which poetry inclines to is analogous to the transformed body of Christ after the resurrection, furiously citing St Augustine's *De Civitate Dei* in support of his leap. After the resurrection, the body will be in continuous 'beo-gheit', life-thrust; it will be total prayer.

Poetry is the relation between essences discovered in an inclination of sympathetic loneliness from one to another. It is the resurrection now, an earthly praying, for things, amidst things. This line of argument of Ó Ríordáin's is entirely at one with the neo-Platonic line of poetic theory, from the Renaissance down: that poetry resurrects a golden world, because it recovers man's creative ability from the fallen state of time. In this aspect the poet becomes a Christ-like person, figuring the potential redemption in things, in time. The poet's measuring, his or her metric, imitates the measuring, the mathematics, of creation itself, the basic mathematics ordained in being. For the poet not to travel outwards seeking those other 'dwellings' 'indoors' is damnation, *the* sin, false creation. Ó Ríordáin moralizes this:

> And the damned person what happened to him? I think he belied the truth: that he refused to humble himself to the forms of truth and that he continued to create his own pseudo-forms like an anti-Creator, so that he stayed inside himself always, like a badger.[8]

He quotes the poem of Séamus Dall Mac Cuarta on people who stay underground in themselves, tunnelling away in their egos:

> It's the badger's way to tunnel away
> In darkness day and night:
> He does not come out to all
> That was created in heaven and earth.

If the creative spirit is not to be turned in on itself it must seek realization of otherness, and that involves the kind of intense sympathy evident in the Diary entry describing his feelings after he took the dog to the dogs' home, bathetic as this instance might first seem. It also involves the self-scrutiny that comes about when this action of sympathetic reaching fails, or is aborted.

It is Ó Ríordáin's view that *everything* will have its own prayerful instinct, deriving from its basic pattern. That includes a family, a village, a town, a city, a people, a language. Language and the tradition of the people to whom that language belonged mattered intensely to Ó Ríordáin. His poetic would lead him to think that way; or it may be that it was the importance of language and tradition to Ó Ríordáin, specifically the Irish language, Irish tradition, which led him to create a poetic which linked language, psychology, aesthetics and theology in the way that he did.

To be yourself you need to lose yourself into your tribe, your *dúchas* (tradition), your language, uncovering their basic patterns and in doing so discovering your own. Of Seán Ó Riada, the Irish musician who turned his back on the busy artistic life of Dublin to find his own place and his own quiet in the West Cork Gaeltacht, he wrote:

> He recognised his own ego in the accomplishment of the [Irish] language. He wanted to achieve his own completed self. . . . The mind of the language, the mind of the music was older than the mind which was created with him . . . until he could come into full possession of this older mind his actions would be pastiche and futility, each one separated from the other.[9]

To achieve integrity involved integration, with the tradition, with the language, with the people. Not to do so is to lose the basic pattern, never to experience 'beo-gheit'; to be lost in the sterile tunnelling of Séamus Dall Mac Cuarta's 'broc' (badger) in the labyrinth of the personal ego, one of the damned. Modern democratic notions of personal freedom, that set at nought integration with a larger entity, are illusory. He excoriates freedom, in this sense, in the poem 'Saoirse' in *Eireabaill Spideoige*:

I'll go down amongst the people
On foot,
And I'll go down tonight.

I'll seek release
From the venomous freedom
That's howling here.

I'll chastise the pack of thoughts
That snarl about me
In the loneliness.

And I'll find the chapel
That's full of people
At fixed times.

I'll seek out people
Who've never hankered
To be free or lonely.

I'll listen to shilling-thoughts
Being exchanged
Like cash . . .

The mind that fell into the deep slough
Of freedom's exhausted.
The hill that God created's not there,
But there are abstract hills, fantasias,
Each one full of cravings
Scaling in futility.
There's no limit to freedom
Or to fantastic mountains;
And there's no limit to craving,
Or relief
To be had.[10]

This slough ('iomar' in Irish, linked to 'iomar na h-aimiléise' – the slough of despond) is not the sea floor of the preface to

Eireabaill Spideoige, where the basic patterns can be come upon; this is the mindlessness of self-betrayal and damnation.

In 'Saoirse' he talks of going 'down amongst the people', but what people, where? His own people came from Baile Bhúirne in West Cork, but as a Gaeltacht that was an area where Irish as a spoken language had been steadily contracting since his youth. Dunquin, in West Kerry, however, became for him a haven, a solace, a place alive with significance.

His feelings about Dún Chaoin are revealed in a poem called '*An Feairín*' in his second volume of verse, *Brosna* (*Kindlings*) (1964). A previously unpublished account of how the poem originated during a night in Dunquin is given in Ó Coileáin's biography. 'An Feairín', 'The Little Man', is someone called Pound:

> One night we were night-visiting in John O'Connor's house. They were debating about the resettling of the people from [the Blaskets]. [The Blasket islanders were settled on the mainland in the 1950s.] The woman of the house, referring to Pound, said that the poor little man would want his own house and land like any other islander. I took particular notice of how she said the word 'feairín' and 'little man'. I composed this:[11]
>
> 'He'd want a house and land
> The little man,' she said, of Pound;
> Pound sank into her word
> And settled there.
>
> I never saw him plain until she said it.
> I studied him, fully,
> In the light of what she called him
> And her meaning was correct.
>
> She's nabbed Pound in her word,
> Because Pound's a little fellow,
> All his living frame concurred with her
> From tip of head to toe.
>
> Pound's tenured in those words,
> He's peaceful there;
> And whoever else's insecurity may occupy
> Our minds, it won't be Pound's.[12]

The way the woman of the house spoke the ordinary word 'feaírn' was poetic, because it touched the quintessence of Pound himself and in so doing it awoke; the word was, in her syntax, and with reference to the man, and the islands, the land round about, a 'thrust of joy': 'geit áthais'. For Ó Ríordáin such an awakening comes out of a live relation between essences; each essence is a basic pattern or form which has its own means of prayer, a potential activated when the relation is made between one pattern and another in the loneliness of time. The word, according to St John, was God; the open mind of a child, the sympathy of a woman, the attentiveness of a poet can return the word, in the play of art, to God, as a figuring of the resurrection.

Dún Chaoin (Gentle Fortress), Dunquin, became a golden world for Ó Ríordáin, a figure of resurrected life. In an unpublished lecture describing the landscape around Slea Head, and the view of the Blaskets and the Three Sisters, he writes 'You'll be startled (again he uses the Irish word 'geit') with the life and vigour of the pattern. . . . This country brings to mind miraculous days when God was with us.'[13]

The rational commonsensical mind knows that Dunquin is an underprivileged area, that the Irish language is dying out, that the glimmerings of insight may be, to some, only fancy or romantic self-indulgence. Ó Ríordáin fully admits all of this, indeed it torments him, and this torment is one of the factors that gives his poetry edge and attentiveness, but nevertheless he asserts that there is something there, something basic, ancient, authoritative and *true*. This essential truth, which, if poetry can achieve it, puts the mind in touch with transfigured life, is seen as totally upsetting the normal commonsensical, matter-of-fact truth in 'Na Blascaodaí', a poem on the Blaskets and Dunquin, in which Peig Sayers, a famous Blasketwoman and a renowned storyteller, completely usurps everyday consciousness, replacing it with the basic, the prayerful, the ancient, the sea floor of the unconscious. The pattern stands out, revealed, in radical presence, in strangeness:

A white subterranean house
Dreams at the edge of Dunquin
Where I listened to the ancient speech
Of a bed-ridden woman, blinded with age;
And the deep mind was up on the surface
While reason was sent to the bottom.

Peig Sayers' mind, a currach,
Carried us over the waves;
The froth of the intellect submerged
While the undermind brightened like foam,
Our voices were seized with a strangeness,
Their sound acquired echo and substance.

We'd only heard this kind of echo
From strange mountains out in the distance,
But here is the broadcasting station
Transmitting this resonant sound.
Remoteness is near us,
Order's transformed in the air.[14]

Ó Ríordáin here celebrates integration and unity. The isolated twentieth century intellectual from Cork city, who works in the Motor Taxation Department of the City Hall, where what he described as the 'hollow men' (following Eliot and punning on *Halla* na Cathrach) walk about with papers in their hands, is integrated in the artistic statement with Dún Chaoin, Peig Sayers, the sea, the mountains, the Gaelic tradition itself: *dúchas*. Community becomes communion; things are more completely themselves in the golden world of the poem. Its rhythmic drive (inadequately imitated in the translation) conveys a sense of abundant life. Such a saying as he makes for Dún Chaoin is a prayer in Ó Ríordáin's sense.

'Siollabadh' ('Syllables') is a poem with an entirely different setting – the ward of Sarsfield's Court Sanatorium outside Cork city – but the quality of prayerful realization of the presence of life is very like that in 'Na Blascaodaí'. A nurse comes into a ward to take the pulse of the patients. Her femininity, life and sexuality are conveyed in what is one of Ó Ríordáin's most perfect poems. The patients, their beds, the movements of the nurse, her expertise in taking the pulse, the pulse itself in each patient, the afternoon, the excitement and delight of life suddenly presenting itself, and the mysteriousness of the pulse of being itself; all these are gathered together and orchestrated in the rhythmic pulse of the saying of the different lives that the poem integrates in *its* own life. 'Ní insint dán ach bheith' – 'Poetry is being, not telling.'[15]

A nurse in a hospital
On a bright afternoon;
Arteries in dormitories
Effortlessly pulsing;
And she stood at each bedside
Waiting and counting,
Writing down the metric
Of the syllables in her fingers;
And she syllabled rhythmically
Out of the room,
Leaving a symphony
Of arteries counting;
Syllables and murmurs,
And Amen all concluded
In a whisper in the sick room;
But the chanting continued
In the monastery of flesh,
Arteries like acolytes
Murmuring the nones.[16]

For sensual pleasure in the rhythmic possibility of words, for the frank unintellectualized delight in the existential presence of the moment, for life re-presented as blessing, this poem can stand alongside the miraculous moments of joy and celebration to be found in Rilke's 'Ninth Duino Elegy', Hopkins's 'That Nature is a Heraclitean Fire of the Comfort of the Resurrection', or Yeats's astonishing openness in 'Vacillation IV':

My fiftieth year had come and gone,
I sat, a solitary man
In a crowded London shop,
An open book and empty cup
On the marble table-top.

While on the shop and street I gazed
My body of a sudden blazed;
And twenty minutes more or less
I seemed, so great my happiness,
That I was blessed and could bless.[17]

Poems like 'Siollabadh', in which the isolated self moves out of the labyrinths of the ego to confer with otherness, can be found throughout Ó Ríordáin's work from beginning to end. In *Línte*

Liombó (1971) there is a poem which translates the aesthetic and theological principles underlying his theory into political terms. In Irish the poem is 'Ní Ceadmhach Neamhshuim' ('Indifference is not Acceptable'). The demand made by the poem is total: no indifference of any kind is acceptable; we must aspire to total commitment to Christ in others and in all else:

Indifference is not Acceptable

No fly, or lion nor bee
Nor man or woman
That God has made
Whose good is not our duty.
Indifference to their fear
Is not acceptable. No lunatic
In the madhouse whom
We shouldn't sit or walk with
While they carry in their hands
Our suffering for us.

No place, no stream or bush
Or flagstone, however lonely,
Whether north or south or east or west
That we shouldn't think about
With love and tender feeling;

Though South Africa's a world away
And the moon's beyond our reach
There's nowhere in all this life
Where we haven't been.[18]

The thinking here may owe something to Irish Christian tradition, but it entirely belongs with the approach to art and literature to be found in Ó Ríordáin's theoretical and discursive writings. If the open mind of a child is basic to the discovery of what is essential in experience, then all experience should, ideally, be approached in openness. Only in this way can there be a prayerful interaction between the individual mind and the rest of being. Such interaction is a figuring of Christ's presence, and all of life should be approached as if it contained him, potentially. False conscience, opinionatedness, the 'Galway Bray' of the bishops of Galway and elsewhere, all these blaspheme against the creative interaction there should be between people in a proper community. Ó Ríordáin's outrage and disgust at the blasphemy of the blithely assured and corrupt is expressed in another powerful poem, 'To My Friends', in *Línte Liombó* immediately following on from 'Ní Ceadmhach Neamhshuim':

> You make me sick, and not without reason,
> Your total statements,
> Your authoritative opinions,
> Your support for your own puny sort
> Stand for the wrong done to the weak
> By the strong in this world, today,
> And for thousands of years;
> And done under cover of the lying treachery
> You still promulgate in the name of truth,
> In the name of the Christ you've lost.
>
> I will fight you to the death,
> Though you're my friends
> Because I can hear, through the corridors
> Of history the reverberations of your speechifying,
> Trampling and making carnage.[19]

Ó Ríordáin's aesthetic, moral and philosophical credo is absolutely simple and absolutely demanding: honour the thing as it is; do not intellectualize it; hear its essence speak to you through you; then you may share its being in communion. There is, perhaps, an Eastern element in this thinking, but it is also to be found in the European existentialist philosopher of the presence of being: Heidegger. Ó Ríordáin once said of himself: 'Bím i láthair' – 'I am *present*.'[20] He was himself conscious of an Eastern element in his Christian aesthetic which is playfully acknowledged in the first poem of his posthumous book *Tar Eis Mo Bháis (After My Death)* (1978), 'Piscin' ('Kitten'):

> In the West it's not enough
> For words to spring from things;
> Words deepening to themselves won't
> Do; we have to act.
>
> I saw a kitten under the stool
> Tonight, perfectly framed.
> Terrified, he fled from
> The racket, the poor thing . . .

In the East the limit's enough;
That kitten there suffices,
Not like here, because
Paul expounded Christ.

To Westerners, he says:

A kitten under a stool, is not
A fully legitimate kitten.[21]

Though simple, Ó Ríordáin's poetic is utterly demanding. Life is there before him, he wishes to honour it and to gain access to its prayerfulness, but there is darkness as well, and terror. In a Diary entry for 26 April 1940 he has the following account of an encounter in Cork city with a girl who was suffering from TB:

> I saw a girl on the South Mall. I took off my hat immediately, out of courtesy. We stopped. Maria O'Mahoney. A handsome young girl, with fine sturdy legs on her. But she has T.B. I saw her before in Heatherside (a sanatorium). I hardly knew her. . . . She was the most beautiful girl in the place without a sign of ill health. . . . I think myself that one of the doctors used to be looking out for her. I used to be looking on, too, – the old story. . . . But she frightened me. 'This Maria O'Mahoney was not the Maria O'Mahoney that was here before. . . .' She was much reduced. She was no longer a fine strapping girl. 'Consumption hath no pity for blue eyes or golden hair.' A slight redness was in her cheeks. That redness had a deadly meaning. Some of my fellow-patients are now in St. Patrick's Hospital. She had news about most of them. We parted. It is a terrible, sorrowful and bleak story. A beauty, in the vigour of her youth and goodness, rotting. The germs are powerful. You can't oppose them. Poverty caused a lot of this disease. And people are scared that Hitler will destroy this civilisation. If he does he didn't come soon enough. Well-fed Christianity, without a scruple![22]

The writing here is halting because it is heartsmitten. The rage that mounts towards the end of this passage is the rage against the confident complacent values that allow people to rot in poverty and disease through indifference. Charity and compassion have the same root, in Ó Ríordáin, as does the imagination, in real sympathy for the rest of life. But Maria O'Mahoney, the one he met on the street, was not the Maria O'Mahoney he knew in the sanatorium. Death had got a grip on her and transformed her. How can there be a basic pattern to anything or anyone if they can change so drastically? How can there be a prayerful exchange between essences, if those essences are unstable? How can there be the 'thrust of joy' in so much suffering? Might it not be better to have evil fully out, Hitler dominant, so-called civilization gone, than to continue in our overstuffed complacent lives?

In one of the most searching of all of his poems 'Oileán agus Oileán Eile' ('An Island and Another Island') in *Eireabaill Spideoige,* he meditates on the holy site of Gougane Barra, where St Finbarr settled, and built a tiny monastery, on a tiny island in the lake. The informing idea of the poem is the old one that each person is an island, in the sense that each person has his own authentic territory, and that the attempt to uncover and reveal that is what inspired the saint and what should inspire us now. But is the whole activity just 'frantic illusion' in a time when words and life have gone 'vapid'?

Words without verve,
The imperiousness of years,
Their grey film,
Fell on my thoughts . . .

Finbarr and the saints
Are years in the earth;
Enthusiasm's no more
Than frantic illusion.

I'm sick to heart
Of words gone vapid.
Illusion or demon.
Let them distract me.[23]

But bravely, the writing turns aside from this gloomy langour and moves into a section called 'An Bíogadh', 'The Stirring', in which the 'beo-gheit', the 'life-thrust', is attempted, and the saint's presence is attributed to the air, the wind and birdsong:

Saintly intimations stir the air
And the wind moves all through them.

An ancient prayer's submerged in my mind
Which thought now strives to breathe on.

In this fold of saintly thought
A sudden proposition took me,
Enunciated in the bird's fierce song
I heard a scorn towards the world.

The birds' own island was in
The music he flung at things;
Without islands no-one lives
Pity those men who've left them.[24]

Each person, then, must turn away from the clamour to his own special island, which was 'composed as a white prayer/On the lips of the Son of Man'. But this is easily enough said. How do you make poetry out of this? What Ó Ríordáin records is the struggle of the mind, in doubt, searching out the narrative of its experience at Gougane, trying to find a stillness and a central focus. The bleakness is there, the doubt, the search, and the looking for the basic pattern, whereby he and Finbarr can find at-one-ment:

St. Finbarr's Island

At Gougane, on a bad afternoon,
Fog whitened out the sheer
Cliffs. I search the island for
A sign, found it in the trees.

Around me, their contorted growth,
The entangled order.
They'd been driven into any shape
Like a body burnt alive.

Or like writing on a page
With other writing over it.
I saw knee and nostril, back and foot,
And then I saw Mahatma Gandhi . . .

Freedom's zest, love for the turned
Eye, are in the treeshapes; love
For all that's crooked and bent,
And for the soft and straight, contempt . . .

Every man's island is:
His narrative of Heaven,
The Christ that's leaping in his blood,
The implication in his words.[25]

This Gougane Barra poem is a poem of the ascetic will, intent on discovering a relation between the self, the past and place; and also intent on conveying a sense of spiritual continuity. The sign is found; the stirring of the uncovering of its significance is recorded. But what of the two Maria O'Mahoneys? What if there is only the here and now and what if our insistence that there is a centre is pure invention? This doubt is the theme of a poem of intense metaphysical and spiritual anguish in *Brosna,* called 'Moths'.

The moths are creatures whom he wishes to realize, to present them in their pure aspect of integral form. Instead they remain moths, what they are, in exterior reality, and they threaten and terrify. So strong does their pressure become that they threaten to devour the identity of the speaker, whose job it is to control, order, possess and realize them. The trick is, of course, that the poem, while confessing failure to realize the essential 'mothness' of the moths, realizes, profoundly, the experience of the anguish of being excluded from any sense of integral identity. And yet what is being composed in this poem is the formation of identity in the experience of not being sure that there is such a thing. It is a poetry wrung from the beseeching heart, beset by all the circumstances of its doubt:

Flutter of a delicate moth, turning of a page,
Crushing of the small wingspan,
In the bedroom of an autumn evening
Something fragile is being crazed.

Another night, in a dream, I saw
A pair of clothesmoth's wings,
They were extensive as an angel's
And fragile as a woman.

I had to hold them,
Not let them go astray,
And to possess without destroying them
And deliver them to complete delight.

But I spilled the holy dust
Powdering each wing,
And I knew then I hadn't the numbers
Of masculinity, and would never have.

The ten digits marched out of the mess
Authority greater than ever before,
And generations were heard arguing arithmetic
And everyone heard but me.

Flutter of a delicate moth, turning of a page,
Destruction of a wing membrane;
This autumn evening I need the small
Agitation of the hovering moths.[26]

This is a poem of failure, of creative failure, and yet it is also a powerful piece of writing. He has 'spilled the holy dust' but the magic remains in the poem's attentiveness, patience and suffering.

Such a poem as 'Moths' achieves a convincing realization of metaphysical anguish because it is conveyed in an entirely direct manner. Even the obscurity of the 'numbers' does not really matter. They are a private symbol, and it is clear enough that they refer to male sexuality and creative power.

Ó Ríordáin began his career as a published writer with a statement, the preface to *Eireabaill Spideoige*, in which he argued that sympathy was crucial to creativity, because it was the means by which the imagination could contact the pattern of something else, thereby moving towards the realization of itself. This poetic linked theology, instinct, ordinary human feeling and language. But it will be evident by now that Ó Ríordáin was not a programmatic writer; he did not write to justify an intellectual conception. As time went on his doubt about whether or not there really was a central meaning, a central pattern, increased; he did not repress that. As always is the case, the doubt increased the tension so his belief in the basic pattern of each thing, each creature was tested. In some poems, such as 'Moths', the doubt is very great, and the writing arises directly from uncertainty. In a late poem 'Oíche Gealái' ('Moonlit Night') light and dark interplay. There is a mixture of serenity, terror, openness and resignation here that is like something in Hölderlin's later poems:

Through the sky's cloudy
The full moon's
An eye of light
Pouring down.
Where it is in the sky
is war. Light's
Declared war on dark.
As much as it can
This carnage of light
Spreads and reveals itself.
In that place, which is
Neither light nor dark
Huge mountains,
Sea distances,
And remote sunsets
Are eaten by light out of dark.
Terror resides
In the unbearable beauty
Of these reaches of light.
This sudden loveliness
Should be hidden.
Nothing can stop it,
All shapes obey it.
Hide it in a cloud.
Let us go in.[27]

The mind opens to a not-knowing, a terrible openness, in a language, Irish, which, common sense tells us, is at the margin of European linguistic culture. But the margins are often where the activity is. In Rome who thought of Nazareth?

12

BRIAN FRIEL

'Isn't this your job to translate?'[1]

At one point in *Volunteers* (1975), there is a particularly bravura piece of invention, during which a fantastic yarn is woven about the skeleton that dominates the archaeological site where the action is set. The volunteer who tells the story admits it is all pure improvisation and, as he breathlessly concludes, tells his audience (those on stage, those in the theatre) that he 'didn't know how that was going to end'. The tale he tells tempts us to allegorize: it is a tale of exile, hanging, sacrifice; a tale which is all too Irish. As Keeney interjects, during the unfolding of the story: 'Ah, shure I can shmell dishaster comin.' But when the tale concludes, Keeney, tired and worldly-wise, alive to the vices of allegory and the dreariness of the predictable message, says to Pyne, the narrator:

> Not bad, Pyne. Fairly trite melody but an interesting sub-theme. Not bad at all.[2]

The core of a story takes good care to keep itself hidden; it does not yield its secrets to the facile probe of the allegorizing mind, that aspect of our uncertainty that reaches out for meaning and explanation, for the facts. If a story has a core it will have sub-themes or sub-texts relating it to other stories with their own undercurrents. It is those interrelations that are interesting, not the surface entertainment of the so-called 'story'. The sub-theme or sub-themes of a set of stories create reverberations that stir us, as possibilities interweave, meanings multiply; the thing that contains the stories, the form itself, acquires its fling, its ramification, its identity.

Friel is a dramatist with an impressive technique which he uses, expertly, to create that multiplying fling and ramification.

If we go back to that scene in *Volunteers*, where Keeney questions Pyne's leaden predictability (who wants unthinking rhetoric about graves, exile, sacrifice?) we find Friel twisting the action around into another tale, immediately following this one, this time invented by Keeney, save that Keeney's narration is participatory, and funny. It's a tale, which is acted out, about two American matrons, who hugely enjoy their holiday in an Ireland unsettled by civil commotion because it allows them to be frisked with tremendous zeal on all kinds of occasions by security men: 'It was just frisk, frisk, frisk day and night for almost a week.'[3] Theatrically this is a superb turn, from the lugubrious to the carnivalesque; and Friel's theatre is asking you to test your reaction to these two narratives, not necessarily to spot the hidden connection, but primarily, simply to enjoy them; while at the same time delighting in the fluid variousness of which this art is capable. There is a connection, of course, but, for this writer at least, it cannot be sorted by means of a theoretical construct; the connection is rather that which obtains between quite different elements mutually coexistent in a unified field of cultural awareness.

Each of these two voices attempts to create a world. On this occasion the stories do not strive against each other for dominance, as they sometimes do in Friel; they are set side by side in the evolving physical relationship that only theatre can provide. And that relationship is often one of disjunction. The forces and tensions of those disjunctions, and the efforts language makes to express, repress, or heal them: these are the matters which concern us here.

Within a cultural system, the story itself, with its contents, themes, characters and so forth, while interesting enough in its own right, only serves as a vehicle for the conveyance of the complex of hidden contradictions, the tensions of which keep the system active. A story, therefore, if it is a significant one for a culture or an occasion, does not come cellophaned in transparent material, bearing a tag declaring its intent. It involves us and moves us precisely because it is resistant to easy formulation; we cannot readily translate its secrets. And we cannot do that because the story, if again, it is a powerful one, is various, manifold and in a crucial sense, uncertain. It can only carry its charge if the elements are active, which will mean they are mobile, shifting, impatient of the tired mind's desire to close down this uncertain activity. But although it may be a vehicle, a story can only be effective as such if it discovers a form which may hold these contradictions. A vehicle conveys nothing if it is crazy; a story needs must articulate, put together; it cannot be haphazard. Only then can it translate the contradictions and the disjunctive active elements, which is not to say that it explains them or sorts them out. A story translates the interior elements of a culture most effectively when the form the translation discovers for the articulation encompasses the broadest possible scope. Time and again Friel's theatre holds in play the complexity of contemporary Irish culture: with its bleak parishes; its vociferous and timorous assertions; its hatred; its heartbreaking gentleness and affection; its obsession with the past; its ghoulish materialism and indifference; its fierce and casual passions.

An early short story of Friel's, 'Among the Ruins', gives us a clue to his understanding of the relationship between the form an artist creates, and the interior depths and labyrinths which it seeks to translate. A family, husband and wife, little boy and girl, travel back to the father's native place near Errigal in Co. Donegal. The house is in ruins, the past a jumble of memories. The little boy, Peter, goes missing, and Joe, his father, eventually finds him in a small cluster of trees engrossed in play:

> He was on his knees at the mouth of a rabbit hole, sticking small twigs into the soft earth.
>
> 'Peter! What the hell!'
> 'Look, Daddy. Look! I'm donging the tower!'[4]

The past is, to a large extent, unknowable; its conflicts and terrors, including those of childhood, are often unresolved and hidden. There is a darkness. But the child's instinct, to create a frail interlocking structure over the dark hole, is that of the artist too. In the Elizabethan theatre the wooden structure of the stage itself had a door which opened into an area which, by convention, was recognized as hell. The little boy's grid of twigs is itself a tiny story with its own, semi-comic name; its image reverberates in the father's mind as he drives home. The child's structure over the unknown hole has entered into the network of human communication. The unknown is still not known, but the structure which would not be there without it, and which to some extent it articulates, translates, has entered the arena of human reason and feeling.

> He would ask him in the morning, but Peter would not know. Just out of curiosity, he would ask him, not that it mattered. . . . And then a flutter of excitement stirred in him. Yes, yes, it did matter. Not the words, not the game, but the fact that he had seen his son, on the first good day of summer, busily, intently happy in solitude, donging the tower.[5]

A crucial (perhaps *the* crucial) preoccupation in Friel's work, which has both moral and technical dimensions, is announced in these lines: something internal and hidden, which is related to the past, has been made manifest in the child's activity in the trees. It vibrates with meaning for the father: this construct signifies; it is a vehicle for connecting the past with the present, inner with outer, the inarticulate with form. But Friel's own writing, his own prose, is performing this function for that which the story is carrying for us: the writing is a translation for us, involving us.

Friel is an entirely social writer, in that his work remains always attentive to the minutiae of ordinary everyday life; but his calm and lucid realism is, in effect, born out of a responsibility to translate those interiors that are dark and hidden into a language that incorporates the world as we perceive it under normal conditions. The given world, the social contexts of family, politics, love affairs, administration, running a touring theatre company, are amongst the locations in which the private worlds of feeling are tested. So that Friel's art has a powerful interior charge which is socialized by his classic realism. He was, inevitably, drawn to the theatre, because the theatre is the form which, above any other, tests the interior against the world of fact; and it does so in a way which holds up, for the audience's gaze and contemplation, the disjunctions between the stories people tell about themselves to themselves, and their actual conditions. We see people like ourselves inventing stories and so translating themselves; and we are asked to adjudicate on those narratives. The theatre is the most effective arena for contemplating the disjunctions narratives generate as they translate the varieties of individual and collective experience.

In *Philadelphia, Here I Come* (1964) the disjunctions between inner and outer are effectively dramatized by splitting Gar O'Donnell into public and private versions of his personality. Private Gar continuously underlines the difficulty of adequately conveying, in the social context of life in a huxter's shop in Ballybeg, the complexity of a human narrative. People need to 'save the appearances', as when the 'lads' come round to visit Gar before he sets off to Philadelphia in the morning. No one can face the reality of the departure, and the tension is resolved by bravado and heroic narratives of 'Greenock pieces' and two Dublin skivvies who, they say, chased one of the lads naked along the beach. Private's narrative clashes with this, now orthodox, fabrication:

> We were all there that night, Ned. And the girls' names were Gladys and Susan. And they sat on the rocks dangling their feet in the water. And we sat in the cave, peeping out at them. And then Jimmy Crerand suggested that we go in for a swim; and we all ran to the end of the shore; and we splashed about like schoolboys. Then we came back to the cave, and wrestled with one another. And then out of sheer boredom Tom, you suggested we take the trousers off Crerand - just to prove how manly we all were. But when Ned started towards Jimmy - five-foot nothing remember? - wee Jimmy squared up and defied not only the brave Ned but the whole lot of us. So we straggled back home, one behind the other, and left the girls dangling their feet in the water. And that was that night.[6]

None of the characters in the play can find a language capable of conveying their own view of how they are to any other character. They cannot 'translate all this loneliness, this groping, this dreadful bloody buffoonery'.[7] But Friel's theatre *does* translate it, by making evident the gap between the realm of desire and that of necessity and by making that gap the object of our contemplation. We then see that the interaction and mutuality of social necessity is that by which the interior is constrained, and that it finds a voice in Friel's art.

We cannot but speak in our social context, but to speak is almost invariably to distort. It is extremely difficult, if not impossible, to find a just correspondence, a perfect 'congruence' between the words used and the material being expressed. Again, Friel's theatre is an arena for observing these lacks, so that it is, like Synge's and Beckett's, a theatre obsessed with language; but unlike its predecessors this theatre conveys the difficulty of communication by underlining the normality of failure rather than the failure of normality.

Heidegger says 'that it is language, not man, which speaks,'[8] and Friel's theatre shows us men and women tangled in the net of languages which speak them rather than the other way around. The theatre is a space in which we observe men and women at a critical edge: they are creatures whose pasts are intersecting with the present during each moment of intensified time that is theatrical time. From these various pasts they bring the gear and baggage of languages, stories, narratives, and in this critical present they are engaged in the testing of those languages as they seek to make them congruent with the facts as they evolve. They want to hold the line, they want to make or find 'a matching of hope and past and present and possibility',[9] but invariably things will not cohere with the languages they bring with them. And those languages themselves are easily distorted or betrayed. Mistranslation is endemic.

In *Volunteers* Desmond, the young untenured academic who is supervising the prisoners engaged on the dig, finds out that the site is to be closed that evening because the developers want to get on with the building programme. The work isn't properly finished and the prisoners must return to gaol. Desmond is outraged, and in a speech from the verandah overlooking the hole where the prisoners are working (which is the stage floor itself) indulges himself in a bit of nationalist/Marxist rhetorical elevation:

> I personally will write to every newspaper in the country and expose this act for what it is - a rape of irreplaceable materials, a destruction of knowledge that the Irish people have a right to inherit, and a capitulation to moneyed interests.

The self-aware Keeney's acid comment on this is: 'That's good. That's impressive. God but I'm a sucker for that sort of stuff.' Stimulated now by the situation, by his own afflatus, by the intoxicating sense of being right and true and brave Dessy the Red climbs to even greater heights; the language of politics takes over:

> As for you men, no one knows better than myself how much toil and sweat you have put into this dig and I know you are as angered by this news as I am. As to what form your anger will take, that is up to you.[10]

And so on. There is a perfect convergence here between Desmond's politics, the language, his view of himself; what is incongruous is the *fact* that he speaks to them of rights while they are prisoners without will. They are 'volunteers' only in the joke sense of that word; and their compliance with necessity will probably lead to their deaths (they will almost certainly be put to death when they return to prison as collaborators with the state). Desmond's rhetoric, a language of power, translating his desire, promising to translate that into action, is out of touch with actuality. It isn't *real.* This disjunction is shown up later when Desmond returns. He went off intending to disrupt the board at the university which was discussing the dig, but when he got there the meeting had concluded. He also has to admit he didn't know the full facts and that there is no alternative but to close. Now the men pretend to have taken him at his word, and there is much fun at his expense when they tell him they have written to the papers, so inspired were they by his speech, and his stand for them. The last thing he wants now is a convergence between word and deed. He is like them in that he is a victim; and like them that which victimizes him is, at root, language. They are, in Keeney's words, casualties of language: 'which one of us here isn't?'[11]

Desmond fails to stay in touch with his audience, the men, and vanishes into indignation's closed circle. Cass in *The Loves of Cass Maguire* (1966) is insistent that she will unfold her story in the way she wants to and tells the audience in the theatre that that is what she is going to do. She is emphatic that she lives in the present, the 'here and now'; 'Who the hell knows what happened in the past!' she exclaims to the audience later. But the past is all she can talk about; in a way what else can happen in a theatre except talk about various pasts?

Cass Maguire is in Eden House, a rest home for the elderly, or a workhouse, as she bluntly put it. Her narrative frames the action and when her memory flares the scenes from the past will not stay away: they are enacted on stage. This flashback technique adroitly indicates how her narrative control, her language, breaks down and shows that she is overwhelmed by that which she would command. Her return to Ireland and her family, both of which she has idealized for years in the Bronx, is a terrible disappointment. Now, in Eden House, the scenes of her humiliation will not go away; they keep interrupting her attempt to hold the audience with her immediate vitality, her lavish, stage-Irish-Americanisms. Hers is a theatre for the voices she cannot keep under.

In the home there are two who have resolved the problem of accommodating the interior with the facts of actuality by creating an entire fantasy world of private invention. It is, needless to say, based on a story, the story of Tristan and Iseult. These two, named appropriately Trilbe and Ingram, are pathetic extensions of the storytelling 'lads' in *Philadelphia, Here I Come*; or of Gar O'Donnell's hopeful citations from Edmund Burke in the same play. They are related to Fox in *Crystal and Fox* (1968), Casimir in *Aristocrats* (1979), everyone in *Faith Healer* (1979), Yolland and Hugh in *Translations* (1980), Senator Donovan in *The Communication Cord* (1982), Lombard in *Making History* (1988), and so on. Storytellers, narrators, talkers abound in Friel's theatre. But what marks Trilbe and Ingram is that their fiction is allowed, for once, to travel free and unchecked. And, in the end, they draw Cass into this mode of 'truth': 'our truth, our truth' they intone, which Cass at last picks up, giving up the struggle to keep in touch with reality, which, for her, is the audience in the theatre. As, in the third Act, she gravitates closer to the point where she will enter fiction, she loses contact with the auditorium. A stage direction reads: '*She takes a few steps towards the footlights, shades her eyes, searches the auditorium. She sees nobody*':

> And I could ov swore there were folks out there.
> (*Shrugs*) What the hell.[12]

At last she joins the Trilbe and Ingram 'rhapsody' (Friel's word) to the strains of the 'Liebestod' from Wagner's *Tristan und Isolde*. She has sunk into the 'winged chair', reserved for these sterile flights, which is Friel's powerful critique on the danger of the autonomous imagination. It must be put to the test, otherwise the world of everyday experience, the actual, will cease to be real, to cite a distinction made by Seamus Deane in a discussion of the short stories which underlines Friel's moral intelligence.[13] Friel distrusts the storyteller, the maker of fictions, the word-spinner. In *The Loves of Cass Maguire* and to some extent in *Aristocrats* he is kinder to them in that he allows them dignity while at the same time making evident their pathos.

Cass Maguire, despite her desire for total presence, cannot stop the past from obtruding on to the space she wants to keep for herself, from which she projects to the audience, the playing area itself. Eden House is a place of voices, tales from the past or untrammelled dislocated fictions, which latter 'truth' she enters at last with relief, surrender and dignity. In *Aristocrats* Friel takes one of the most haunting symbols in Irish writing, the Big House, and locates it in Ballybeg. The Hall is saturated with history, narratives; it is a 'bloody minefield' of stories: Yeats, Hopkins, Cardinal Newman, G.K. Chesterton – all have objects associated with them. The *chaise-longue* 'is Daniel O'Connell', the candlestick 'is George Moore'.[14] Casimir is the anecdotalist of these relics for the benefit of Tom Hoffnung, an American academic who is writing a history of the Catholic Ascendancy families. Casimir exhausts himself on his enthusiastic narration, and in making sure everything is in place. He desires that there be a complete 'congruence' between the past, his narration and the present. He is fiercely active in the latter realm, which is of course that of the play, trying to keep everything under control, fully remembered and explained. Claire, the youngest sister, is getting married, and he rushes about, trying to make sure that everyone is relaxed and happy. Historical forces, presences and personalities have been reduced to objects: Yeats's cushion, Moore's candlestick. Curiously, his sick father's voice is also 'objectified' by the installation of an intercom, so that his needs can be attended to at once in the event of any emergency. That history may not be easily controlled is made powerfully evident at the end of the first Act when Casimir, as he brings a tray out into the garden for an al fresco lunch with the rest of the family, is struck rigid with terror as he hears his father's senile authoritarian blare from the ironically titled 'baby-alarm':

FATHER. Casimir!

(*Casimir jumps to attention; rigid, terrified.*)

CASIMIR. Yes Sir!

FATHER. Come to the library, at once. I wish to speak to you.

(*Casimir now realizes that the voice has come from the speaker.*)

CASIMIR. Christ! . . . Oh-oh-oh my God . . . Ha-ha . . .

Judith, the eldest sister, comes in.

FATHER. At once, Sir! And bring your headmaster's report with you. I intend to get to the bottom of this.
CASIMIR. Judith?
JUDITH. What is it?
CASIMIR. Judith?

(*She goes quickly outside, gets down beside him and takes him in her arms. He is crying now.*)

CASIMIR. I'm sorry – I'm sorry – I'm very sorry.
JUDITH. It's all right.
CASIMIR. I'm very sorry, very sorry.
JUDITH. Everything's all right – everything's fine.

Act II opens with Casimir still gamely trying to create a convergence between the present and the past: he is crawling around on his hands and knees trying to find the old and hidden croquet holes in the lawn. The story that Casimir wants to tell is that the past can be relived, just like that: 'hey presto' it's there again. The trouble is that the past contains within it terror and uncertainty, whereas Casimir's language tries to be cheerful and objective. He is enthusiastic and emphatic about each identification he makes, whether he is naming the Chopin pieces Claire plays, or finding the holes in the overgrown croquet lawn, or naming the places where famous people damaged themselves in Ballybeg Hall.

His narratives are challenged by Hoffnung in the last Act, when the American points out that Casimir could never have seen Yeats, whom he claims to remember so vividly, because Yeats died before Casimir was born. Tom walks off and Casimir, in nightmarish uncertainty, starts to relate to Eamon, his brother-in-law, what they both have just participated in, his father's funeral. But even that now he begins to doubt:

All that happened, didn't it, Eamon? All that happened? Oh, yes, he would have been so gratified.[15]

His uncertainty leads him to tell Eamon a story, yet another story, about the past; this time of a childhood humiliation by his father when Casimir began to realize, he tells Eamon, that he could live within 'smaller, perhaps very confined territories, without exposure to too much hurt'. These are territories, however, that are maintained at great cost, involving, as they do, incessant narratives which try to retain a connection between past and present, inner and outer.

Ballybeg Hall itself is a fiction sustained by the various narratives of the play: Casimir's, even Eamon's, the local man who has married into the family. The latter's devotion to the Big House is, he acknowledges, grounded in 'all that is fawning and forelock-touching and Paddy and shabby and greasy peasant in the Irish character'. That is why, he concludes, 'we were ideal for colonizing'. Judith, who has had the responsibility of looking after the house as well as taking care of father, reveals, at the end, that the house is no longer an economic proposition, nor has it been for a long time. All the complex historical narratives, the ghosts of Newman and Hopkins, are contradicted; but, strangely, at the play's end there is a curious air of jubilant relaxation. The stories are all over; or at least the frantic need to sustain ones that cost dear. The characters are all to move, but as the curtain falls they do not stir. The people in the play have been brought into a secular, non-fantastical world where what is actual is real; and it is no accident that Uncle George has started to speak again after years of silence. They sing at the close:

> They have fitted a slab of granite so grey
> And sweet Alice lies under the stone.[16]

As if to imply that death puts all narratives into perspective. Sombre, enigmatic and curiously hopeful, *Aristocrats* brings a great deal of frenetic invention and interpretation to a strangely pacific conclusion on this minor chord.

In *Faith Healer* (1979) Friel completely aligns his technical concerns to his moral preoccupation with language. Starkly functional, the play consists of four monologues which recount, from their various perspectives, the story of Frank Hardy, faith healer. They all differ; names change, crucial events are told in drastically different ways; the same person is said to be from different countries. Narration is unstable; language and memory distort. How can there be an accurate translation of events, feeling, personality? But all are agreed on one thing: Hardy had a gift, a power to transform actuality, which functioned according to a law of its own. Hardy's art, though not linguistic, answers to a need, mute and unexpressed, in the people he ministers to, although it is as unpredictable and unstable as the narration through which it is conveyed. The audience in the theatre never *see* Hardy performing; thereby avoiding scenes which would be unworkable theatrically, while at the same time reminding them how power is constructed in language.

Hardy's art of healing is put to the test of actuality in Donegal on the night he meets his death. Though it is not linguistic, this art is conveyed to us through language; it is a story which people need. As ever with Friel's theatre the story is tested against other stories and against and in actuality. But this actuality, as conveyed in the words Friel gives Hardy in the last monologue, is both phenomenal and numinous; and entirely mysterious:

> And although I knew that nothing was going to happen, nothing at all, I walked across the yard towards them. And as I walked I became possessed of a strange and trembling intimation: that the whole corporeal world - the cobbles, the trees, the sky, those four malign implements - somehow they had shed their physical reality and had become mere imaginings, and that in all existence there was only myself and the wedding guests. And that intimation in turn gave way to a stronger sense: that even we had ceased to be physical and existed only in spirit, only in the need we had for each other.[17]

Hardy's art, which is going to fail, is tested against actuality. He is attempting, futilely, to translate that interior capacity he has for access to wholeness into the world of phenomena and he won't be able to do it. But that world is spoken of as mysterious in itself, one in which there is no difference between Hardy and his executioners. Friel, here, is creating a language for the ultimate translation of two terms into each other, a complete and secular sharing, a communion purged of liturgy.

Faith Healer, at the close, envisages a crossing of boundaries, of the limits between consciousness and other(s). In *Translations* (1980) the crossing of boundaries is explored in linguistic and cultural terms. Technique is most carefully attuned to function: a major source of pleasure in the play is the invigorating quasi-illusion Friel creates about the language the characters are

supposed to be speaking. Apart from Latin and some Greek the only language the audience hear spoken is English, yet they accept a convention that for most of the play the language they are hearing is meant to represent Irish. So the audience are engaged in a translation game where they have all the pleasure and none of the effort.

The action revolves around the Ordnance Survey of the 1830s, during which Irish place names were translated into English and Ireland was mapped and surveyed. Lieutenant Yolland, the young English officer, and Maire, the local girl, cross boundaries in their affection for each other; but Yolland has identified completely with Ireland, the Irish language and Irish tradition. One of the thematic cruxes of the play comes, appropriately enough, when Owen, the hedge schoolmaster's son, and Yolland, are working on the translation of the name of a crossroads, Tobair Vree. Old Hugh, Owen's father, has just left, on a wonderful exit line where he says that 'it can happen that a civilisation can be imprisoned in a linguistic contour which no longer matches the landscape of . . . fact!'[18]

That statement is a very clear-sighted summary of what has happened. The landscape of fact is the one that is going to be created when Yolland and Owen have done their work. The language is changing, but Yolland is romantically attached to the old forms. Owen, just as realistic as his father, but no more so, points out that no one, apart from him, knows how the crossroads Tobair Vree got its name: a man called Brian, who had cancer, fell into a holy well *near* the place where the crossroads is and drowned; but the well is now gone, and no one remembers the man.

Translation, the carrying over of the depth of association, is a difficult business, because languages have quite different systems of awareness. People may not, but languages do. Maire and Yolland wave at each other across the fields, but the fields that lie between them are the fields of language, of discourse, and it takes a great deal of work to make the translation, before a field day is possible. They rush headlong, at each other and to disaster. Joyce gave it to the fatuous Englishman Haines to say in *Ulysses*: 'it seems history is to blame';[19] but Joyce knew, as does Friel, that the difficulty lies with language. Far from being a lament for the disappearance of the Irish language, *Translations* embodies an awareness of cultural differences, and the tragedies and violence they generate. It is an unsentimental analysis of the politics of language.

The Communication Cord (1982) is the farcical re-enactment of these concerns, as if Friel had felt the need to emphasize them by repetition, variation and modulation into an outrageously comic mode.

The central image of the play is the set itself, an 'authentic' Irish country cottage, rebuilt to look exactly like the real thing. Like Ballybeg Hall this cottage is eloquent: it has a wealth of historical association, and rootedness; it is, in the words of Senator Doctor Donovan, 'the touchstone . . . the apotheosis'. It strikes a chord in every Irishman's breast; and it is the umbilical cord connecting us to the past. The trouble is everybody is using it for his (or her) own ends. The plot has the required complexity of farce, but to put it simply, everyone is confused and ends up, literally, in the dark when the light is blown out. The Senator, curious about the old-world implements attached to the wall, manages to lock a cow halter around his neck, thereby well and truly tying himself back into the umbilical cord. The confusion and mayhem arise because of the opportunity for exploitation the languages of tradition provide. The Senator is freed but at the end of the play as the young academic linguist, Tim, is making love to Claire ('Maybe silence is the perfect discourse'[20]) their friend Jack also gets the cow halter around his neck. At the final black-out the whole house, the prison-house of language, is falling down.

Language itself and the traditions, the 'images of the past'[21] it embodies may enslave us: the communication cord, the means of transmitting messages, the entire network of understanding, can become the halter of victimage. There is in Friel a profound distrust of language, because he understands its power.

In *Making History* (1988) O'Neill is someone who tries to resist this power. His situation is that of someone who is surrounded by people with very strong languages, who are trying to translate him into their terminology or into one they recognize. He doesn't have a stable language himself. He speaks with an English accent for most of the play, except in moments of anger, when he breaks into his native Tyrone. He is Irish but is also a product of the English and European High Renaissance, having been brought up in the Sidney House at Penshurst, deliberately idealized in the play. He marries an English girl, Mabel, to the chagrin of

Lombard and O'Donnell. Lombard, the Archbishop, has *his* version of O'Neill which is determined by the Roman Catholic politics of the Counter-Reformation; as has O'Donnell, who is deliberately depicted as a patriotic enthusiast. O'Neill wants to stay out of these 'cords' although he does want to retain some inalienable right to be Irish in the country which is his. The trouble with that is that none of the available models will quite do. However, affectionate as he is in his memories of the pleasures and culture of Penshurst he cannot forget the racial slur delivered by Sir Henry Sidney, the evening of his departure, after all the years of generosity and kindness, when he was again, even if only for an instant, the 'Fox O'Neill', the traitorous unreliable Irishman.[22] But this does not mean that O'Neill is a victim of romantic or atavistic impulses. In a passage where, using a typical Renaissance trope, he translates various friends and allies into the language of flowers, he figures O'Donnell as borage and therefore as 'inclined to excessive courage, even recklessness'. This tropic set piece intervenes in another, larger discourse, which explores and attempts to translate the networks of opposition between Irish and English culture, 'two deeply opposed civilizations'. Maguire of Fermanagh is in rebellion and pressure is mounting on O'Neill to join him. Harry Hovedon, his secretary, asks: 'are you going to betray your old friend, Maguire?'

> O'NEILL. (*Roars*) 'Betray my old – !' For Christ's sake don't you start using language like that to me, Harry! (*Softly*) Maguire is a fool. He's determined to rise up and nobody can stop him and he'll be hacked to pieces and his people routed and his country planted with Upstarts and safe men. It happened to Fitzmaurice. And McDermott. And Nugent. And O'Reilly. And O'Connor. And O'Kelly. Their noble souls couldn't breathe another second under 'tyranny'. And where are they now? Wiped out. And what did they accomplish? Nothing.[23]

They are 'casualties of language', of words like 'tyranny', 'nobility', 'soul'. But the irony of all of this is that immediately after this outburst O'Donnell, the enthusiast, rushes in, afire with excitement, with the news that the Spanish have, at last, agreed to invade, with the consequence that O'Neill himself will indeed join Maguire.

The rebellion is crushed, and O'Neill and O'Donnell are, in the second Act, isolated and on the run. Out in the Sperrins O'Neill writes his submission to the Queen and a most powerful and moving scene occurs when he recites the submission to O'Donnell, a submission couched in the most elaborate and courtly English, a language of total abnegation, self-surrender and self-obliteration:

> Most sorrowfully imploring her gracious commiseration and appealing only to her princely clemency, without presuming to justify my unloyal proceedings against her sacred majesty.[24]

O'Donnell, at first, enjoys this recitation and makes fun of the baroque extremism of the language of surrender but the mood darkens as it comes home to him how real, how *true* this language now is. There is now a perfect 'congruence' between word and situation. This language of victimage describes a situation which has come about because one culture, one language, has defeated another. So extreme is O'Neill's self-excoriation that one becomes aware that Friel is alive to the possibility that after defeat self-laceration may begin to have its own terrible attractions. The victim longs for the cord to tighten round his neck. Language may be not only a prison-house but a torture chamber where the complex transactions between victim and oppressor include masochism, self-disgust, self-contempt, acquiescence.

Lombard is a busy *naïf*. He wants to write the history of O'Neill as a champion of the Counter-Reformation, and as an Irish patriot. He is not interested in the 'truth', which O'Neill insists he must write. He wants to tell 'a story' which will make O'Neill a hero for 'a colonized people on the brink of extinction'.[25] O'Neill protests that he wants the truth, but when Lombard offers him the chance to make any changes in the outline he cannot or will not. He responds with silence.

The 'truth' the play has revealed is that there are different sets of cultural awareness which are conveyed in different languages: this truth relies upon the totality of those languages the play has set before us, its structure an arrangement of fragile interlinkings over the gulf between cultures and individuals. The end of the play is powerful in its unremitting focus on a man who is distrustful of all language, which means he is trustful of no one, even Harry, who sells a pair of shoes to buy a cheap bottle of Chianti for his drunken master.

Friel's theatre is one in which language is held up for scrutiny. It reveals the power it has over people as individuals; and it shows that intensity and passion are, more often than not, created by language. He was drawn to the theatre because there the audience can see very clearly those disjunctions between the language someone displays and the contexts in which it is transacted. It is the place for realizing the *lack* of congruence between the word and the situation. The languages people use (or, more provocatively, by which they are used) embody sets of cultural awareness, which are translated or transacted as they speak. Friel's theatre is a laboratory of translations of different cultural and individual awarenesses interacting in a framework in which each strand is separate; but together, these strands are the interwoven form (the text or tissue) which stands before us in the theatre, just like the structure of twigs the little boy creates in 'Among the Ruins'. We are; and we are in the void, in the theatre, looking at that frail luminous structure which clings, with unremitting fidelity, to the formations of recognizable social life. But it is not social realism that Friel is interested in; he is obsessed by its making and unmaking in language.

Friel's theatre is concerned with many issues, such as, for instance, cultural identity or conflict. But these do not have a static presence in his work: they are taken up into the weave of the various languages that the plays hold in tension, and they become mobile, elusive, and all the more interesting for that. They are brought into the realization of the intervoicings of the plays but they still retain complexity, a 'hiddenness', despite the fact that they are being explored. So that there is a sense in Friel's theatre of people or cultures *not* being reduced to formulae, an air, if one wishes, of spiritual generosity.

There is, as has been said, in Friel, a distrust of language, a preference for silence; yet he approaches language with a kind of reverence too. His dialogue is impacted with awareness; and he writes an English cadenced like Burke's, and like his, one attentive to the need to control while at the same time retaining the potential for surprise. His English is also spare and suspicious, written by someone intensely aware of the presence of a hidden language in modern Ireland: Irish.

13

SEAMUS HEANEY

'Leaving everything'[1]

A technical and emotional problem for the artist is getting the right angle on his material. If it's a botched stroke then the stone will split all kinds of ways revealing sheets of useless contours, interesting maybe, but distracting. Or the artist will find himself wandering in a wasteland of association and anxiety, inventing, circumventing. When Samuel Beckett wrote of contemporary Irish poetry in the 1930s, and praised the work of Denis Devlin, what he liked in Devlin was that he had a 'mind aware of its luminaries' and avoided the fashionable Cuchulainoid clichés of the day. The 'centre', Beckett mordantly says, 'isn't that kind of girl'.[2] It is not possible to strike into the centre by preoccupations which take you off out into the circumference, blethering away about Fionn and the Fenians; the wet weather of the west, lost heroes, lost heifers, while all the time the centre remains unvisited, unsaid.

Beckett became a master of circling around the centre, because the bleak conviction of his own writing is that there can be no saying of the centre, or that any such saying is in itself a fiction created to appease the restless mind by closure. Beckett's technical and emotional problem was to find forms of language which would remain faithful to the desire to speak of what matters without rushing in and usurping the secrecies of the centre.

Seamus Heaney is very different. From start to finish he wants to speak of the source; and he wants his language to have the weight, drive and authority that poetry originating in a source should have. His conviction is that such a poetry will be fresh, powerful and strong, and capable of giving pleasure and delight to a community, for whom the source is culturally and emotionally relevant. It is necessary, then, to get the angle, or the line of approach, right. It's not often possible to approach the material head-on; skill, craft and instinct are required in order to strike the seams that will open into the rich interiors. The dedicatory poem to 'Clearances' in *The Haw Lantern* says it all. The poem and the sequence are in memory of his mother Margaret Kathleen Heaney:

> She taught me what her uncle once taught her:
> How easily the biggest coal block split
> If you got the grain and hammer angled right.
>
> The sound of that relaxed alluring blow,
> Its co-opted and obliterated echo,
> Taught me to hit, taught me to loosen,
>
> Taught me between the hammer and the block
> To face the music. Teach me now to listen,
> To strike it rich behind the linear black.[3]

But what is the richness behind the linear black of the lines on the page? What wealth does it open into? 'Thatcher', an early poem from *Door into the Dark,* evokes the kind of golden world that Renaissance art claimed, often, to deliver:

> Couchant for days on sods above the rafters
> He shaved and flushed the butts, stitched all together
> Into a sloped honeycomb, a stubble patch
> And left them gaping at his Midas touch.[4]

Sir Philip Sidney writes:

> Nature never set forth the earth in so rich tapestry, as divers poets have done, neither with so pleasant rivers, fruitful trees, sweet smelling flowers, nor whatsoever else may make the too much loved earth more lovely. Her world is brazen, the poets only deliver a golden . . .[5]

Things are transformed, translated, through the touch of art; they are brought into conformity with some standard of perfection, they are measured against it. Such a golden measuring has deep attractions for Heaney, which he reveals when writing of the Polish poet Zbigniew Herbert in *The Government of the Tongue.* Herbert delights in the strict exact geometry of Greek architecture, which was 'organised in the sun' itself and was a reflection in the temporal world of the '*lucidus ordo* – an external order of light and balance'.[6] The thatcher in the poem shapes light, brings the ordinary into correspondence with an exact and exacting geometry, which is also functional.

But the title of the book from which the poem comes is *Door into the Dark*, and we are much more accustomed to Heaney as the poet of darkness, water, bog and shadow, than as a celebrant of light, clarity and geometry. The two things of course belong together. The black seam opens to richness and to Midas; and in some hidden way release and delight belong together with suffering and penance.

But we are going ahead of the story. From the start Heaney's writing is concerned with the gaining of access; access to tradition, place, language, the self, the collective, the tribe, the dead, woman and so on. Any artist will feel that there is a buried world to which he or she wants to give voice, and when the right words start to come there will be an experience of relief, of rightness, of (to use a word no longer much in critical favour) justice. In *Preoccupations* he writes of how he felt when he had written the poem 'Digging' in 1964:

> This was the first place where I felt I had done more than make an arrangement of words: I felt that I had let down a shaft into real life. The facts and surfaces of this thing were true, but more important, the excitement that came from naming them gave me a kind of insouciance and a kind of confidence. I didn't care who thought what about it.[7]

('Insouciance', by the way, is one of Heaney's favoured words: it counters another one that haunts him – 'obedience'.) He tells us that he felt that he had made contact with 'reality', a subterranean reality that gave a charge to the detail of the surface, in the same way that the intentness of the water diviner is charged in the poem about him by the drive from beneath. The real life is underneath, stored in richness, structured and lovely. The thatcher's 'sloped honeycomb' reveals a golden world because his structure is alive to the patterns hidden in things, the *lucidus ordo*. Getting the angle right matters because if you do you strike it rich; you open the seam. But if the reality of the gold light is subterranean, then the approach will not be obvious. The approach will be ritualized and organized, and will work against the given nature of language and experience: hence verses (from Latin *versus*, meaning against) and form. Poetry pulls against the inertia of the given; it is a digging in its effort and virtue; it is a travelling away from the known to the hidden; and it involves a kind of search, pilgrimage or quest.

The first volume, *Death of a Naturalist,* chronicles the dying away of the conventional mind with its sets of attitudes: that things are out there, that the world divides into good and evil, that bad dreams are just bad dreams, and that fear is a symptom of immaturity, to be set aside with other childish things. The writing is looking for trouble, for difficulty; or, rather, wishes to acknowledge trouble and difficulty. 'Personal Helicon' uncovers the instinct for depth and self-discovery, and speaks of the way poetry may search out the interiors of the personality, but the activity is seen as dangerous, obsessive, and at odds with conventional wisdom:

> As a child they could not keep me from wells
> And old pumps with buckets and windlasses . . .
> . . . one
> Was scaresome for there, out of ferns and tall
> Foxgloves, a rat slapped across my reflection.
>
> Now, to pry into roots, to finger slime,
> To stare big-eyed Narcissus into some spring
> Is beneath adult dignity. I rhyme
> To see myself, to set the darkness echoing.[8]

Echo. Its resonance sounds again and again in Heaney, and the notion of echo encapsulates something very important to him; that is, if the right note is struck, the correct tone found, then the material itself, all the buried knowledge of tradition, all the intricate weave of language, will respond and thereby give authority, justice and '*steadfastness*' to the articulation.[9]

Towards the end of *Door into the Dark* there is one of the most moving poems in all of Heaney, 'The Given Note'. A fiddler goes out on to 'the most westerly Blasket' to find the real thing, the ethereal music, which he gets out of the strange, confused 'loud weather' of the night. Others follow and can't hear the music; but he brings back 'the whole thing'. Now

> The house throbbed like his full violin.
> So whether he calls it spirit music
> Or not, I don't care. He took it
> Out of wind off mid-Atlantic,

Still, he maintains, from nowhere
It comes off the bow gravely,
Rephrases itself into the air.[10]

The aspect of this lovely poem-music I want to concentrate on at the moment is the idea that to 'take' music of this quality of resonance you have to go out of the ordinary way of things; the artist needs to go at a tangent to the main stream. The 'broad road of the journalist', in Yeats's phrase, will not take the artist to the source; it won't lead to those darknesses where the tradition still transmits its signals, where the ancients interrogate the present. 'Stay clear of all processions,' Simon Sweeney says in 'Station Island';[11] 'keep at a tangent' Joyce advises in the same poem.[12] To get at the 'whole thing' needs resolution and the courage to search out the connections between the personal world of feeling and the larger cultural and tribal one. Too close a concentration on the personal leads to atrophy and solipsism; too entranced a subjection to the tribal means that the energy is dispersed over too wide a range. For authority the personal and tribal must be reconciled:

Once, clearing a drain
I shovelled up livery slicks
Till the water gradually ran

Clear on its old floor,
Under the humus and roots
This smooth weight. I labour
Towards it still. It holds and gluts.[13]

'I labour' and 'it' holds and gluts; the water runs clear on the old floor. It is sometimes argued that Heaney's transactions with the tribal are merely a fascination with the myth-kitty, and that by indulging this he is opportunistically identifying with the stereotypes of Irish cultural nationalism. Such a view seems wholly to miss the point, which can be stated simply: Heaney *is* engaged upon a cultural and tribal exploration; he *is* testing out his cultural inheritance to see where the significant deposits are located; but he is *not* engaged upon a mindless submission to the old tradition or the goddess or whatever. Heaney is interested in individuation, in the way that Jung explained it, as being a holding in balance of the sense of the self with the sense of larger cultural archetypes or entities. Again, it should be said, Heaney is concerned with balance rather than passionate intensity for its own sake; the *lucidus ordo* rather than the savage god. This enterprise is difficult and needs to be pursued with caution, intelligence and utmost precision. In this area of psychic and cultural excavation blunders are extremely dangerous and presumption may literally be mortal.

The poem just quoted, 'Bann Clay', precedes, in *Door into the Dark*, the poem 'Bogland', which announces a theme which is to dominate Heaney's writing for years, that of lost and neglected areas of memory and understanding, tribal and psychological: the ground itself is kind, black butter

> Melting and opening under-foot,
> Missing its last definition
> By millions of years.
> They'll never dig coal here,
>
> Only the water-logged trunks
> Of great firs, soft as pulp.
> Our pioneers keep striking
> Inwards and downwards.
>
> Every layer they strip
> Seems camped on before.
> The bogholes might be Atlantic seepage.
> The wet centre is bottomless.[14]

This knowing, this realization, is not stereotypical; it is secret, haunted, and the writing conveys the atmosphere of strenuous effort applied to a hidden secrecy, now opening at last. Those engaged in this activity are 'pioneers'; they are not reciters of the litanies handed out by schools, courts or churches. They work.

The title of *Wintering Out* was meant to be 'comfortless enough, but with a notion of survival in it'.[15] The volume itself carries a powerful atmosphere of exposure and bleakness. Objects, places and people stand out, are foregrounded, in a strange and resonant presence. Always there is the sense of difficulty at getting at the core of the thing, the scene, the person, the situation. The poems themselves use the short curt line that Heaney has made his own device for meditative presence, to create a tense quatrain that is a kind of bardic modernist stanza. These densely weighted and measured syllabics are seeking tradition, not affirming it. There are no 'oak groves' left, as he writes in the poem 'Bog Oak'. He is aware that Celtic tradition linked the oak wood to inspiration and healing (Druid is linked with 'doire', meaning oak, which gave its name to Derry), but all that order is gone, well gone, and the person who seeks intimations of it courts the risk of romantic infatuation and presumption as well as facing into a great deal of hard work:

> The softening ruts
> lead back to no
> 'oak groves', no
> cutters of mistletoe
> in the green clearings.
> *Perhaps I just make out*
> *Edmund Spenser.* (my italics)[16]

Spenser was amongst the first of the linguistic imperialists, to use a crude terminology, who equated the Gaelic language with sedition, and who argued for the establishment of the English language, understanding very clearly the total interrelation between discourse and power.

So, for Heaney to search out a live connection with this old world he has to go against the given discourses, hence the syllabic art of these terse quatrains, working against the confident drive of English iambic. For this reason does *Wintering Out* contain that group of poems which search out the inner feel of place-names ('Broagh', 'Toome' and so on) which are like divination mantras to get in touch with the charge of the original, trying to bypass Spenser and his language. Heaney attempts to follow the trail of the 'servant boy', in the poem of that name, and in a superb and daring rhythmic move he repeats the phrase 'your trail', as if trying to catch the trace of the servant boy's 'meaning' as he moves from 'haggard to stable':

> Old work-whore, slave-
> blood, who stepped fair hills
> under each bidder's eye
>
> and kept your patience
> and your counsel, now
> you draw me into
> your trail. Your trail
> broken from haggard to stable.[17]

He puts himself to school to these paths, these dark tracks, so that he may find a way into, so that he may 'untousle'

> a first dewy path
> into the summer grazing.[18]

His own learning and the given discourses are no use. Heaney's poetic procedure involves a kind of deschooling of the 'world-schooled ear' used to the usual confabulations. He wants to

> Cock my ear
> at an absence.[19]

This simple statement will flood into realizations which are metaphysical, in particular in *Seeing Things* (1991). For the time being he knows he's looking out for signs to pluck out of the emptiness. Towards the end of the poem just noted, 'Gifts of Rain', the river Moyola itself is evoked, the river of Heaney's childhood. But not just the river; the sound of the river, and the river's name; all are worked into the movement of the verse which is itself a rediscovery of the river's presence, a poetic event reconciling personal feeling and historical tension:

> The tawny guttural water
> spells itself: Moyola
> is its own score and consort.

It plays itself and is translating itself now into the realizing capacity of Heaney's openwork meditative procedure. This creativity is a deschooling of mind and sensibility so that a new and different attentiveness can (re-)emerge:

> bedding the locale
> in the utterance,
> reed music, an old chanter
>
> breathing its mists
> through vowels and history.

We hear an old music in these lines, a sense of permanence sounds in the continuo of the assonantal movements. It is as if we hear a shift in the harmonics over the bass tone of vowellings in the drift of consonants, and nowhere more so than in the lovely modulation on the word 'history', where the 'st' sound drifts forward more emphatically than in 'mists' because of the open 'o' which follows. And then:

A swollen river,
A mating call of sound
rises to pleasure me, Dives,
hoarder of common ground.[20]

Something complete happens here. The poem is a total event in itself. But *what* happens? Crudely, perhaps, the Moyola, in its original strangeness, and the network of relationships in which it is bedded, is redelivered, is *translated* into English. The world of language the poem creates is complete, is 'golden'. But such an activity involves a deschooling, involves a departure from the fixed, tired ways of seeing and knowing. In this way, poetry may be properly thought of as the 'breath and finer spirit' of knowledge, in Shelley's phrase, in that it vivifies understanding by movement. This Moyola poem, 'Gifts of Rain', is, fittingly, a prelude to two poems which mediate placenames into depth, vividness and complex association; and these are followed by 'Oracle', a tiny but massively significant piece and one which is also very moving. The oracle is the willow, in which Heaney used to hide as a child on the family farm, Mossbawn. In *Preoccupations* he writes: 'In that tight cleft, you sensed the entrance of light and branches, you were a little Atlas shouldering it all, a little Cernunnos pivoting a world of antlers.'[21] The poem reads:

Hide in the hollow trunk
Of the willow tree,
its listening familiar,
until as usual, they
echo your name
across the fields.
You can hear them
draw the poles of stiles
as they approach
calling you out:
small mouth and ear
in a woody cleft,
lobe and larynx
of the mossy places.[22]

Again, the world of listening is hidden, away from the big strenuous voices. The oracle is in a neglected spot, and the pathways to the places where recoveries may be made are overgrown; they have to be 'untousled', or as in 'Midnight':

> The pads are lost or
> Retrieved by small vermin.

Who are the small vermin? Fickle commentators; crude agitators for cultural probity? Whoever they are they

> listen and scent.
> Nothing is panting, lolling,
> Vapouring. The tongue's
> Leashed in my throat.[23]

Watch the introduction of the first person, its only usage in the poem. The tongue is governed by loss, and by a sense that to recapture the lost 'pads' (another one of Heaney's favoured words) may, simply, be impossible. A pathway connects point A to point B. Point A is where the moving intelligence of a culture may be at any given time; point B is the source, the origin; the movement along the pathway, the pad, is a movement of translation, along which the living moment vibrates with the trouble and touch of the past, the dead. The tongue is leashed, in 'Midnight'; there is nothing to be said; and then the Tollund Man surfaces, from prehistory, a gift from archaeology, but also a reward for persistence and tense waiting. A spirit of insouciance breathes in the lift and swing of the opening line of that, now well-known, poem:

> Some day I will go to Aarhus.

He makes his vow to visit Silkenburg where these Iron Age sacrificial victims are on display, and at the close of the poem he imagines himself driving (nearly always a sign in Heaney of definite connection between point A and point B, between moment and source) through the places associated with Iron Age Celtic ritual in Denmark, saying the names, not knowing the tongue, but reaching through to some kind of core:

> Tollund, Grabaulle, Nebelgard,
> Watching the pointing hands
> Of country people,

Not knowing their tongue.

Out there in Jutland
In the old man-killing parishes
I will feel lost,
Unhappy and at home.[24]

'Out there', beyond schooling, beyond the limits of the given discourses, he will be at home. In *Preoccupations* he tells us that he felt that when he had written this poem he knew that if he was not deeply in earnest about what he was saying he was invoking dangers for himself.[25] The attempt to follow the trail of the servant boy, to 'untousle' the old pads, had to be made, but that meant it had to be objectified in poetry. In *The Government of the Tongue* Heaney quotes Jung on the process whereby an insoluble conflict may be overcome by outgrowing it, and by developing a 'new level of consciousness':

> One certainly does feel the affect and is tormented by it, yet at the same time one is aware of a higher consciousness looking on which prevents one from becoming identified with the affect, a consciousness which regards the 'affect' as an object, and can say 'I know that I suffer'.[26]

Heaney equates the higher level of consciousness with poetry, and Jung's 'affect' with 'insoluble conflict'. The 'affect' in 'The Tollund Man' is the emotional knot, the 'insoluble conflict', which violence creates. The process of the poetry is the means of the objectification of this conflict; the naming of names ('Grabaulle, Nebelgard') gives a 'sad freedom', which translates something of an ancient sadness. Somehow a continuum of human suffering is established; an atmosphere of pity is engaged; and the sombre event of the poem is alive both to past and present.

In *Memories, Dreams, Reflections* Jung makes it clear that one aspect of the process of individuation, the aim of which is to achieve a balanced psychic freedom, is that whereby the person finds the courage to speak out his or her own view of things and to trust the guidance of his or her own dreams, nightmares and fears. Taking your own path requires courage and daring. Imagine Heaney trying to explain to, say, the average literary critic in 1972 that he was planning a series of poems about bogs and about their powers of preservation! And then saying that the whole point of such an enterprise was to find emblems of continuity, while at the same time maintaining a steely awareness that continuity may well be an illusory concept. Surely (one can hear the voices) the last thing an Irish poet should be writing about now is bogs? And talk of a tradition, core and all of that went out with Corkery. Cop on, man; cop out.

But Heaney did not and does not. He kept his ear cocked at an 'absence'; and his mind alert for the 'sunlit absence'[27] even though there were no longer any 'oak groves'. He would (to use a Heaney-type optative) follow the advice of the 'swimming tongue' of the longship in 'North', a tongue ungoverned and confident:

> Compose in darkness.
> Expect aurora borealis
> in the long foray
> but no cascade of light.
>
> Keep your eye clear
> as the bleb of the icicle,
> trust the feel of what nubbed treasure
> your hands have known.[28]

Trust in what *you* know, this tongue says; selve yourself. Keep out of the thronged dictions that crowd in on you. Keep to the 'abrupt self', in the phrase of Hopkins, a poet he admires; or as the same poet has it in 'As Kingfishers Catch Fire', each 'mortal thing'

> Selves – goes itself; myself it speaks and spells.[29]

The drive of the individuating self in *North* is very powerful. He has now gone to the comfortless scholium of *Wintering Out*; he has learnt the technique of fearful open attention; and the ambition in *North* is to bring the self and the collective unconscious into some kind of harmonious relation, and at the same time and in the same breath translate past and hidden memory out of absence into the immediacy of linguistic play in the verse itself. There is little doubt that Heaney knew precisely what he was doing ('My eye has known what my hand did,' in the words of Robert Lowell, one of his master spirits[30]) in all of this. *North* was a response to the fact of violence in Ireland in the

1970s, but one which complicated that response psychically. Nowhere in this volume is there any identification with one camp or the other, as has sometimes been argued. The hurt is there, and the hurt and anger are felt in specific ways, but the poetry achieves objectivity.

Consider that weird and strange poem 'Bone Dreams', exactly the poem Heaney should or could not write if he is obscurely or otherwise an apologist for nationalist violence, for it is a love poem *to England*. A bone is found, then it is flung at England (Heaney's bony quatrains fired at the English lyric). But the poem turns to meditate on itself, on language, specifically the English language, starting from the word 'bone':

> Bone-house;
> a skeleton
> in the tongue's
> old dungeons.
>
> I push back
> through dictions
> Elizabethan canopies.
> Normal devices,
>
> the erotic may flowers
> of Provence
> and the ivied Latins
> of churchmen
>
> to the scop's
> twang, the iron
> flash of consonants
> cleaving the line.[31]

This sudden switchback, to Anglo-Saxon, the 'scop's twang', is a celebration of the layered richness of English. The poem, as its concentration intensifies, becomes a free space for the Irish bone-thrower to lie down with English in a 'dream-bower', a 'love-nest':

> Come back past
> philology and kennings,
> re-enter memory
> where the bone's lair

is a love-nest
in the grass.
I hold my lady's head
like a crystal

and ossify myself
by gazing; I am screes
on her escarpments,
a chalk giant

carved upon her downs.
Soon my hands, on the sunken
fosse of her spine
move towards the passes.

V

And we end up
cradling each other
between the lips
of an earthwork.

There is a conflict between Ireland and England; it often seems insoluble to the mind trained in the discourses of politics, negotiation, opposition. It may be, in fact, insoluble. But a poem such as this witnesses to a space human creativity can create where history is set aside and the problem is viewed objectively. The 'affect', to use Jung's term, is there, but viewed from a 'higher level of consciousness', poetry.

At the centre of *North*, taking pride of place in the collection, is 'Kinship', Heaney's paean to bog-knowledge. It is an estranging poem, and is meant to be forbidding. Listen to the complex oral ogham of the opening consonantal music of plosives and stops:

Kinned by hieroglyphic
peat on a spreadfield
to the strangled victim
the love nest in the bracken,

I step through origins.[32]

This place, of dark secrets, incisions, process, ritual, victimage, cannot be sounded by the 'naked eye'. Sheer looking will not do. The gaze is needed, so the process of moving along the strange pads will realize itself and the 'outback of the mind'[33] may be approached. In this place the water 'lisps'; when an old turf-spade is found, 'hidden under bracken', the green fog of moss around it speaks when he lifts it up:

As I raised it
the soft lips of growth
muttered and split,
a tawny rut
opening at my feet.

And later:

This is the vowel of earth
dreaming its root.[34]

The bog is translating itself into language, into an English that has been opened out to accommodate glimmerings of Celtic origin. Tacitus, who wrote of the Celts, is invoked towards the close:

And Tacitus,

observe how I make my grove
on an old crannog
piled by the fearful dead:
a desolate peace . . .

Come back to this
'island of the ocean'
where nothing will suffice.
Read the inhumed faces

of casualty and victim;
report us fairly,
how we slaughter
for the common good

and shave the heads
of the notorious,
how the goddess swallows
our love and terror.[35]

Tacitus is invoked, and the shade of Yeats is here as well ('when may it suffice': 'Now shall I make my soul'), but the point of these allusions is not mere referential thickening; they are part of the movement that the poem enacts. Heaney wants to gain access to the outback of the mind, which involves working through this strange bog-ritual. The aim is poetic objectivity, by means of which the 'affect' of Ireland's tormented history and violent present, can be distanced. Personal feeling and tribal archetypes are drawn together. Neglected hiding places are visited with unexpected traces of emotion; and Heaney's tense quatrains are enlivened with sudden and sharp recognitions. The act is a balancing act between the individual and collective, the imagination and communal emotion. The voice moves hesitantly, but full of slow deliberate authority as well; it is a living voice seeking the knowledge and wisdom of the dead. And this is why Tacitus and Yeats (and others, too) appear. Poetry is a right kind of judging; the felt experience of justice is the movement of speech. Only the dead can judge because their collectivity is, it may be hoped, outside the clamant self-interest of the living, who are full of strife and self-justification. 'Wisdom', wrote Yeats, 'is a property of the dead';[36] or at least the notion that it is so is a good stick to beat the presumptuous assertions of the living with. Heaney seeks conference with the dead. This hankering for their impeccable tribunal is what leads him into bogland, into Dante, into the tale of Sweeney, and into the pilgrimage of *Station Island,* one more pathway to the 'outback'.

All of this sombre gravity and thoughtfulness is not conducted without wit and self-mockery. He knows he's like

> a weeping willow
> inclined to
> the appetites of gravity.[37]

It is possible to be greedy for seriousness. And in 'Hercules and Antaeus' he knows he has bequeathed 'all' his mental equipment to 'elegists'; a forlorn but bitterly satisfying teat to suck. Sadness has its morose delectation, as Stephen Dedalus knew. He craves, too, a more active style, something more rapid than the gloomy syllabics of the *North* quatrains:

> I sit here with a pestering
> Drouth for words at once both gaff and bail
>
> To lure the tribal shoals to epigram
> And order. I believe any of us
> Could draw the line through bigotry and sham
> Given the right line *aere perennius.*[38]

The 'right line' is a line of poetry, and of tradition: we speak of someone in the line of Pope, or Dryden or Donne. It is also the line that separates true from false, a line of judgement, of geometry, from point A to point B. It may help create lucidity, adduce the *lucidus ordo* of Herbert. It may be a line of pure clear light, quick with awareness, unlike the weighty dictions of most of the *North* poems, fretted with gravity, turning towards the dead for tribunal.

In 'Oysters', the poem which opens *Field Work*, a new tone is struck, a clear light enters, but wished for, not achieved:

> I saw damp panniers disgorge
> The frond-lipped, brine-strung
> Glut of privilege
>
> And was angry that my trust could not repose
> In the clear light, like poetry or freedom
> Leaning in from the sea. I ate the day
> Deliberately, that its tang
> Might quicken me all into verb, pure verb.[39]

The verb connects subject and object, A to B; this poetry wishes for an increased activity, a poetry of clear light and freedom, 'pure verb'.

Field Work contains a number of exquisitely worked elegies, each one an attempt at a proper relation between the living voice and the dead friend, a verbal adjustment between subject and object. Dante prefaces the elegy to a cousin, Colum McCartney, and in the Lowell elegy he writes

> The way we are living,
> timorous or bold,
> will have been our life[40]

the proverbial terseness of which gets at the stark truth at the core of Dante's vision. What we are doing is going to be what we will have been. Poetry's judgement is to set the concerns of life against the fact of death and test them for reality. Death interrogates the complacency of the living, so those who do not know how to 'eat the day/deliberately' do not have clear light. Yeats, in 'The Leaders of the Crowd' says that the lamp of Truth shines 'from the tomb'.[41]

The 'Glanmore Sonnets', the centrepiece of *Field Work*,

celebrate the day's process, and the variousness of living, but the pleasure they register, 'deliberately', is linked to the fact that the poet, in choosing the sonnet form and in praising marriage by a form closely associated with the fury of erotic love, is going against the grain.

Biographically, too, the time at Glanmore was a new departure for Heaney along his own pathways. He left his post at Queen's, went south, out of the northern tangle and complexity into the risky exposure of being a full-time writer. He was ploughing his own ground:

> Vowels ploughed into other: opened ground . . .
>
> Now the good life would be to cross a field
> And art a paradigm of earth new from the lathe
> Of ploughs. My lea is deeply tilled.
> Old ploughsocks gorge the subsoil of each sense.[42]

'Gorge' is used in a way which alludes to its uncommon meaning of 'to plough' (St George is the ploughman), so the ploughshares of tradition (poetic form itself, the trope of the 'good life', the *locus amoenus*) open the subsoil of sense, being, daily life. The steady hand, which is the sign of the individual will, holds the pull of the craft into the depth of tradition, thereby aligning language to history, *translating* history into a renamed reality. Language, tradition, will, emotion: all go together here in an activity of verse which is sheer blessing. The writing is packed with awareness.

In 'Field Work', the sequence which gives its title to the volume, he returns to the 'outback' of the mind, to meditate upon a totally open vowel, the vowel 'O', through which may breathe mist and history. This space is open, a prelude to the astonishing free spaces of the later books; it is the boghole too, but lifted out of the muddy strata into the air for the spirit to whistle through. It is, also, a vaccination mark on the arm of a woman:

> Where the sally tree went pale in every breeze,
> where the perfect eye of the nesting blackbird watched,
> where one fern was always green
>
> I was standing watching you
> take the pad from the gatehouse at the crossing
> and reach to take a white wash off the whins.

I could see the vaccination mark
stretched on your upper arm, and smell the coal smell
of the train that comes between us, a slow goods,

waggon after waggon full of big-eyed cattle.[43]

This is a writing that is totally open and totally attentive. Deliberately the pace is slowed so the full scene opens out to the eye of the mind. It has a quality of presence related to what Rilke described in the ninth 'Duino Elegy':

Are we, perhaps, *here* just for saying: House,
Bridge, Fountain, Gate, Jug, Fruit tree, Window, –
possibly: Pillar, Tower? . . . but for *saying*, remember,
oh, for such saying never the things themselves
hoped so intensely to be.[44]

In the next section of the sequence the mark of the vowel is on a woman's thigh:

But your vaccination mark is on your thigh,
an O that's healed into the bark.

The 'Field Work' idea operates as a kind of framing conceit: having taken the strange pad to the field of individuation, the work that goes on there will cohere, will be a round open circle, complete in itself and entirely human. Getting the angle right will take you into the field of force where the work can be done, and where past and present, life and art can interact. Melville, Lowell, Donne, Yeats, Pound all peer at one another in the heartlifting bravery that concludes section II:

Our moon was small and far,
was a coin long gazed at

brilliant on the Pequod's mast
across Atlantic and Pacific waters.

Section III proceeds through negatives (Not the, Not the, No) to the marvellously actual sunflower, an open vowel, all yellow and fiery brown:

in a still corner,
braced to its pebble-dashed wall,
heavy, earth-drawn, all mouth and eye,

the sunflower, dreaming umber.

The sequence concludes with a poem charged with secrecy and with the tension of some intimate and powerful rite:

Catspiss smell
the pink bloom open:
I press a leaf
of the flowering currant
on the back of your hand.

These doings, ordinary, careless, are translated into a different order of experience by the aura of mystery, and the slow openwork of the first three poems of the sequence. A rite is being enacted, a vaccination by means of the leaf itself; the open O is being crossed and anointed:

for the tight slow burn
of its sticky juice
to prime your skin,
and your veins to be crossed
criss-cross with leaf-veins.
I lick my thumb
and dip it in mould,
I anoint the anointed
leaf-shape.

The leaf is already crossed; the rite confirms the imprint of nature; the poetry becomes a space where nature and human action are balanced: field work.

The field poem in *Field Work* follows Dante's pathway through the circle of Hell; it is a translation of the Ugolino episode in the *Inferno* where the dead interrogate the living, and the living question the dead. Ugolino and his four sons are starved to death in 'that jail which is called Hunger':

when I saw
The image of my face in their four faces
I bit on my two hands in desperation;
And they, since they thought hunger drove me to it,
Rose up suddenly in agitation
Saying, 'Father, it will greatly ease our pain
If you eat us instead, and you who dressed us
In this sad flesh undress us here again.'
So then I calmed myself to keep them calm.
We hushed.[45]

Then follows Dante's curse on Pisa. Even though Ugolino had betrayed the city

> the sins
> Of Ugolino, who betrayed your forts,
> Should never have been visited on his sons.

This translation, charged with relevance to the human suffering created by the situation in Ireland, carries the force of a moral reality. Dante's conversations with the dead revolve around what right action in life is, because the way we are living will have been our life. Poetry aspires to be a field of force in which human motivation and action will be weighed and measured. A simple, direct and powerful insight reveals itself in Heaney's version of Dante: that there are limits to punishment; that certain excesses are evil; and that their effects go on and on: Ugolino is hasped on to the back of his enemy in a frozen hole of ice, eating out his brain forever.

When Heaney moved south to Wicklow in 1972 he began working on a translation of *Buile Shuibhne, The Madness of Sweeney,* which he eventually published in 1983. Sweeney is the poet-king from Dál Araidhe (Heaney's own area) who went mad after he had been cursed by a powerful saint. This translation is linked to the fascination with Dante, in that Sweeney, like the figures in the *Inferno* and the *Purgatorio,* is in an aftermath. He is also suffering through, again and again, his offences and sins; and in the depth and clarity of his awareness, he acts as a kind of critic of safe lives and trivial understandings. But most significantly, perhaps, he embodies a sense of freedom and release. He has the power of flight, and can move, like imagination itself, over impossible distances. His apartness from the rule-bound lives of the sane gives him a closeness to the world of nature. The verses celebrating the harsh landscapes of exposure weigh the difference between this open world and the closed internal worlds of betrayal, power and lust. The discourse of nature works against and is measured by the discourse of culture, but to say this does not convey the clean lift and pleasure of Sweeney's chafing vision:

> The sough of the winter night,
> my feet packing the hailstones

as I pad the dappled
banks of Mourne.

Or lie, unslept. in a wet bed
on the hills by Lough Erne,
tensed for first light
and an early start.[46]

A 'double note of relish and penitence' was the way Heaney described the literary attraction of the original Irish. But this translation, like his other translations, is no mere literary exercise: it is a further advance in a process of learning which involves 'deschooling' the mind, freeing it from the false languages and ready-made opinions in which it is good at trapping itself. Sweeney's trail is another one he follows, like that of the servant boy in *Wintering Out*. In the introduction he tells us Sweeney had been with him from the start, and that he was associated in his mind with tinkers, called Sweeney, who used to camp in the ditchbacks 'along the road to the first school I attended'. Another learning was in the ditches. Sweeney, the tinker, true to his code, shouts to him at the beginning of 'Station Island' to stay clear of all processions.

Station Island is a volume about the search for freedom, but freedom is now so abused a word as almost to be meaningless. Heaney tries to measure out his understanding of it in this volume and in *The Haw Lantern*.

'Chekov on Sakhalin' is based on the journey Chekov took to the prison island, a journey away from the Moscow literary set into the uncomfortable unknown, the penitentiary. The first night there he drinks a bottle of cognac given him by his friends before he left, and smashes the empty bottle on the stones.

In the months to come
It rang on like the burden of his freedom

To try for the right tone – not tract, not thesis –
And walk away from floggings. He who thought to squeeze
His slave's blood out and waken the free man
Shadowed a convict guide through Sakhalin.[47]

'A Bat on the Road' recalls Joyce and Stephen Dedalus's meditation on: 'A batlike sound waking to consciousness of itself in darkness and secrecy and loneliness'.[48] This phrase recapitulates the entire Heaney learning process towards freedom, and Joyce is to be a powerful voice at the end of the search poem which is the centrepiece of the volume, 'Station Island' itself. In this poem the soul/bat breaks for freedom:

> don't
> bring it down, don't break its flight again,
> don't deny it; this time let it go free.

This volume, *The Haw Lantern* and *Seeing Things* try to describe places, moods and spaces, an openness on a plane which is tilted at an angle to the surface of what happens, so that the quotidian splits right into the rich seams within. These spaces are clearings ('Clearances') in *The Haw Lantern*; in *Station Island* the thought and word-work circle round and round, alert, vigilant and tense with the expectation of free flight, of which there are many glimmerings. But *Station Island* is part of a process which is more fully developed in *The Haw Lantern* and *Seeing Things*.

Station Island's learning involves a multiple attentiveness. 'Sheelagh na Gig' admonishes the imagination:

> 'Yes, look at me to your heart's content
> but look at every other thing.'[49]

Just before the poem 'Station Island' comes an alluring and strange poem 'The King of the Ditchbacks', which recalls Sweeney the tinker, and links him to Sweeney the mad king. All of Heaney's marginal figures gather here: the one who takes the stray pads, the last mummer, the servant boy, the one who stays clear of processions and who 'untousles' the corn. A threshold is crossed, untaken paths are opened up:

> As if a trespasser
> unbolted a forgotten gate
> and ripped the growth
> tangling its lower bars[50]

(think of the shaft lifted from the green 'fog' in 'Kinship')

> just beyond the hedge
> he has opened a dark morse
> along the bank

(think of 'Broagh')

a crooked wounding

of silent, cobwebbed
grass. If I stop
he stops
like the moon.

Heaney is following a spoor again, on the track of mad Sweeney, a translator. The 'small dreamself' was in the branches of the middle Irish poem, which he now interrogates in an extraordinary and moving series of 'invocations':

- Are you the one I ran upstairs to find drowned
  under running water in the bath?
- The one the mowing machine severed like
  a hare in the stiff frieze of harvest?
- Whose little bloody clothes we buried in the garden?
- The one who lay awake in darkness a wall's
  breadth from the troubled hoofs?

'Station Island' is a search for clearer self-definition; it is an attempt 'to come into his own', to individuate and to belong at one and the same time. The pilgrimage poem is also Dantesque: St Patrick's purgatory at Lough Derg was known thoughout medieval Europe, and the technique Heaney uses is inspired by Dante. 'Station Island' gives voice to the dead who interrogate the living. The writing, like Dante's, is concerned with right judgement, with measuring the value of human action, and with searching for a truthful order of speech, a glimmering of the *lucidus ordo*. What is it, the poem asks, to take the true paths? How do you weigh and measure human experience? Is there a standard; is there a point of origin? Carleton, whom he sights in his driving mirror as he is parked at the roadside, gives advice and it is typically down to earth:

'. . . You have to try to make sense of what comes.
Remember everything and keep your head.'

In section III of the poem, Heaney meditates on his memory of a seaside trinket, a toy grotto made of shells, with cockles glued upon it, then upon

pearls condensed from a child invalid's breath
into a shimmering ark, my house of gold.

Absence here is dwelt upon, strengthened into a kind of power:

I thought of walking round
and round a space utterly empty
utterly a source, like the idea of sound;

like an absence.

Or like an open O for the mind to blow through, a circular clearing for memory to vanish into. The phrases quoted above are of the utmost significance in the late Heaney - they are repeated in the eighth poem of 'Clearances' in *The Haw Lantern* - and they are baffling and simple at once. Space which is utterly empty and which is also a source does not make commonplace sense, but it is Heaney's ambition to move beyond the enclosures of the known and given to different clearings. Paradox and contradiction are part of the deschooling needed. But also it is very simple; the memory of the invalid child is only that, a memory, an absence, but this absence is totally a source. All art conjures out of emptiness, 'is re-begot/Of absence, darkness, death, things which are not.'[51] Translation, which to some extent all art is, arises from a sense of absence and the related longing for a source, the desire to connect the moment, A, to the source, B.

'Station Island' as well as circling round and round a space both emptiness and source, also 'does the rounds': it takes a pathway along with others in a procession, but a procession now outdated and from another time. The poet, as well as being intent on individuation, is also active as a conscience which has, as Heaney puts it in *The Government of the Tongue,* a possible etymology meaning 'our capacity to know the same thing together'.[52]

One of the ways of testing for such a co-knowing is to go on a poetic pilgrimage in which the pathways are open to the dead and tradition. Present being unfolds in and through the past: the present *translates* the past. Carleton is translated into the present tense, as are Dante, Colum McCartney, Barney Murphy, Francis Hughes and Joyce. The poetry becomes an arena of conscience and translation. Take section VI, which recollects an early erotic experience. The mood is translated from an absence into presence; sexual frustration is recalled and then its release:

all that ever opened
was the breathed-on grille of a confessional

Until that night I saw her honey-skinned
Shoulder-blades and the wheatlands of her back
Through the wide keyhole of her keyhole dress
And a window facing the deep south of luck
Opened and I inhaled a land of kindness.

And now, into this writing comes Dante, whose knowing and understanding speak to the developing presence and freedom of this moment of blessedness opened and shared. Dante and Heaney write together, as follows:

As little flowers that were all bowed and shut
By the night chills rise on their stems and open
As soon as they have felt the touch of sunlight,
So I revived in my own wilting powers
And my heart flushed, like somebody set free.

Heaney's own comment on this follows:

Translated, given, under the oak tree.[53]

'No oak groves' any more? There are or can be if life turns to renew itself:

The dazzle of the impossible suddenly
blurred across the threshold, a sun-glare
to put out the small hearths of constancy.[54]

This dazzle can work anywhere, a metaphysic Heaney has schooled himself in, and one in which his master is Kavanagh. It is possible 'to re-envisage the zenith',[55] to put a new face on the golden rule of the sun, and of light. The translation of base metal into gold can take place in the forged conscience of verse. 'Translate me something by Juan de la Cruz' an old Spanish priest once gave him as a penance, which he does. The ordinary bread is the living source of the light:

This eternal fountain hides and splashes
within this living bread that is the life to us
although it is the night.[56]

Joyce, another insouciant master, enters at the end of 'Station Island'. Individuate, is what he says, keep your eye clear, take your own soundings, and they will put you in touch with the whole thing, like the fiddle player in 'The Given Note':

'You lose more of your self than you redeem
doing the decent thing. Keep at a tangent.
When they make the circle wide, it's time to swim

out on your own and fill the element
with signatures on your own frequency,
echo soundings, searches, probes, allurements,

elver gleams in the dark of the whole sea.'[57]

'Let go, let fly, forget,' he says and Heaney, using the Sweeney persona in 'Sweeney Redivivus', the concluding section of *Station Island,* tries to do just that. These poems enact strange surges of freedom, full of rage, loss, sex, strangeness. One heartbreaking poem is 'Sweeney's Returns', when the bird-man comes back home, perches on a suburban windowsill to look in at his wife's bedroom, to find she is gone. This place is a place, which, like any other, can become a source, an absence that can become charged:

when I perched on the sill
to gaze at my coffers of absence
I was like a scout at risk behind lines
who raises his head in a wheat field
to take a first look, the throb of his breakthrough
going on inside him unstoppably:

the blind was up, a bangle
lay in the sun, the fleshed hyacinth
had begun to divulge.
Where had she gone? Beyond
the tucked and level bed, I floundered
in my wild reflection in the mirror.[58]

The Haw Lantern, a densely argued book of poetry, combines alert divinatory power with nonchalant mastery. The book opens with an open vowel, an O, and recalls how Marsilio Ficino, the Florentine neoplatonist, hung from his ceiling a coloured figure of the orb of the world, so that the order of the universe and 'not just single things' would meet him when he walked abroad.

The *lucidus ordo* of Ficino is also to be seen in the parabolic 'From the Republic of Conscience', where things may be known together, not singly. You have to be cleared at immigration and the clerk is a kind of Diogenes, who tests and clears people by the 'haw lantern' in the poem of that name. In this republic you carry 'your own burden' and 'symptoms of creeping privilege' disappear. Leaders weep 'to atone for their presumption to hold office'. This place is a place which the conscience of poetry seeks to open; it is a clearing ground for being true:

> I came back from that frugal republic
> with my two arms the one length, the customs woman
> having insisted that my allowance was myself.[59]

This release to the self is a way of conveying a recovered or restored sense of freedom. One of the ways the poetry has of registering this freedom is in an imagery of emptiness, where the emptiness is a totally open space, the O sensed internally as an expanse and limit of the soul:

> After the bowstring sang a swallow's note,
> The arrow whose immigration is its mark
> Leaves a whispered breath in every socket.
> The great test over, while the gut's still humming,
>
> This time it travels out of all knowing
> Perfectly aimed towards the vacant centre.[60]

Against this openness and working through it and in it is the astonishingly heartsmitten brilliance of 'Clearances', where all clutter is cleared away so that people and things stand out in sacramental presence. This clarity is out of Kavanagh, but it is learnt in the moral being, by a deschooling of the shattered and lame discourses of human exhaustion at the end of the twentieth century. He writes as if in response to the Angel's need in Rilke's 'Ninth Elegy':

> When all the others were away at Mass
> I was all hers as we peeled potatoes.
> They broke the silence, let fall one by one
> Like solder weeping off the soldering iron:
> Cold comforts set between us, things to share
> Gleaming in a bucket of clean water.
> And again let fall. Little pleasant splashes
> From each other's work would bring us to our senses.[61]

Total absorption and trance, a world transformed and translated from singleness and separateness, to integrity.

This knowledge is poetic knowledge, an order of understanding capable of a sense of wholeness, an open O filled with attention:

> This space we stood around had been emptied
> Into us to keep, it penetrated
> Clearance that suddenly stood open.
> High cries were felled and a pure change happened.[62]

Seamus Heaney has arrived at his own ground. Angular and riddling his verse has often been but it is clear that his track was, since the outset, the unbeaten one. He has gone to places in the psyche, both personal and collective, which are sometimes shameful and often risky. He has known that what he undertook he could not have done without utmost seriousness. His search for poetic freedom has meant departures, from outmoded styles, settled habits of thinking and, not least, from comfortable habits of life. It is this last which marks him out as a master-poet, the readiness to accept the frightening but exciting challenge of Rilke's, that he has cited himself, and which he has said the mind becomes adept at evading: 'You must change your life.'[63]

Pure change happens in the poetry of Seamus Heaney. Things are really seen in his renewing light.

14

MOVEMENT AND AUTHORITY

'Suddenly you're through'[1]

In 1989 I was at a poetry reading at the Institute of Irish Studies in Dublin. Seamus Heaney was reading a series of poems called 'Shelf Life' from *Station Island.* He explained and commented upon a phrase in the first poem of that series. The phrase is *'An union in the cup I'll throw'*. He said that the phrase, which comes from *Hamlet,* is one which has always haunted him. Not surprising, perhaps, that the word 'union' in Shakespeare would have struck a boy at school in Northern Ireland studying *Hamlet* with a peculiar and mysterious force. Might there be some hint in the word itself? Might there be a hint from the context in the play *Hamlet* about what union means in England and to the English? There is a hint in the play, and it is a very dark one, because the union that is thrown into the cup is Claudius's kingly ring, and it is poisoned, in order to kill Hamlet when he rests in the swordfight, just in case Laertes doesn't. The union is death to protect a dynasty, founded by killing the true sovereign, Hamlet. Hamlet is to be killed again; the true king is to be killed a second time.

Union is deeply interconnected with the notion of sovereignty. Because the Falkland Islands were part of the union of the British Empire, the invasion of the Argentinians could not be tolerated. It was an invasion of sovereign territory, and so the affront to a part, even a tiny and very remote part, was an affront to Britain and to her Queen, and had to be answered with force. What was overlooked at the time, particularly in the popular press coverage of the war, was that the concept of union has to change, as indeed sovereignty does, to accommodate itself to new circumstances. In 1800 an Act of Union, with the consent of the Irish parliament in Dublin, created a union of the kingdoms of Britain and Ireland.

But in 1922 a part of that union separated and acquired autonomous status: the Irish Free State was created, which in time became the Republic of Ireland. This meant that the notion of a sovereign unity of Great Britain and all of Ireland had to be adapted in order to accommodate the new reality: that there now was a sovereign state, with rights, institutions and freedoms, which was not constitutionally in place before. In 1922 the Union was a union between Great Britain and Northern Ireland, the United Kingdom. There might be now a few, a very few, who would still argue that the establishment of the Irish Republic, and prior to that the Irish Free State, was an illegal and unconstitutional act, and that for Lloyd George and his government to tolerate Irish seccession from the Union was something that no individual statesman or government had the power to do. But the notion of sovereignty has to change to adapt to new circumstances. After all, the Glorious Revolution of 1688–9 was 'Glorious' because it got rid of one king, James II, in order to install a new king, William III, to protect (so the argument of that high constitutionalist, Edmund Burke, runs) the true spirit of the constitution, the true sovereignty of the British crown. The trouble is that the notion of sovereignty remains a very fixed one for people who have a keen interest in things remaining always the same. Claudius throws a union into the cup to keep things as they are, to accomplish which he has to kill Hamlet. George Moore in *The Lake* writes that 'the law of change is the law of life'; to keep things the same you have to kill the new life emerging.

The sovereignty of Ireland has always been a problem from the very earliest times. And the Irish mythographers, poets and lawgivers, who were often combined in the same person in the traditional Gaelic world, had an interesting way of dealing with this problem.

Irish legendary history is a tangle. Many people are familiar with the accounts of the waves of successive invaders: those led by Cessair, then Partholan, then Nemed, followed by the Fir Bolg, the Tuatha Dé Danann, and the Clanna Míl, the Milesians. This is the account assembled in the *Leabhar Gabhála* (*The Book of Invasions*), the twelfth century compilation about the invasions of Ireland, accumulated over the previous centuries and given form in a sustained narrative. The *Leabhar Gabhála* contains many interesting and entertaining stories; but one thing emerges more clearly than anything else, and that is that Ireland was a country which was being constantly invaded and resettled. Who are the original Irish?

This is a question which cannot be answered, of course, and the old Irish mythographers knew that very well. What they did was to use tradition to create some order for the tangle of stories, claims and counter-claims about ancestral rights that were made all over Ireland in the pre- and post-Christian periods.

Before the Celts there were other people, the people who built Newgrange, and the neolithic burial chambers, for example, but baffling as are the different waves of Celtic invasions, these pre-Celts are a closed book to us, as they were to the early Irish poets and mythographers. These latter made the pre-Celtic tumuli and burial-places the habitations of the old Celtic deities and called them the Tuatha Dé Danann, a fiction to 'save the appearances'. But the Celts themselves are confusing enough to be going on with. There were the Cruithin, who were the first Celts, according to T.F. O'Rahilly in his *Early Irish History and Mythology*; followed by the Fir Bolg, also known as the Érainn (whence Ériu) who came from Britain. Then there were the Laigin (whence Leinster), also known as the Gaileóin (from Gallia or Gaul) and they turn up among the Connacht forces in the *Táin Bó Cuailnge*, Ireland's composite legendary epic. Finally according to O'Rahilly, there are the Gaels, or the Goídels, who called themselves the Féni, and they were the latest of all.

I am not competent to speak of the accuracy of O'Rahilly's account and sequence of these peoples, but it looks convincing enough. One thing is clear; with these peoples and tribes and variant languages (the Goídels or Gaels were Q-Celts whereas all the others were P-Celts: i.e. they said 'cenn' for head; whereas the Cruithin would have said 'penn', as do the Welsh) the question as to whom the sovereignty of Ireland should devolve was always a vexed one. And not just the sovereignty of Ireland, but of provinces, and local kingdoms.

Sovereignty is a concept crucial to kingship through all the peoples of Europe, indeed throughout what linguists would term the Indo-European peoples. Proinsias Mac Cana in *Celtic Mythology* points out that it is even older than Indo-European society itself:

The notion of a mystical or symbolic union between

> the king and his kingdom is older than Indo-European society. And where the kingdom was conceived anthropomorphically as a goddess, the latter then symbolised not merely the soil and substance of its territory, but also the spiritual, and legal dominion which the king exercised over it, in other words his sovereignty.[2]

The sovereignty of Ireland is symbolized as a woman. We are told that three goddesses presided over Ireland at the coming of the Gaels or Goídels – Ériu, Banba and Fódla – and these are versions of the sovereignty goddess. The Goídels or Gaels had to marry these women, who are really all one woman, Ireland herself, and this marriage was, in fact, kingship. MacCana continues:

> Nowhere was this divine image of sovereignty visualised so clearly as among the Celts, and more especially in Ireland, where it remained a remarkably evocative and compelling concept for as long as native tradition lasted. . . . It is closely implicated in all the various epiphanies of the Celtic goddess referred to; in a sense it is the factor which integrates them into a unity.

Wherever the Celtic goddess of fertility appears, however she appears, sovereignty is implicated. It is often said that Celtic deities are not specialized, in the way that Graeco-Roman ones tended to be (think of Venus, goddess of love, for example) and this is certainly the case with Ériu, Banba, Fódla. She turns up in all kinds of situations and in many different guises. One of these was Medhbh.

In a tale called *Baile in Scáil* (*The Phantom's Frenzy*) the phantom Lugh (from whom Lyons in France, and he is also the sun god Lugh Lámhfhada) reveals to Conn of the Hundred Battles all his successors down to 1022. Lugh takes Conn into a rath where a maiden called 'flaitheas Éireann' is seated on a crystal couch, wearing a golden crown, and with a vat of red beer before her. In the cup she pours a drink and gives it to all the kings of Ireland ('An union into the cup I'll throw'). The drink is red in all kinds of ways: 'derglaith', meaning 'red beer', punning on 'derg-fhlaith', 'red king', or 'red kingliness', or 'royal blood'. P.L. Henry, in his study of Old Irish wisdom and learning, *Saoithiúlacht na Sean-Ghaeilge* has drawn attention to this tense punning on red beer and kingliness.[3] Red is a colour associated with the otherworld in Irish tradition, and is therefore linked with the otherworld from which sovereignty emanates. The sign of kingship is the drink given.

Medhbh is linked to the effects of this drink. The relation with mead is obvious: Old Irish 'mid' is mead, linked with Welsh 'mead', old English 'meodo' and Sanskrit 'máhdu'. The word Medhbh means, literally, we are told, 'intoxication'. To quote P.L. Henry: 'she is the goddess who dispenses the drink of sovereignty to the one who is to be king and who marries him.'[4] (In this light Claudius is an antagonist of Medhbh, if you like, in that he gives the poison which kills the true prince.) In the *Book of Leinster* she is described as 'clever, wise, harsh and merciless'.

Medhbh is the great queen of the *Táin Bó Cuailnge,* and there she carries with her implications of her status as a goddess of sovereignty. And in other stories too. The early Irish, aware of the confusion of claims about sovereignty, personified her in all sorts of different ways, so that at times she was in Temhair, at other times in Cruachan in Connacht, and yet again among the Ulaid in present day Ulster. The stories, in other words, stay away from a definite identification of sovereignty with one tribe, one people, one place. Indeed, all may be seen to have a claim upon her. Sovereignty itself as a concept remains fixed; that is a unifying notion. But it can be adapted and changed depending on circumstances and need.

At one time Eochaidh Feidhlech (meaning 'steadfast ploughman') defeats Fachtna, king of the Ulaid, *and* high king of Ireland, and kills him. According to the sources Eochaidh Feidhlech was a Goídel; Fachtna, being of the Ulaid, would have been associated with an earlier people, the Érainn, or the Fir Bolg. So here, in this tale, we have a translation of a dynastic or tribal conflict which may have taken place over hundreds of years, or over ten years: we do not know. Or at least to the best of my knowledge, we do not know. The point of the story is simple: one tribe replaces another in the ascendancy. Fachtna, according to tradition, was the father of Conchobhar, and according to the account in a tale called *Cath Bóinne* (*The Battle of the Boyne*) Eochaidh, Fachtna's slayer, gave to Conchobhar, as éric (a recompense under Brehon law) his three daughters, among them Medhbh, and the kingdom of Ulster, retaining to himself the high kingship, located at Temhair (Tara). Medhbh, however, leaves Conchobhar, and returns to Temhair, where the real king resides. According to *Cath Bóinne* this betrayal is the basic reason for the enmity between her and Conchobhar that is the subject of *Táin Bó Cuailnge.* Having left Conchobhar and returned to Temhair (known often as Temhair Érainn, showing that it was recognized that the Érainn, of whom the Ulaid were a branch, were once a powerful dynasty) she goes with a number of other men until she resides at Cruachan in Connacht. It is clear that the storytellers are associating her with as many of the provinces and kingships as possible: Temhair, the Ulaid (who resided at Emhain Macha, about which more later) and Cruachan in Connacht. Everyone is getting a bit of the action; or everyone is given a sip of the cup containing the red beer of kingly intoxication, Medhbh, sovereignty.

Her father, Eochaidh Feidhlech, 'steadfast ploughman', calls together Feis Temhrach, i.e. the ceremonial sleeping with the goddess sovereignty that the king does after his installation. This looks like Eochaidh, one of the Goídels, asserting high kingship over all the other kings in Ireland, unifying them. Many do come to the Feis (literally 'sleeping with': the king slept with his country, the goddess, in or after the sacral installation), even Conchobhar from the Ulaid, but Medhbh stays away at first. She does come in the end. She goes to the Boyne one day to bathe. Conchobhar of the Ulaid, obviously discontented at what Eochaidh is up to with all the ceremonial, follows her, spies upon her, then rapes her. All the other sub-kings, when they hear of this, attack the Ulsterman but he defeats the lot of them at the Boyne and pushes them back as far as the Shannon. He has taken sovereignty by force, asserting again the claims of the Ulaid over the steadfast newcomer at Temhair. What is being revealed to us in this cluster of stories? That sovereignty is mobile; that it is (she is) a goddess, but that she cannot be totally tied to one place or one manifestation. There are, indeed, a number of Medhbhs; Medhbh of Cruachan, and Medhbh Lethderg (of the red side, i.e. from the otherworld) at Temhair. No one dynasty has a monopoly.

Bronislaw Malinowski, the anthropologist, argued that myths were often charters, by means of which a people or tribe told themselves a story to enhance or justify their right to a particular piece of land, inheritance or heritage; and there seems to be some basis for this. Edmund Leach summed up the Malinowski view of myth as a 'legitimation of social arrangements'.[5] But these tales also show how the human mind can recognize that an inheritance or a right may not belong to any one people, and that rival even conflicting claims need to be accommodated, without in any way infringing the principle of sovereignty itself and its unifying power. Lévi-Strauss's view of myth, as a system of signs whereby contradictory elements in life are resolved or at least held in balance, seems more in touch with the way these ancient stories unfold their entangled meanings.

Macha is another of the Celtic goddesses associated with sovereignty. She is cognate with Medhbh. She was the wife of Nemhedh in the third of the invasions recounted in *Leabhar Gabhála*. She gives her name to Emhain Macha, where Conchobhar presided over the Ulaid, and to Ard Macha, Armagh. She was the daughter of Midhir of Bri Leith, according to some accounts. Midhir and Eochaidh Feidhlech are equivalent (O'Rahilly says that Eochaidh is 'ultimately Midhir's double'[6]) so Medhbh and Macha are also linked in this entanglement of relationships. Medhbh is the daughter of Eochaidh, Macha of Midhir; if Midhir and Eochaidh are each other's double, so are their daughters. Macha is another way of the storytellers getting at the complex of claims that government, authority, order and unity involved.

Who is this Macha and what does she do? There's a tale about her in the *Book of Leinster* which P.L. Henry has commented upon.[7] Three kings ruled Ireland together; these were Díhorba, Aedh and Cimbaeth (the latter is a Pict, i.e. one of the Cruithin). Again we are dealing with different claims to sovereignty. They agree to share the kingship between them, each having seven years as king, in rotation. Aedh dies and his daughter Macha (here she is his daughter, not Midhir's) asks to take his place in the rotation. The others refuse but she defeats them and gets her way. Then Díthorba dies, and his five sons Baeth, Bras, Bétach, Uallach and Borbchas want to take over his term. This time she refuses them and defeats them in battle. Then she marries the remaining partner, Cimbaeth, the Cruithin. When the marriage is concluded she pursues the sons of Díthorba (misfortune) into Connacht. One night she catches up with them. They are seated around a fire roasting wild boar. (Roasting is an aristocratic form of cooking, according to Lévi-Strauss, and closer to nature than boiling.) Macha comes to them in the guise of a leper: she has reddened her cheeks with red clay (again the symbol of the otherworld) and has stuck a dough made of rye flour on her face.

> 'Doesn't the hag have a lovely eye?', says one of them, 'let's lie with her.' He takes her to the wood with him, but Macha ties him up and leaves him devoid of strength. She comes back to the fire.
>
> 'Where's the man who went with you?' they ask.
>
> 'He's ashamed that he went with a leper.'
>
> 'No need for that. We're all going to do the same.'
>
> Each one takes her to the wood, but she ties them up and then she takes them all in one tangle to the Ulaid.
>
> 'Kill them,' says the crowd.
>
> 'No, because then I'd lose real kingliness. I'll keep them as slaves; and they'll build a rampart for me that'll be the chief city of Ulster forever.' With that she marked out the limits for the fort with her neck brooch or *eo-muin*. From that Emhain Macha took its name, the neck-brooch, or *eo-muin*, of Macha.

Here, in this tale, we see that sovereignty is again being described: it's divided, fought over, secured and protected. Macha does not kill the five sons of Díthorba because to do so would not be an action in keeping with her royalty: instead she makes use of them as builders of the exterior symbol of her authority.

In the story of Macha which forms one of the pre-tales to the *Táin Bó Cuailnge*, Macha comes to an isolated farmer in Ulster, called Crunnchu, whose wife has died. She looks after him and in time becomes pregnant by him. A fair is held in Ulster in which nothing can beat the horses of Conchobhar. Crunnchu says, however, that Macha can outrun them. She does so, but the race brings her to her time and she dies in childbirth. She gives birth to twins, Fír and Fial, Truth and Generosity (the two traits of kingliness), and before she dies lays a curse on the Ulaid that in times of crisis they will be laid low with the pangs of childbirth. This is the famous *ces*, which Cuchulain did not have, as he, being of British extraction, was not a true Ulsterman. Because of this Cuchulain, whose original name Setanta links him with the Setantii of Britain, becomes the hero of the Ulaid, and in time the central figure of the *Táin Bó Cuailnge*. His father is none other than the Lugh who shows Conn of the Hundred Battles the sovereignty of Ireland in *Baile in Scáil* (*The Phantom's Frenzy*).

Cuchulain is the protector of Conchobhar, the Ulaid, and of the sovereignty of Ireland, as it is revealed in Ulster at Emhain Macha. Nevertheless we have seen that Conchobhar has himself offended against his own sovereignty by allowing Macha to race against his horses; and at the Boyne, as we saw in the stories of Medhbh, he behaved badly as well.

The stories of sovereignty as they cluster around Medhbh and Macha are tangled, and strands from one narrative are to be found in the other: Macha is, in a sense, the same person as Medhbh. What the storytellers are doing is creating narratives which reveal part of the huge structural arrangement that is the central core of the various versions of the sovereignty story, the unity that underlies all the diversity. The entire structure, the total unit of the myth can never be apparent or actual, nor will it ever be; but each story reveals part of the pattern, just as each ruler, king, tribe, people, race can embody part of the unity that is in the cup extended to Conn Cétchathach.

The unity of the country of Ireland, figured in the goddess, may show here and there in the accidents of time and change. The man who wants to fix her for himself will fail, because she is mobile and elusive; and no one can possess her totally. She may be in Emhain Macha amongst the Ulaid, in Temhair Érainn in Meath, in Cruachan, in Temhair Luachra in Munster; and she may be in all these places at once. The storytellers of ancient Ireland do not fix her; they take great care to underline her ubiquity, her harshness, her beauty, her foulness. They are, in a way, diametrically opposed to the modern propagandist mind, which wants to say Ireland, the true Ireland is this, or that, or the other. Ian Adamson, for example, recently argued that the authentic Irish were the Cruithin, and I heard him say in Oxford that their suppression is the cause of the melancholy in the true Gaelic-Scottish nature, to be found in the Presbyterian people. Or we hear it argued that the real Irish are Catholic and republican and that their legendary origin can be figured in the Fianna of Fionn mac Cumhail, hence Fianna Éireann. But the ancient mythographers knew better than to use stories to make things cut and dried; a story with a meaning that is cut and dried is a dead story. Macha marries Cimbaeth, the Cruithin, but she is also associated with Temhair Érainn, Eochaidh Feidhlech and Cruachan in Connacht. She is multivalent and intertribal. The danger, said Samuel Beckett, is in the neatness of the identifications, and the Old Irish mythographers knew this as well: Medhbh cannot be identified too closely with one sect; she must belong to all.

There is something for everybody in the Old Irish stories. My people, on my mother's side, for example, are Kearneys, and come from North Cork. In working through the material for this chapter I came across the statement that the king of Temhair Érainn in Meath was also known as 'rí Chearnaí'; this refers to Conall Cernach (Cernunnos of European tradition) but the Kearneys get a look in as well. All are linked in.

It was often said that you could not trust what the Irish will tell you because they will make sure that they tell you what you want to hear. At its worst the racial slur here is that the Irish cannot tell truth from falsehood. But in another sense there is a vital cultural manoeuvre going on: it is most important that strangers feel at home, that they be accommodated within the structure, and that means adapting the elements of the structure to take account of the new presence. Strangers too must be given part of the total unity, they too must be given a sip from the cup of flaitheas Éireann, so the concept of unity must be sufficiently flexible to take them in. They must be told what they want to hear; not to do so leaves them outside and therefore dangerous. They are here, so they must become part of what is here before them; they must be articulated, that is *joined into,* the pre-existing arrangement. For this articulation to take place the pre-existing arrangement needs to be multivalent, interactive, mobile and rotating. Constantly changing.

The word 'réim' means reign. It comes, according to Henry, from the Indo-European stem **réidh* – meaning *movement.* The authority of a king was expressed in the movement, the swift progress, of a chariot. Macha, in the story of the race, defeats Conchobhar's chariot team, again drawing into question his legitimacy. In her agony she gives birth to the two aspects of kingship, Fír and Fial. Her movement, her 'réim' is more authentic than 'réim Chonchubhair', naturally enough, because she is what he has violated, as he violated Medhbh at the Boyne. The driving of a chariot symbolized kingship. In an account of a test at Temhair we have a description of a chariot drive ('réim') which would test the prospective king and whether he was fit to reign ('teacht i réim'). The chariot would rise up in front of anyone for whom sovereignty was not destined, and a cloak, lying in the chariot, would be too big for him. There were two stones at Temhair, called Blocc and Bluicne (now in the Church of Ireland graveyard nearby) and for the sovereign king these two stones, which abutted together, a hand's breadth between, would swing open and allow the moving chariot to pass through. Ahead of him then, at the terminus of the chariot run, was Fál, the penis. (A stone, said to be Fál, still stands on one of the mounds at Temhair.) Fál would shriek against the chariot base for everyone to hear for him who was acceptable to the sovereignty of Temhair. The two stones, Blocc and Bluicne, would not open for anyone not acceptable to sovereignty, nor would Fál shriek against the bottom of the chariot.

The parting of Blocc and Bluicne emphasizes the maleness of the person acceptable to sovereignty; the shrieking of Fál against the bottom of the chariot emphasized his femininity. Interestingly, we are told in the *Book of Leinster* that Fál did not shriek for Cuchulain. This Fál is, of course, the Lia Fáil.

The point to be emphasized here is that the rule of a king acceptable to sovereignty is encapsulated in movement, a rush, a mobility, a rotation; and as such it corresponds with the mobility already attributed to the concept of sovereignty itself. The concept must move and change if it is to accommodate contradiction; the chariot in the test-race at Temhair accommodates male and female.

It is time to return to the Heaney poem in which the phrase '*An union in the cup I'll throw*' occurs.

Granite Chip

Houndstooth stone. Aberdeen of the mind.

Saying *An union in the cup I'll throw*
I have hurt my hand, pressing it hard around
this bit hammered off Joyce's Martello
Tower, this flecked insoluble brilliant

I keep but feel little in common with –
a kind of stone age circumcising knife,
a Calvin edge in my complaisant pith.
Granite is jaggy, salty, primitive

> and exacting. *Come to me*, it says
> *all you who labour and are burdened. I*
> *will not refresh you.* And it adds, *seize*
> *the day.* And, *you can take me or leave me.*[8]

It is difficult to figure out what is going on in this poem. The granite chip hammered off the Martello Tower in Dublin is the union. It is an 'Aberdeen of the mind', linked with Scotland, unified with Britain since 1707, a union which, in Swift's phrase, made Ireland 'an injured lady'. The granite chip is also, he imagines, in him, a 'Calvin edge' in his 'complaisant pith', the spelling 'complaisant' reminds us of 'aisyness', 'Be aisy'. What the granite chip says is mysterious. It is associated, one presumes, with British power, in that it is a chip off the block of one of the Martello Towers, which were built during the Napoleonic wars as lookouts. Is it, perhaps, history, conceived of as hard fact; the 'insoluble brilliant' facts of oppression, violence, wrongs done on all sides? Whatever it is it gives no release: '*I will not refresh you*'; and its doctrine is '*Seize the day*', enjoy yourself while you can. There's no escaping the harshness of historical fact, so take ease in the sensuality of bitterness. This tiny chip is the union, the jewel that poisons the entire cup and murders Hamlet. And is there a suggestion that the Union is the hard fact that has poisoned all the life of Ireland, creating sensualities of indifference, intolerance, bitterness, despair, comfort?

These conclusions or suggestions about this poem have to be tentative. But it seems clear that the granite chip signifies the sombre dreariness of historical determinism. It is in a different mood entirely to the mobility of those early stories we spoke of. The Union referred to here is that accomplished by Act of Parliament, the Act of 1800. Such a union cannot have the flexibility and rotation of the concept of sovereignty conceived of as *movement*. This is fixed, a chip off a granite block, the grey Aberdeen of material reality in the nineteenth century. This is the Union which moved government to Westminster, from where the Irish would experience the shame of being considered a non-people. Sir Samuel Ferguson, a Unionist, in an address to the Protestant Repeal Association in May 1848, quoted a typical slurring remark from the House of Commons: 'If Nigger were not Nigger, Irishman would be Nigger.'[9] When in the same House it was suggested that Charles J. Haughey was angry in

Brussels when he met Mrs Thatcher because of the Stalker affair, there were guffaws from the Tory benches, as if the idea of Irish outrage was in itself hilarious. But examples of this kind could be multiplied pointlessly: this Union is insoluble; it doesn't move. The poem on the granite chip gets nowhere. In any case its life is only 'Shelf Life', the title of the series from which it comes. It is a kind of fossil.

I want to conclude by citing another poem of Heaney's, from *The Haw Lantern*.

From the Frontier of Writing

The tightness and the nilness round that space
when the car stops in the road, the troops inspect
its make and number and, as one bends his face

towards your window, you catch sight of more
on the hill beyond, eyeing with intent
down cradled guns that hold you under cover

and everything is pure interrogation
until a rifle motions and you move
with guarded unconcerned acceleration –

a little emptier, a little spent
as always by that quiver in the self,
subjugated, yes, and obedient.

So you drive on to the frontier of writing
where it happens again. The guns on tripods;
this sergeant with his on-off mike repeating

data about you, waiting for the squawk
of clearance; the marksman training down
out of the sun upon you like a hawk.

And suddenly you're through, arraigned yet freed,
as if you'd passed from behind a waterfall
on the black current of a tarmac road

past armour-plated vehicles, out between
the posted soldiers flowing and receding
like tree shadows into the polished windscreen.[10]

This story is about breaking through. Tightness and nilness, numbers, inspection, interrogation; all these convey the feeling of entrapment. The driver is being categorized; his movement, his 'réim', is being halted; his gallop is being stopped. First one obstacle, then the next; Blocc and Bluicne, in a way, then the Lia Fáil. Movement is regained; the border guards, presiding over fixed categories, flow and recede 'into the polished windscreen'. Heaney enters the country of writing, which is beyond the fixed categories of the border sentinels, who would 'hold you under cover'. The country of writing is the country of movement, of 'réim': is réimse saoirse í. The sovereignty of Ireland, Medhbh or Macha, for the mythographer, was not fixed, and because of that a unity could be envisaged, in which everyone had a part. Outside of this country, outside the frontiers of writing, 'everything is pure interrogation'. Inside it things flow together in a unity which can accommodate Ulaid, Cruithin, Goídel, Fir Bolg, Catholics, Presbyterians.

What does it mean in contemporary terms if we follow the logic of the old mythographers, and Heaney, who follows them? An Irish person wants the sovereignty of Ireland to be preserved; that means it must be capable of accommodating *everything, all* traditions. The Irishman or woman who wants to protect sovereignty will be characterized by movement, he or she will move across borders and be at home anywhere. Catholicism will take on Presbyterianism; Presbyterianism will become Catholic. Maleness will take on femaleness and the other way around. For love of Ireland, you will leave her, only to find her.

Two quotations, the first from Tadhg Camchosach Ó Dálaigh:

> Dá grádh do fhágbhus Éireann
> im bráthair bhocht beigléighinn
>
> For love of her I left Ireland
> as a poor unlearned scholar[11]

The second quotation is a translation of a Gaelic poem on Patrick Sarsfield, who fled Ireland after the defeat of the Boyne, Aughrim's great disaster and the (dishonoured) Treaty of Limerick. The translation is by James Clarence Mangan:

> I'll journey to the North, over mount, moor, and wave.
> 'Twas there I first beheld, drawn up in file and line,

The brilliant Irish hosts – they were bravest of the brave.
But, alas! they scorned to combine![12]

CODA
Seers and dancers

'Roof it again. Batten down. Dig in.'[1]

So does one of the twelve-line curtal sonnets in 'The Squarings' section of Seamus Heaney's *Seeing Things* (1991) open. This slow, self-instructional mode, a kind of rigour of the mind, is one that presents itself strongly throughout the book. It is saying: go steady, look, look deep, look again, think, feel, experience, let the words become instinct with awareness, fretted with thought. Make them so intensely alive to things that they share to some extent in the nature of the things they represent. Let poetry be a scope for wonder, for the opening of being; think, but think through. The process working here in this book is an enactment of the tense pressure of utter collectedness that Martin Heidegger alerts us to in his dialogue on language with D.T. Suzuki, where each philosopher courteously refrains from literalness in order that the thinking can show the beauty of language itself, the glorious fact of its existence.[2] Heaney in this book creates a poetry of decorous waiting, of readiness to receive impressions, a poetry capable of seeing things in the gold light it itself is capable of shedding.

And strike this scene in gold too, in relief,
So that a greedy eye cannot exhaust it:
Stable straw, Rembrandt-gleam and burnish

Where my father bends to a tea-chest packed with salt,
The hurricane lamp held up at eye-level
In his bunched left fist, his right hand foraging

For the unbleeding, vivid-fleshed bacon,
Home-cured hocks pulled up into the light
For pondering a while and putting back.

That night I owned the piled grain of Egypt.
I watched the sentry's torchlight on the hoard.
I stood in the door, unseen and blazed upon.[3]

The demeanour here is steady and composed, utterly alert, and yet totally solid, even nonchalant, if the word be stripped of associations of frivolity and reacquire its sense of collectedness and sanity, of refusal to usurp the privacies of things by presumptuous urgings and strivings. This poetry is a praying with, through, and for things. Letting them be, but seeing them, really seeing them. The discipline is Heaney's own alert power of patient waiting, of letting be, but it comes out of a hard school, where he has learnt to restrain his intellectualizing streak, and to keep clear of interferences, whether political, or personal, or cultural. It is also brilliantly ordinary, a love poem to his father, and behind the poem are kindly tutelary spirits: Rembrandt, of course, but also the Patrick Kavanagh of 'A Christmas Childhood'; Beckett, from whom he has learnt restraint; Yeats, who has taught him how to cope with irreconcilable personal conflicts; Joyce, who has shown him how to awaken the soul to and in its own light; Denis Devlin, who has taught him the vanity of ego; and so on, not to mention Dante's power of registering the shock of moral realizations, or the penitential cleanliness of medieval Irish syllabic verse. Heaney is encyclopaedic, learned, but profoundly in touch with things-as-they-are. This learning is carried very lightly: as Michael McLaverty once said to him, 'don't let the veins bulge in your biro.' The writing is superbly attentive to ordinariness, but the metaphysical and psychological groundwork is elaborate and most carefully prepared. We can get a glimpse of what is going on at the deepest levels, of the harsh school Heaney put himself to, and of his total relatedness to the full complexity of the Irish tradition in a poem like 'Field of Vision', which could also be read as an exploration of the kinds of possibilities now opened up for Irish writing and Irish culture. There is a sense that, to quote a phrase of Pearse Hutchinson's, 'the frost is all over,'[4] that the colonial, or post-colonial, or post-post-colonial repression is over and done with. And one of the reasons it is finished is because of the thought and the work Heaney, Friel, Nuala ní Dhomhnaill and Pearse Hutchinson himself have put in, and the ways in which their efforts have brought forward to fuller realization the work of Joyce and Beckett and Yeats and Stuart, as well as reworking their appraisals of tradition for the late twentieth century.

This poem is a kind of education process in itself, an opening up to new ways of thinking. What it says is shattering but utterly true, that you can see things better, more deeply, by what bars the field of vision:

> I remember this woman who sat for years
> In a wheelchair, looking straight ahead
> Out the window at sycamore trees unleafing
> And leafing at the far end of the lane.
>
> Straight out past the TV in the corner,
> The stunted, agitated hawthorn bush,
> The same small calves with their backs to wind and rain,
> The same acre of ragwort, the same moutain.
>
> She was steadfast as the big window itself.
> Her brow was clear as the chrome bits of the chair.
> She never lamented once and she never
> Carried a spare ounce of emotional weight.
>
> Face to face with her was an education
> Of the sort you got across a well-braced gate –
> One of those lean, clean, iron, roadside ones
> Between two whitewashed pillars, where you could see
>
> Deeper into the country than you expected
> And discovered that the field behind the hedge
> Grew more distinctly strange as you kept standing
> Focused and drawn in by what barred the way.[5]

Immobility, fixity, stasis; but then the learning from that. The bleakness of inaction, of futility, gone through, faced up to, not rejected, is an 'education': in distress, trauma, patience, waiting, steadfastness. There can be no articulation without emptiness; no rhetoric without the driving energy of its antiself, its antibodies; no health without the balancing of forces that, ungoverned, usurp stability. There is no nonchalance without tension; no learning without incompetence. Seamus Deane, Heaney's schoolfellow and friend, in a defence of the *Field Day Anthology* (1991), published in the *Guardian* newspaper, quoted Walter Benjamin as saying that there is no mastery where there has not first been incompetence. Paradoxical but true. Think of the lumbering English drama of the 1570s, then think of the total mastery of the 1590s. So with Irish writing: think of the vapid ironies of Mangan's worst, or the grim determination of Ferguson's fearsome epics; then think of Yeats's powerful but beautifully organized mathematics, whereby the conical energies of history and personal fate interact, and in the interaction throw out fiery visions of states of being.

Heaney's poem is a calm, collected meditation on the shift from futility to power, from misery to full life. And, the poem is saying, full life arrives in and through the contemplation of all that prevents it. There can be no liberty without the acceptance of oppression, and the going beyond it. To speak of this is to speak, maybe, of the emergence of a higher form of consciousness through the acceptance of suffering, a region of the spirit which Stuart's novels and Kinsella's poems explore in depth. The negativities of loss and trauma, the 'bars', allow the 'field of vision' to grow 'more distinctly strange'. Heaney is deliberately unspecific about all of this, but the bars framing the scene, the criss-cross of iron, is the whole sorry story of human loss, Ireland's pain, the cavings in of guilt and fright, the feeling that you can't go in or on. This poem lifts the whole preventative psychosis out of its fixed inactivity, and makes it into, translates it into that by which the vision is attained. Aubrey de Vere, the Irish Victorian pietist, tried in *Inisfail* (1861) to do the same thing, by explaining Ireland's pain in sacrificial terms, but he sought to impose a system on the suffering, that of Catholic theology, thereby losing touch with things-as-they-are.[6] Heaney's poetic unites an essentially Christian temperament with a secular phenomenology, which allows him to dance amidst things.

When I saw Brian Friel's *Dancing at Lughnasa* in the Phoenix Theatre in London in the summer of 1990, I came out during the interval to the bar almost unable to control my feelings. Tears were in my eyes. Something magnificent was taking place, had taken place, in the flour dance of the women in the first Act. These women, 'these five brave Glenties women' of the dedication had, in spite of all their trouble, disgrace, impending doom, danced, wildly, to music coming from the wireless set. They dance with intensity, but also convey 'a sense of ordinary order being consciously subverted';[7] shouting and singing, bootlaces flying, the women are 'caricaturing themselves' within the release of the dance. All of a sudden the wireless goes dead; but the moment of ceremony has occurred. The dramatic impact of this dance was (is) extremely powerful. In spite of all difficulties - uncertainty about income, an illegitimate child, a retarded girl, a priest returned from the missions who has gone native and become deranged - the women dance. They are not, all the time, victims of their culture. Something exists whereby people can get outside their history, their given, fated narratives.

Towards the end of the play there is a formal set piece, whereby the crossing over of cultural boundaries (seeing through the gate in Heaney's terms) is explored. Jack, the returned missionary, comes in wearing the crumpled white tropical uniform of the British army chaplain which he had been during the First World War. He has agreed to swap hats with Gerry, the Welsh father of Michael, the narrator, by Chris, one of the women. Gerry is joining the Popular Front in the Spanish Civil War. There is a crossing of boundaries on all fronts. Jack tells Gerry to put his hat on the ground:

> anywhere - just at your feet. Now take three steps away from it - yes? - distancing of yourself from what you once possessed. Good. Now turn round once - like this - yes, a complete circle - and that's the formal rejection of what you once had - you no longer lay claim to it. Now I cross over to where you stand - right? And, you come over to this position I have left. So. Excellent. The exchange is now formally and irrevocably complete. This is my straw hat. And that is your tricorn hat. Put it on. Splendid! And it suits you! Doesn't it suit him.[8]

They have changed states.

NOTES

1 CHANGE AND STASIS IN IRISH WRITING

1 Bernard Shaw, *Back to Methusalah: A Metabiological Pentateuch* (London, 1928), pp. xvi–xvii.
2 Thomas Kinsella, *Davis, Mangan, Ferguson: Tradition and the Irish Writer* (Dublin, 1970), p. 67.
3 Translation by the author.
4 See William Blake, *Jerusalem*, chapter 2, plate 31.
5 W.B. Yeats, *Collected Poems* (London, 1950; repr. 1958), pp. 227–8.
6 ibid., p. 400.

2 LANGUAGE AND TRADITION IN THE NINETEENTH CENTURY

1 Thomas Kinsella, *Davis, Mangan, Ferguson: Tradition and the Irish Writer* (Dublin, 1970), p. 67.
2 Edmund Burke, 'A Second Letter to Hercules Langrishe' in Matthew Arnold (ed.) *Letters, Speeches and Tracts on Irish Affairs by Edmund Burke* (London, 1881), p. 339: 'A third point of Jacobin attack is on *old traditionary constitutions.*'
3 Desmond Fennell, *Beyond Nationalism* (Dublin, 1986), *passim*.
4 Edmund Burke, *Reflections on the Revolution in France*, edited by Conor Cruise O'Brien (Harmondsworth, 1968), p. 171.
5 ibid., p. 120.
6 *The Letters of Thomas Moore*, edited by Wilfrid S. Dowden (Oxford, 1964), vol. I, p. 143.
7 *The Poetical Works of Thomas Moore*, edited by David Herbert (Edinburgh, 1872), p. 438.
8 *The Poetical Works of Thomas Moore*, collected by himself (London, 1853–4), vol. IV, p. vii.
9 *The Poetical Works of Thomas Moore* (London, n.d.) pp. 226–7.
10 ibid., p. 271.
11 ibid., p. 209.

12 ibid., p. 364.
13 John Windele, 'Memoir of the Late Mr. Callanan', *Bolster's Quarterly Magazine,* vol. III (1829), p. 292.
14 J.J. Callanan, *The Poems* (Cork, 1861), p. 112.
15 Douglas Hyde, *The Love Songs of Connacht* (Dublin, 1893), p. 94.
16 Samuel Ferguson, 'Hardiman's *Irish Minstrelsy* - No. III', *Dublin University Magazine,* vol. IV (1834), p. 448.
17 Samuel Ferguson, 'The *Dublin Penny Journal*', *Dublin University Magazine,* vol. XV (1840), pp. 115–16.
18 Samuel Ferguson, 'Hardiman's *Irish Minstrelsy* - No. IV', *Dublin University Magazine,* vol. IV (1834), p. 516.
19 *The Penguin Book of Irish Verse,* edited by Brendan Kennelly (Harmondsworth, second edition, 1981), p. 208.
20 *Poems of Sir Samuel Ferguson,* edited by Alfred Percival Graves (Dublin and London, 1918), p. 208.
21 W.B. Yeats, *Collected Poems* (London, 1958), p. 214.
22 *Poems of James Clarence Mangan,* edited by D.J. O'Donoghue (Dublin and London, 1903), p. 11.
23 ibid., p. 152.

3 GEORGE MOORE

1 *A Drama in Muslin* (London, 1886; repr. Gerrards Cross, 1981), p. 69.
2 *The Lake* (Gerrards Cross, uniform edition, 1932), p. 160.
3 *Esther Waters* (London, uniform edition, 1947), pp. 162–3.
4 ibid., p. 382.
5 *Sister Teresa* (London, 1901), p. 207.
6 See Richard Cave's discussion of Moore's 'Since the Elizabethans' in *Cosmopolis* (October 1896) in *A Study of the Novels of George Moore* (Gerrards Cross, 1978), chapter 7, which explains the significance of the terms 'underlife' and 'illuminations' for Moore's aesthetic.
7 *Ave,* in *Hail and Farewell* (repr. Gerrards Cross, 1976), p. 223.
8 ibid., p. 223.
9 ibid., p. 208.
10 ibid., p. 257.
11 See Joseph Hone, *The Life of George Moore* (London, 1936), p. 224.
12 *The Untilled Field* (repr. Gerrards Cross, 1976), p. 99.
13 *The Lake,* p. 202.
14 ibid., p. x.
15 ibid., pp. 171–4.
16 ibid., p. 173.
17 *Hail and Farewell,* p. 548.
18 ibid., p. 559.
19 *The Brook Kerith* (London, uniform edition, 1931) pp. 145–6.
20 ibid., p. 457 *et seq.*
21 ibid., p. 111.
22 *Aphrodite in Aulis* (London, uniform edition, 1931), p. 35.

4 W.B. YEATS

1 *Collected Poems* (London, 1958), p. 241.
2 ibid., p. 285.
3 ibid., p. 166.
4 ibid., p. 56.
5 *Addresses to the German Nation*, translated by R.F. Jones and G.H. Turnbull (Chicago and London, 1952), p. 60.
6 ibid., pp. 215–16.
7 See Paul R. Sweet, *Wilhelm von Humboldt: A Biography* (Columbus, Ohio, 1980), vol. II, pp. 469–70.
8 *Collected Poems*, p. 285.
9 *Uncollected Prose*, edited by J.P. Frayne (London, 1970), vol. I, p. 81.
10 *Collected Poems*, p. 182.
11 *Mythologies* (London, 1977), p. 331.
12 *Essays and Introductions* (London, 1969), p. 552.
13 *Explorations* (London, 1962), p. 263.
14 *Mythologies*, p. 339.
15 *Collected Poems*, p. 180.
16 *Mythologies*, p. 341.
17 ibid., p. 347.
18 *Essays and Introductions*, p. 195.
19 ibid., p. 509.
20 ibid., p. 510.
21 *Collected Poems*, p. 57.
22 ibid., p. 375.
23 Lady Gregory, *Cuchulain of Muirthemne* (Gerrards Cross, Coole edition, 1970), p. 15.
24 *Essays and Introductions*, p. 520.
25 ibid., p. 512.
26 *Collected Poems*, p. 378.
27 ibid., p. 375.
28 A.N. Jeffares, *A New Commentary on the Poems of W.B. Yeats* (London, 1984), p. 412.
29 *A Vision* (London, 1937), p. 253.
30 *Essays and Introductions*, p. 409.
31 ibid., p. 518.
32 *Collected Poems*, p. 369.

5 J.M. SYNGE

1 Quoted in Declan Kiberd, *Synge and the Irish Language* (London, 1979), p. 106.
2 W.B. Yeats, *Collected Poems* (London, 1958), p. 274.
3 J.M. Synge, *Collected Works*, general editor, Alan Price, vol. II (Oxford, 1966; repr. Gerrards Cross, 1982), p. 350. All subsequent references to *Collected Works*, 1982 repr. with volume number and editor.

4 ibid., p. 1.
5 ibid.
6 ibid., p. 10.
7 William Wordsworth, *The Prelude*, Book I (Harmondsworth, 1978), p. 56.
8 *Collected Works*, vol. II (ed. Alan Price), p. 10.
9 ibid., p. 350.
10 *Collected Works*, vol. IV (ed. Ann Saddlemyer), p. 53.
11 'The Vagrants of Wicklow' in *Collected Works*, vol. II (ed. Alan Price), p. 208.
12 ibid., pp. 235–6.
13 ibid., p. 236.
14 Quoted from TCD MS 4379, F.84 in Mary C. King, *The Drama of J.M. Synge* (London, 1985), p. 105.
15 See Yeats's preface to the first edition of *The Well of the Saints*, *Collected Works*, vol. III (ed. Ann Saddlemyer), p. 63.
16 *Collected Works*, vol. II (ed. Alan Price), p. 100.
17 ibid., p. 130.
18 ibid.
19 ibid., p. 132.
20 *Collected Works*, vol. IV (ed. Ann Saddlemyer), p. 53.
21 *Collected Works*, vol. II (ed. Alan Price), p. 269.
22 *Collected Works*, vol. III (ed. Ann Saddlemyer), p. 71; and Mary C. King, op. cit., p. 107.
23 *Collected Works*, vol. III (ed. Ann Saddlemyer), p. 117.
24 ibid., p. 23.
25 See Paul F. Botheroyd, 'J.M. Synge's *The Aran Islands, Riders to the Sea* and Territoriality' in Dapo Adelugba (ed.) *Studies on Synge* (Ibadan, 1977), pp. 75–86.
26 *Collected Works*, vol. III (ed. Ann Saddlemyer), p. 7.
27 ibid., p. 23.
28 ibid.
29 See Martin Heidegger, 'Das Ding' ('The Thing') in *Vortrage und Aufsatze* (Neske, 1954), p. 177. 'Death is the shrine of nothingness, namely of that which is never in any respect something merely existent, but which nonetheless essentiates, and indeed is the mystery of Being itself. . . . Death is in the shrine of nothingness, the mountain-range of Being.' Translation supplied by Dr Joseph O'Leary, Sofia University, Tokyo.
30 Adrienne Rich, *The Dream of a Common Language: Poems 1934–1977* (New York, 1978), pp. 74–5: 'But there come times - perhaps this is one of them - / when we have to take ourselves more seriously or die; / when we have to pull back from the incantations, / rhythms we've moved to thoughtlessly, / and disenthrall ourselves, bestow / ourselves to silence, or a severer listening, cleansed / of oratory, formulas, choruses, laments, static / crowding the wires.'
31 *The Collected Letters of John Millington Synge*, edited by Ann Saddlemyer, vol. I (Oxford, 1983), pp. 286–7.

32 *Collected Works*, vol. III (ed. Ann Saddlemyer), p. 95.
33 ibid., p. 149.
34 ibid., p. 133.
35 ibid., p. 173.
36 ibid.
37 *The Collected Letters of John Millington Synge*, edited by Ann Saddlemyer, vol. II (Oxford, 1984), p. 56.
38 *Collected Works*, vol. III (ed. Ann Saddlemyer), p. 217.
39 ibid., p. 193.
40 ibid., p. 249.
41 ibid., p. 251.
42 See Declan Kiberd, op. cit., p. 179.
43 *Collected Works*, vol. I (ed. Robin Skelton), p. 66; also see Mary C. King, op. cit., p. 66.
44 See Declan Kiberd, op. cit., pp. 204 *et seq*.
45 See Robert Welch, *A History of Verse Translation from the Irish 1789–1897* (Gerrards Cross and New Jersey, 1988), pp. 147–61.
46 Douglas Hyde, *Love Songs of Connacht* (London and Dublin, 1893; repr. Shannon, 1969), p. 9.
47 'A Nocturnal upon S. Lucy's Day, being the shortest day' in A.J. Smith (ed.) *John Donne: The Complete English Poems* (Harmondsworth, 1975), p. 72.

6 JAMES JOYCE

1 *Ulysses* (London, 1937), p. 697.
2 *A Portrait of the Artist as a Young Man* (Harmondsworth, 1960), pp. 91–2.
3 *Stephen Hero* (St Albans, 1977), pp. 81–2.
4 *Dubliners* (London, 1927), pp. 115–16.
5 See Richard Ellmann, *James Joyce* (London, 1966), p. 218.
6 *Stephen Hero*, p. 73.
7 ibid.
8 W.B. Yeats, *Mythologies* (London, 1959), pp. 306–7.
9 *Stephen Hero*, p. 75.
10 ibid., p. 74.
11 *A Portrait*, pp. 207–8 *et seq*.
12 *Ulysses*, p. 235.
13 ibid., p. 183.
14 ibid., p. 190.
15 ibid., p. 201.
16 *Finnegans Wake* (repr. London, 1964), p. 6ll.
17 *Ulysses*, p. 236.
18 ibid., p. 376.
19 ibid., p. 479.
20 ibid., p. 404.
21 ibid., p. 479.

22 See Frances A. Yates, *Giordano Bruno and the Hermetic Tradition* (London, 1964), p. 250.
23 'A Valediction: Forbidding Mourning' in A.J. Smith (ed.) *The Complete English Poems* (Harmondsworth, 1973), p. 84. 'Moving of th'earth brings harms and fears,/Men reckon what it did and meant,/ But trepidation of the spheres,/Though greater far, is innocent.'
24 Sir Philip Sidney, *An Apologie for Poetrie,* edited by Edmund Auber (London, 1901), p. 25: 'onely the Poet, disdayning to be tied to any subiection, lifted up with the vigor of his own invention, dooth growe in effect, another nature . . . so as hee goeth hand in hand with Nature, not inclosed within the narrow warrant of her guifts, but freely ranging onely with the Zodiack of his owne wit.'
25 *Ulysses,* pp. 659–60.
26 Frances A. Yates, op. cit., p. 256.
27 ibid., p. 208.
28 *Ulysses,* p. 697.
29 See Richard Ellmann, *Ulysses on the Liffey* (London, 1974), p. 164.
30 ibid., p. 175.
31 *Finnegans Wake,* p. 581.
32 ibid., p. 582.

7 JOYCE CARY

1 See Alan Bishop, *Gentleman Rider: A Life of Joyce Cary* (London, 1988), pp. 32–3.
2 ibid., p. 24.
3 *Joyce Cary: Selected Essays,* edited by A.G. Bishop (London, 1976), pp. 66–7.
4 ibid.
5 *The Case for African Freedom* (London, 1944), p. 12.
6 *Joyce Cary: Selected Essays,* p. 19.
7 ibid., p. 49.
8 *Castle Corner* (London, Carfax edition, 1952), pp. 6–7.
9 ibid., p. 147.
10 ibid., p. 152.
11 ibid., p. 154.
12 ibid., p. 172.
13 ibid., p. 266.
14 *A House of Children* (London, Carfax edition, 1951), p. 11.
15 ibid., pp. 14–15.
16 ibid., p. 223.
17 ibid., pp. 234–5.
18 *Joyce Cary: Selected Essays,* p. 117.
19 See Malcolm Foster, *Joyce Cary: A Biography* (London, 1969), p. 285.
20 *To Be a Pilgrim* (New York, 1942), p. 342.
21 *Joyce Cary: Selected Essays,* p. 73.
22 William Blake, *Milton,* Book I, plate 28.

23 *The Horse's Mouth* (London, 1944), p. 90.
24 ibid., p. 91.
25 ibid., p. 136.
26 *Not Honour More* (London, Carfax edition, 1966), p. 203.

8 FRANCIS STUART

1 *Memorial* (London, 1973), p. 217.
2 See Ken Smith, *Inside Time* (London, 1989).
3 *The Pillar of Cloud* (London, 1948), p. 55.
4 ibid., p. 9.
5 *Faillandia* (Dublin, 1985), p. 239.
6 ibid., p. 105.
7 *The Abandoned Snail Shell* (Dublin, 1987), p. 27.
8 *Memorial*, p. 61.
9 Quoted in Daniel Murphy, *Imagination and Religion in Anglo-Irish Literature: 1930–1980* (Dublin, 1987), p. 191.
10 *The Pillar of Cloud*, p. 157.
11 ibid., p. 156.
12 *The Abandoned Snail Shell*, p. 18.
13 *The High Consistory* (London, 1981), p. 67.
14 *Pigeon Irish* (London, 1932), p. 173.
15 *The Pillar of Cloud*, p. 208.
16 *Blacklist, Section H* (London, 1975), p. 45.
17 *The Abandoned Snail Shell*, p. 10.
18 *Blacklist, Section H*, p. 167.
19 C.G. Jung, *Psychology and Alchemy*, vol. XII of the *Collected Works*, translated by R.F.C. Hull (London, 1968), p. 230.
20 *The Abandoned Snail Shell*, p. 42.
21 *Redemption* (London, 1974; original edition, London 1950), pp. 162–3.
22 *Blacklist, Section H*, p. 311.
23 *Pigeon Irish*, pp. 218–19.
24 *The Abandoned Snail Shell*, p. 27.
25 *Memorial*, p. 41.
26 W.B. Yeats, *Collected Poems* (London, 1985), p. 295.
27 Quoted in *Blacklist, Section H*, p. 363.
28 'For if we have been planted together in the likeness of his death, we shall be also in the likeness of his resurrection: Knowing this, that our old man is crucified with him, that the body of sin might be destroyed, that henceforth we should not serve sin (Romans 6: 5–6, Authorized Version).
29 *Memorial*, p. 218.
30 Quoted in W.J. McCormack (ed.) *A Festschrift for Francis Stuart* (Dublin, 1972), p. 10.
31 *Pigeon Irish*, pp. 50–1.
32 ibid., p. 186.

33 *Redemption*, p. 208.
34 ibid., p. 215.
35 ibid., p. 218.
36 *A Hole in the Head* (London, 1977), p. 186.
37 *Faillandia*, p. 344.
38 *The High Consistory*, pp. 98–9.
39 *Faillandia*, p. 223.
40 *The Pillar of Cloud*, p. 147.
41 *Memorial*, p. 84.
42 *The High Consistory*, p. 224.

9 SAMUEL BECKETT

1 Hugh Kenner (ed.) *Desmond Egan: The Poet and His Work* (Maine, 1990), p. 52.
2 *More Pricks than Kicks* (London, Picador repr., 1973), p. 148.
3 See Samuel Beckett, *Company* (London, 1980): 'Pangs of faint light and stirrings still. Unformulable gropings of the mind. Unstillable.' Also see 'Stirrings Still' in *As the Story was Told* (London and New York, 1990).
4 *More Pricks than Kicks*, p. 36.
5 Vivian Mercier, *Beckett/Beckett* (New York, 1977), p. 161.
6 See Samuel Beckett, *Proust & Three Dialogues with Georges Duthuit* (London, 1965), p. 90.
7 See James Joyce, *Ulysses* (London, 1954 repr.) p. 188.
8 *Murphy* (London, Picador repr., 1973), p. 69.
9 ibid., p. 53.
10 See Austin Clarke, *Collected Poems* (Dublin, 1974), p. 547.
11 *Proust*, pp. 65–6.
12 ibid., p. 64.
13 *Murphy*, p. 101.
14 *Proust*, p. 21.
15 *Murphy*, pp. 55–6.
16 Source: conversation with Desmond Egan.
17 *Proust*, p. 90.
18 *Watt* (London, Jupiter edition, 1970), pp. 28–9.
19 ibid., p. 219.
20 See Vivian Mercier, op. cit., p. 163.
21 See *Watt*, p. 207; *Molloy* (London, Jupiter edition, 1971 repr.), p. 44.
22 *Watt*, pp. 41–2.
23 Francis Stuart, *The Abandoned Snail Shell* (Dublin, 1987), p. 27.
24 Richard Ellmann, *along the riverrun* (London, 1989), p. 238.
25 *Watt*, pp. 124–5.
26 ibid., p. 167.
27 *Molloy*, p. 162.
28 ibid., p. 93.
29 ibid., p. 94.

30 Samuel Beckett, *The Complete Dramatic Works* (London, 1990 edition), p. 60.
31 *Molloy*, p. 95.
32 ibid., p. 33.
33 *Malone Dies* (Harmondsworth, 1970 edition), p. 26.
34 ibid.
35 *Molloy*, p. 147.
36 ibid., p. 15.
37 *Malone Dies*, p. 63.
38 ibid.
39 See Robert Welch, *Irish Poetry from Moore to Yeats* (Gerrards Cross, 1980), pp. 76–115.
40 *The Penguin Book of Irish Verse*, edited by Brendan Kennelly (Harmondsworth, second edition, 1981), p. 162.
41 *Molloy*, p. 37.
42 *Malone Dies*, p. 64.
43 ibid., p. 65.
44 *Watt*, p. 217.
45 *Malone Dies*, p. 65.
46 ibid., p. 67.
47 *Company*, p. 47.
48 ibid., p. 67.
49 Vivian Mercier, op. cit., p. 160.
50 W.B. Yeats, *Collected Poems* (London, 1958), p. 142.
51 *The Complete Dramatic Works*, p. 422.
52 *More Pricks than Kicks*, p. 36.
53 *Malone Dies*, p. 74.
54 *Company*, pp. 53–4.
55 In *The Beckett Trilogy: Molloy, Malone Dies, The Unnamable* (London, 1979 edition), p. 66.
56 ibid., pp. 290–1.
57 *Proust*, p. 90.
58 *Trilogy*, pp. 283–4.
59 ibid., p. 332.
60 ibid., pp. 355–6.
61 *How it is* (London, 1964), p. 57.
62 *Murphy*, p. 66.
63 *How it is*, p. 45.
64 ibid., p. 141.
65 ibid., p. 86.
66 ibid., p. 95.
67 ibid., p. 148.
68 ibid., p. 148.
69 ibid., p. 147.
70 ibid., p. 17.
71 See Paul Davis, *The Ideal Real: Imagination and Knowledge in the Prose of Samuel Beckett*, D.Phil thesis (Reading, 1988), p. 252 and *passim*.

10 MÁIRTÍN Ó CADHAIN

1 An tSr. Bosco Costigan, *De Ghlaschloich an Oileáin* (Béal an Daingin, 1989), p. 33. All translations in this chapter are the author's, save where otherwise specified.
2 ibid., p. 327.
3 Máirtín Ó Cadhain, *Páipéir Bhána agus Páipéir Bhreaca* (Baile Atha Cliath, 1969), p. 26.
4 *An Braon Broghach* (Baile Atha Cliath, 1949), p. 36.
5 ibid., p. 47.
6 ibid., p. 48.
7 *Cré na Cille* (Baile Atha Cliath, 1949), p. 38.
8 ibid., p. 25.
9 W.B. Yeats, *Collected Poems* (London, 1958), p. 295.
10 *Cré na Cille*, p. 102.
11 George Moore, *The Lake* (1921 edition; repr. Gerrards Cross, 1980), p. 173.
12 Seán Ó Tuama, 'A Writer's Testament' *Ériú* XXIII (1972), pp. 245–6; and see Gearóid Denvir, *Cadhan Aonair: Saothar Liteartha Mháirtin Uí Chadhain* (Baile Atha Cliath, 1987), p. 48, where this view is discussed.
13 See W.B. Yeats, *A Vision* (London, 1937), p. 68: 'Here the thought of Heraclitus dominates all: "Dying each other's life, living each other's deaths." '
14 *An Braon Broghach*, p. 112.
15 ibid., pp. 135–6; translation based on Eoghan Ó Tuairisc's in *The Road to Brightcity* (Swords, 1981), p. 70.
16 ibid.; translation based on Ó Tuairisc, ibid., p. 78.
17 *Páipéir Bhána agus Páipéir Bhreaca*, p. 41.
18 *An tStraith dhá Thógáil* (Baile Atha Cliath, 1970), pp. 80–1.
19 Samuel Beckett, 'Gnome' in *Collected Poems in English and French* (London, 1977), p. 7.
20 *An tStraith dhá Thógáil*, p. 89.
21 ibid., p. 99.
22 ibid., p. 100.
23 ibid., pp. 14–15.

11 SEÁN Ó RÍORDÁIN

1 Seán Ó Coileáin, *Seán Ó Ríordáin: Beatha agus Saothar* (Baile Atha Cliath, 1982), pp. 389–90. The translation is mine, as are all translations in this chapter. Seán Ó Tuama's study of Ó Ríordáin in *Filí faoi Sceimhle* (Baile Atha Cliath, 1978) is essential reading.
2 *Línte Liombó* (Baile Atha Cliath, 1971), p. 30.
3 W.B. Yeats, *Collected Poems* (London, 1958), p. 267.
4 Seán Ó Coileáin, op. cit., p. 125.
5 *Eireaballl Spideoige* (Baile Atha Cliath, 1952), pp. 9–11.

6 *The Poems of Gerard Manley Hopkins,* edited by W.H. Gardner and Norman MacKenzie (Oxford, 1970), p. 90.
7 *Eireabaill Spideoige,* p. 12.
8 ibid., p. 18.
9 Seán Ó Coileáin, op. cit., p. 189.
10 *Eireabaill Spideoige,* pp. 100–2.
11 Seán Ó Coileáin, op. cit., p. 190. The Diary extract is from Ó Coileáin's biography; the poem is taken from *Brosna.* See note 12.
12 *Brosna* (Baile Atha Cliath, 1964), p. 15.
13 Seán Ó Coileáin, op. cit., p. 100.
14 *Eireabaill Spideoige,* p. 96.
15 See the comments by Ó Coileáin in his study, p. 100: 'Beirthe air na rithimí bhreise, rithim an dáin ina dtéann siad chun suaimhnis. Comhrithim, comhbhualadh, cómheadaracht.'
16 *Eireabaill Spideoige,* p. 111.
17 Yeats, op. cit., pp. 283–4.
18 *Línte Liombó,* p. 40.
19 ibid., p. 41.
20 Seán Ó Coileáin, op. cit., p. 72.
21 *Tar Eis Mo Bháis* (Baile Atha Cliath, 1978) p. 15.
22 Seán Ó Coileáin, op. cit., pp. 124–5.
23 *Eireabaill Spideoige,* p. 789.
24 ibid., p. 80.
25 ibid., pp. 81–2.
26 *Brosna,* p. 18.
27 *Línte Liombó,* p. 32.

12 BRIAN FRIEL

1 Brian Friel, *Philadelphia, Here I Come* in *Selected Plays* edited by Seamus Deane, (London, 1984), p. 88.
2 *Volunteers* (Dublin, 1989), p. 63.
3 ibid., p. 64.
4 Brian Friel, *Selected Stories* (Dublin, 1979), p. 103.
5 ibid., p. 106.
6 *Selected Plays,* p. 73.
7 ibid., p. 88.
8 Martin Heidegger, 'Language' in *Poetry, Language, Thought* (New York, 1975), p. 198.
9 *Translations* in *Selected Plays,* p. 445.
10 *Volunteers,* pp. 45–6.
11 ibid., p. 28.
12 *The Loves of Cass Maguire* (Dublin, 1984), p. 58.
13 *Selected Stories,* 'Introduction', p. 15.
14 *Aristocrats* in *Selected Plays,* pp. 226–7.
15 ibid., p. 309.
16 ibid., p. 325.
17 *Faith Healer* in *Selected Plays,* p. 376.

18 *Translations* in *Selected Plays*, p. 419.
19 James Joyce, *Ulysses* (London, 1954), p. 18.
20 *The Communication Cord* (London, 1982), p. 86.
21 *Translations* in *Selected Plays*, p. 445.
22 *Making History* (London, 1989), p. 35.
23 ibid., p. 30.
24 ibid., p. 49.
25 ibid., p. 67.

13 SEAMUS HEANEY

1 *Station Island* (London, 1984), p. 58.
2 See Ruby Cohn (ed.) *Disjecta: Miscellaneous Writings and a Dramatic Fragment* (London, 1983), pp. 70–6, which reprints a 1934 essay by Beckett on Devlin.
3 *The Haw Lantern* (London, 1987), p. 25.
4 *Door into the Dark* (London, 1969), p. 20.
5 *Sir Philip Sidney: Selected Poetry and Prose*, edited by David Kalstone (London, 1970), p. 221.
6 *The Government of the Tongue* (London, 1988), pp. 55–6.
7 *Preoccupations* (London, 1984), pp. 41–2.
8 *Death of a Naturalist* (London, 1966), p. 57.
9 See *The Government of the Tongue*, pp. xx, 34, 35 and 139 for different approaches to the word 'steadfast'.
10 *Door into the Dark*, p. 46.
11 *Station Island*, p. 63.
12 ibid., p. 93.
13 *Door into the Dark*, pp. 53–4.
14 ibid., pp. 55–6.
15 Quoted in Neil Corcoran, *Seamus Heaney* (London, 1986), p. 71.
16 *Wintering Out* (London, 1972), pp. 14–15.
17 ibid., p. 17.
18 ibid., p. 20.
19 ibid., p. 24.
20 ibid.
21 *Preoccupations*, p. 18.
22 *Wintering Out*, p. 18.
23 ibid., p. 46.
24 ibid., p. 48.
25 *Preoccupations*, p. 55.
26 *The Government of the Tongue*, p. xxii.
27 *North* (London, 1975), p. 8.
28 ibid., p. 20.
29 See chapter 11, note 6. This poem is a key text for Ó Ríordáin as well.
30 See *Field Work* (London, 1979), p. 81.
31 *North*, pp. 27–8.
32 ibid., p. 40.
33 ibid., p. 42.

34 ibid., pp. 42–3.
35 ibid., p. 45.
36 W.B. Yeats, *Collected Poems* (London, 1958), p. 269.
37 *Field Work*, p. 11.
38 ibid., p. 59.
39 ibid., p. 11.
40 ibid., p. 41.
41 W.B. Yeats, op. cit., p. 208.
42 *Field Work*, p. 33.
43 ibid., p. 52.
44 J.B. Leishman (trans.), *Selected Poems: Rilke* (Harmondsworth, 1967), p. 64.
45 *Field Work*, p. 63.
46 *Sweeney Astray* (London, 1984), pp. 51–2.
47 *Station Island*, pp. 18–19.
48 Quoted in *Station Island*, p. 40, from *A Portrait of the Artist as a Young Man*.
49 *Station Island*, p. 50.
50 ibid., p. 56.
51 *John Donne: The Complete English Poems*, edited by A.J. Smith (Harmondsworth, Penguin, 1975), p. 72.
52 *The Government of the Tongue*, p. 130.
53 *Station Island*, p. 76.
54 ibid., p. 88.
55 ibid., p. 89.
56 ibid., p. 90.
57 ibid., pp. 93–4.
58 ibid., p. 114.
59 *The Haw Lantern*, p. 13.
60 ibid., p. 22.
61 ibid., p. 27.
62 ibid., p. 31.
63 *The Government of the Tongue*, p. 14.

14 MOVEMENT AND AUTHORITY

1 Seamus Heaney, *The Haw Lantern* (London, 1987), p. 6.
2 Proinsias MacCana, *Celtic Mythology* (London, 1973 repr.), p. 94.
3 P.L. Henry, *Saoithiúlacht na Sean-Ghaeilge* (Baile Atha Cliath, 1978), p. 125. This study, a superb integration of complex material, lies behind much of the discussion of legendary material in this chapter. Its learning, its insight into the structure of the Irish mind, and its command of linguistic and literary evidence, is impressive.
4 ibid., pp. 17 *et seq*.
5 Edmund Leach and D. Alan Laywik, *Structuralist Interpretations of Biblical Myth* (Cambridge, 1983), p. 8.
6 T.F. O'Rahilly, *Early Irish History and Mythology* (Dublin, 1946), p. 132.

7 P.L. Henry, op. cit., pp. 28 *et seq.*
8 Seamus Heaney, *Station Island* (London, 1984), p. 21.
9 M.C. Ferguson, *Sir Samuel Ferguson in the Ireland of his Day* (London, 1896), vol. I, p. 250.
10 *The Haw Lantern*, p. 6.
11 T.F. O'Rahilly, *Measgra Dánta* (Corcaigh, 1927), p. 132.
12 *Poems of James Clarence Mangan*, edited by D.J. O'Donoghue (Dublin, 1903), p. 81.

CODA

1 Seamus Heaney, *Seeing Things* (London, 1991), p. 56.
2 Martin Heidegger, *On the Way to Language* (New York, 1971), p. 47.
3 Heaney, op. cit., p. 71.
4 See Pearse Hutchinson, *The Frost is All Over* (Dublin, 1975).
5 Heaney, op. cit., p. 22.
6 See Robert Welch, *Irish Poetry from Moore to Yeats* (Gerrards Cross and New Jersey, 1980), pp. 156–77.
7 Brian Friel, *Dancing at Lughnasa* (London, 1990), p. 22.
8 ibid., p. 69.

INDEX